I0430126

DoD 4145.26-M

DOD Contractor's Safety Manual
For Ammunition and Explosives

March 13, 2008

UNDER SECRETARY OF DEFENSE
FOR ACQUISITION, TECHNOLOGY, AND LOGISTICS

OFFICE OF THE UNDER SECRETARY OF DEFENSE

3000 DEFENSE PENTAGON
WASHINGTON, DC 20301-3000

ACQUISITION,
TECHNOLOGY
AND LOGISTICS

MAR 13 2008

FOREWORD

This Manual is reissued under the authority of and in accordance with DoD Instruction 4145.26 (Reference (a)) and, accordingly, is applicable to all contractual actions entered into on or after the reissue date. The prior DoD 4145.26-M (Reference (b)), dated September 16, 1997, is hereby rescinded and superseded, yet will remain applicable and effective for contractual actions entered into on or after September 16, 1997 and before the reissue date. The Manual provides safety standards common to DoD and private industry ammunition and explosives (AE), operations, and facilities performing AE work or AE services under DoD contracts, subcontracts, purchase orders, or other procurement methods. DoD 6055.9-STD (Reference (c)) establishes these AE safety standards and serves as the primary source document for this Manual. The explosives safety requirements included in this Manual are consistent with Reference (c) so that AE safety standards for DoD Components and DoD contractors are equivalent.

Subpart 223.370 of the Defense Federal Acquisition Regulation Supplement (Reference (d)) requires contracting officers to incorporate this Manual in all AE procurement actions. The purchasing activity may include additional AE or related safety requirements that are not inconsistent with this Manual as it deems necessary. The Manual should be incorporated into AE procurement actions in order to legally bind the contractor to follow the provisions contained therein.

This revision removes the chapter on hazard component data statements and updates quantity distance requirements and basic AE safety principles.

Questions on interpretation of any requirement in this Manual by the contractor should be submitted through the contractor's assigned administrative contracting officer to the procuring contracting officer for further review and resolution.

This Manual applies to the Office of the Secretary of Defense (OSD), the Military Departments (including their Reserve Components), the Office of the Chairman of the Joint Chiefs of Staff, Combatant Commands, the Office of the Inspector General of the Department of Defense, the Defense Agencies, the DoD Field Activities, and all other organizational entities in the Department of Defense (hereafter referred to collectively as the "DoD Components").

This Manual is effective immediately, and is mandatory for use by all the DoD Components as specified in Reference (a).

Forward recommendations for change to this Manual to:

> Chairman
> Department of Defense Explosives Safety Board
> Room 856C, Hoffman Building I
> 2461 Eisenhower Avenue
> Alexandria, VA 22331-0600

RELEASABILITY. UNLIMITED. This Manual is approved for public release. Copies may be obtained through the Internet from the DoD Issuances Web Site at http://www.dtic.mil/whs/directives. An electronic copy can also be obtained by contacting the Department of Defense Explosives Safety Board; Room 856C, Hoffman Building I; 2461 Eisenhower Avenue; Alexandria, VA 22331-0600; telephone at 703-325-2525.

John J. Young, Jr.
Under Secretary of Defense
for Acquisition, Technology and Logistics

TABLE OF CONTENTS

FIGURES

ACRONYMS AND ABBREVIATIONS

AE	ammunition and explosives
ACO	administrative contracting officer
AGM	aboveground magazine
AGS	aboveground structure/site
AGS (H)	aboveground structure, heavy wall
AGS (L)	aboveground structure, light
AP	ammonium perchlorate
ASME	American Society of Mechanical Engineers
°C	degrees Celsius
CFR	Code of Federal Regulations
CG	compatibility group
COCO	contractor-owned, contractor-operated
d	loading density (used in formulae)
D	minimum safe distance (used in formulae)
DCMA	Defense Contract Management Agency
DDESB	Department of Defense Explosives Safety Board
DoD	Department of Defense
DOT	Department of Transportation
ECM	earth-covered magazine
EED	electro-explosive device
EIDS	extremely insensitive detonating substances
ELCG	Energetic Liquid Compatibility Group
ES	exposed site
ESD	electrostatic discharge
°F	degrees Fahrenheit
FO	foreign object
FOE	foreign object elimination
ft	feet
GOCO	government-owned, contractor-operated
H	heavy wall
H/R	heavy wall/roof
HAN	hydroxyl ammonium nitrate
HD	hazard division
HDD	hazardous debris distance
HE	high explosive
HEW	high explosive weight
HFD	hazardous fragment distance
HMX	octogen, nitroamine high explosive

HPM	high performance magazine
IAW	in accordance with
IBD	inhabited building distance
ILD	intraline distance
IMD	intermagazine distance
IR	infrared
JHCS	Joint Hazard Classification System
K	factor that is dependent upon the risk assumed or permitted
kg	kilograms
kPa	kilopascals
kV	kilovolts
ln	natural logarithm
lb	pound
LPG	liquefied petroleum gas
m	meters
MCE	maximum credible event
MIL-STD	military standard
ms	milli second
NAVFAC	Naval Facilities Engineering Command
NEW	net explosive weight
NEWQD	net explosive weight for quantity distance
NFPA	National Fire Protection Association
NG	nitroglycerin
NPW	net propellant weight
OSHA	Occupational Safety and Health Administration
Pa	Pascal
PCO	procuring contracting officer
PES	potential explosion site
PETN	pentaerythritol tetranitrate
PPE	personal protective equipment
psi	pounds per square inch
psig	pounds per square inch gauge
PTR	public traffic route
PTRD	public traffic route distance
Q	net explosive weight for quantity distance expressed in kilograms
QD	quantity distance

R	rear
RDX	cyclotrimethylenetrinitramine
RF	radio frequency
S	side
SG	sensitivity group
SOP	standard operating procedure
TB	technical bulletin
TEA	triethyl aluminum
TNT	trinitrotoluene
TP	technical paper
UL	Underwriters Laboratories
UN	United Nations
W	net explosive weight for quantity distance expressed in pounds
W[Q]	net explosive weight for quantity distance in pounds [kilograms]
WP	white phosphorus

REFERENCES

(a)   DoD Instruction 4145.26, "DoD Contractor's Safety Requirements for Ammunition and Explosives," April 9, 2005

(b)   DoD 4145.26-M, "DoD Contractors' Safety Manual for Ammunition and Explosives," September 16, 1997 (which is hereby rescinded and superseded, yet will remain applicable and effective for contractual actions entered into on or after September 16, 1997 and before the reissue date.)

(c)   DoD 6055.9-STD, "DoD Ammunition and Explosives Safety Standards," February 29, 2008

(d)   Subpart 223.370 of the Defense Federal Acquisition Regulation Supplement, "Safety Precautions for Ammunition and Explosives." December 9, 2005

(e)   DoD Instruction 6055.7, "Accident Investigation, Reporting, and Record Keeping," October 3, 2000

(f)   Parts 1904 and 1910 of title 29, Code of Federal Regulations (CFR)

(g)   Parts 100-199 of title 49, CFR

(h)   Military Standard (MIL-STD)-398, "Shields, Operational for Ammunition Operations, Criteria for Design of and Tests for Acceptance," November 5, 1976[1]

(i)   Technical Bulletin (TB) 700-2/Naval Sea Systems Command Instruction (NAVSEAINST) 8020.8B/Technical Order (TO) 11A-1-47/Defense Logistics Agency Regulations (DLAR) 8220.1, "Department of Defense Ammunition and Explosives Hazard Classification Procedures," January 5, 1998[2]

(j)   National Fire Protection Association (NFPA) Manual 491M.5, "Hazardous Chemical Reactions," current edition[3]

(k)   Department of Defense Explosives Safety Board (DDESB) Technical Paper (TP) No. 13, "Prediction of Building Debris for Quantity-Distance Siting," April 1991[2]

(l)   DDESB TP No. 16, "Methodologies for Calculating Primary Fragment Characteristics," October 17, 2005[2]

(m)   DDESB TP No. 15, "Approved Protective Construction (Version 2.0)," June 2004[2]

(n)   Technical Manual (TM) 5-1300/Naval Facilities Engineering Command (NAVFAC) P-397/Air Force Manual (AFM) 88-22, "Structures to Resist the Effects of Accidental Explosions," November 28, 1990[2]

(o)   DDESB TP No. 10, Change 3, "Methodology For Chemical Hazard Prediction," June 1980[2]

(p)   American Society of Mechanical Engineers Boiler and Pressure Vessel Code, Section VIII, "Rules for Construction of Pressure Vessels," Division 1/Division 2, current version[4]

---

[1] Defense Automated Printing, 700 Robbins Avenue, Philadelphia, PA 19111; Phone: 215-697-2179

[2] Department of Defense Explosives Safety Board (DDESB), Room 856C, Hoffman Building I, 2461 Eisenhower Avenue, Alexandria, VA 22331-0600; Phone: 703-325-0891; Fax: 703-325-6227

[3] NFPA, 1 Batterymarch Park, Quincy, MA 02169-7471; Phone: 617-770-3000; Fax: 617-770-0700

[4] ASME International, 22 Law Drive, Box 2900, Fairfield, NJ 07007-2900; Phone: 800-843-2763; International: 973-882-1167; Fax: 973-882-1717

(q)   NFPA 30, "Flammable and Combustible Liquids Code," current version[3]

(r)   NFPA 70, "National Electric Code," current version[3]

(s)   NFPA 91, "Standard for Exhaust Systems for Air Conveying of Vapors, Gases, Mists, and Noncombustible Particulate Solids," current version[3]

(t)   NFPA 780, "Standard for the Installation of Lightning Protection Systems," current version[3]

(u)   NFPA 77, "Recommended Practice on Static Electricity," current version[3]

(v)   NFPA 10, "Standard for Portable Fire Extinguishers," current version[3]

(w)   NFPA 704, "Standard System for the Identification of the Hazards of Materials for Emergency Response," current version[3]

(x)   NFPA 13, "Standard for the Installation of Sprinkler Systems," current version[3]

(y)   NFPA 15, "Standard for Water Spray Fixed System for Fire Protection," current edition[3]

(z)   MIL-STD-882D, "Standard Practice for System Safety," February 10, 2000[1]

(aa) NFPA 101, "Life Safety Code," current edition[3]

(ab) NFPA 80, "Standard for Fire Doors and Other Opening Protectives," current edition[3]

(ac) NFPA 33, "Standard for Spray Application Using Flammable or Combustible Materials," current version[3]

(ad) Federal Aviation Administration Handbook[5]

(ae) DDESB TP No. 18, "Minimum Qualifications for Unexploded Ordnance (UXO) Technicians and Personnel," 20 December 2004[2]

(af) NFPA 430, "Code for the Storage of Liquid and Solid Oxidizers," current version[3]

(ag) Wilton, C., "Investigation of the Explosive Potential of the Hybrid Propellant Combinations N_2O_4/PBAN and CTF/PBAN," AFRPL-TR-67-124, 1967 (AD A003 595)[6]

(ah) NFPA 251, "Standard Methods of Tests of Fire Resistance of Building Construction and Material," current version[3]

(ai) NFPA 55, "Standard for the Storage, Use, and Handling of Compressed Gases and Cryogenic Fluids in Portable and Stationary Containers, Cylinders, and Tanks," current version[3]

(aj) Zabetakis, M. G. and Burgess, D. S., "Research on the Hazards Associated With the Production and Handling of Liquid Hydrogen," U.S. Department of the Interior, Bureau of Mines Report 5707, 1961[7]

---

[5] Available at http://nasdocs.faa.gov/nasiHTML/FAAStandards/faa-hdbk-006/HDBK006.pdf

[6] Defense Technical Information Center, Fort Belvoir, VA 22060; Phone: 800-225-3842

[7] Chemical Propulsion Information Agency, Accession Number 1964-0291, The Johns Hopkins University, 10630 Little Patuxent Parkway, Suite 202, Columbia, MD 21044-3204; Phone: 410-992-7300; Fax: 410-730-4969

C1. CHAPTER 1

INTRODUCTION

C1.1. PURPOSE

C1.1.1. This Manual provides safety requirements, guidance and information to minimize potential accidents that could interrupt Department of Defense (DoD) operations, delay DoD contract production, damage DoD property, cause injury to DoD personnel, or endanger the public during DoD contract work or services involving ammunition and explosives (AE). The Manual contains the minimum contractual safety requirements to support DoD objectives. These requirements are not a complete safety program, and this Manual does not relieve a contractor from complying with Federal, State, interstate, and local laws and regulations.

C1.1.2. Criteria provided by these Standards are provided in English units (e.g., ft, lb, psi) with metric equivalents shown in brackets (e.g., [m, kg, kPa]).

C1.2. APPLICABILITY. When included in or properly incorporated into their contracts, subcontracts, purchase orders, or other procurement methods and made applicable to the contractor (or to their subcontractors), these safety requirements apply to contractors and subcontractors handling ammunition or explosives. Nothing in this Manual should be construed as making the Department of Defense a controlling employer under Occupational Safety and Health Administration (OSHA) regulations and standards.

C1.3. MANDATORY REQUIREMENTS AND ADVISORY GUIDANCE. This Manual uses the term "shall" or an affirmative statement to indicate mandatory requirements. The terms "should" and "may" are advisory in nature.

C1.4. COMPLIANCE WITH MANDATORY REQUIREMENTS. The Department of Defense requires compliance with mandatory provisions of this Manual and applicable portions of Reference (c). In order to provide consistent and current information to all DoD AE contractors, quantity distance (QD) tables and formulae in Reference (c) are incorporated by reference in Chapter 5 of this Manual. The procuring contracting officers (PCOs) may grant contract-specific waivers to mandatory provisions of this Manual. For government-owned/contractor-operated facilities, requests for waivers of safety requirements shall be processed via the administrative contracting officer (ACO) or PCO through the explosives safety office of the Military Service that owns the facilities for review and approval in accordance with the Military Service requirements. For contractor-owned facilities, requests for waivers from mandatory provisions of this Manual shall be processed through the ACO to the PCO.

C1.4.1.1. In the pre-award phase, during pre-award surveys, noncompliance with mandatory safety requirements normally results in a recommendation of "no award." Any noncompliant condition shall be resolved during the pre-award survey. Contractors may choose to correct the deficiencies immediately, offer a letter of intent to correct the deficiencies (which will become binding upon award of contract), or request that the PCO accept specifically identified existing conditions of facilities (contract-specific waiver).

C1.4.1.2. In the post-award phase, the contractor has 30 days from the date of notification by the ACO to correct the non-compliant condition and inform the ACO of the corrective actions taken. The contracting officer may direct a different time period for the correction of any noncompliance. If the contractor refuses or fails to correct any noncompliance within the time period specified by the ACO, the Government has the right to direct the contractor to cease performance on all or part of affected contracts. When the contractor cannot comply with the mandatory safety requirements of the contract, the contractor may develop and submit a request for a waiver through the ACO to the PCO for the final determination. For DoD-owned, contractor-operated facilities, the PCO coordinates with the explosives safety office of the Military Service that owns the facilities for review and approval in accordance with the Military Service requirements. The request shall contain complete information concerning the requirements violated, actions planned to minimize the hazard, and a proposed date for correction of the non-compliant conditions.

C1.5. PRE-AWARD SAFETY SURVEY

C1.5.1. The PCO will request a DoD pre-award safety survey to help determine contractor capability. DoD safety personnel conduct pre-award surveys to evaluate each prospective contractor's ability to comply with contract safety requirements. While the pre-award safety survey is an opportunity for the contractor to request clarification of any safety requirement or other AE issue that may affect the contractor's ability to comply, any such clarification must be issued by the contracting officer. During pre-award surveys, the contractor shall provide:

C1.5.1.1. Site plans conforming to subparagraphs C1.8.5.1. through C1.8.5.5. for proposed facilities to be used in contract performance.

C1.5.1.2. Evidence of implementation of a safety program containing at least the mandatory requirements described in Chapter 3 of this Manual.

C1.5.1.3. General description of proposed contract facilities, including size, building layouts, construction details, and fire resistive capabilities.

C1.5.1.4. Fire prevention program and available firefighting resources, including local agreements or other documentation demonstrating coordination.

C1.5.1.5. Copies of required licenses and permits or demonstration of the ability to obtain approvals necessary to support the proposed contract.

CHAPTER 1

C1.5.1.6. A safety history including accident experience; safety survey or audit reports by insurance carriers or Federal, State, and local authorities; and any variances, exemptions, or waivers of safety or fire protection requirements issued by Federal, State, or local authorities.

C1.5.1.7. Proposed operations and equipment to include process flow narrative/diagram, proposed facility or equipment changes, proposed hazard analysis, and proposed procedures for all phases of AE operations.

C1.5.1.8. Subcontractor information.

C1.5.8.1. Identification of all subcontractors proposed for the AE work.

C1.5.8.2. Proposed methods used to evaluate the capability of the subcontractor to comply with the requirements of this Manual.

C1.5.8.3. Proposed methods used to ensure subcontractor compliance.

C1.6. PRE-OPERATIONAL SAFETY SURVEY

C1.6.1. The Department of Defense reserves the right to conduct a pre-operational survey after contract award in these situations:

C1.6.1.1. Contractor has limited experience with the item.

C1.6.1.2. After major new construction.

C1.6.1.3. After major modifications.

C1.6.1.4. After an AE accident.

C1.6.2. When these situations occur, the contractor shall provide sufficient notification to the ACO and Defense Contract Management Agency (DCMA) contract safety personnel, to provide adequate time for the Department of Defense to schedule and perform a preoperational survey.

C1.7. POST-AWARD CONTRACTOR RESPONSIBILITIES. The contractor shall:

C1.7.1. Comply with the requirements of this Manual and any other safety requirements contained within the contract.

C1.7.2. Develop and implement a demonstrable safety program, including operational procedures, intended to prevent AE-related accidents.

C1.7.3. Designate qualified individuals to administer and implement this safety program.

C1.7.4. Prepare and keep available for review all hazard analyses used to justify alternative methods of hazards control implemented in order to comply with the mandatory requirements in this Manual.

C1.7.5. http://cyberregs.citation.com/cgi-exe/cpage.dll - pagelist#pagelistProvide access to facilities and safety program documentation to DoD safety representatives.

C1.7.6. Report and investigate AE accidents in accordance with Chapter 2 of this Manual.

C1.7.7. Provide identification and location of subcontractors to the ACO for notification or approval in accordance with terms of the contract.

C1.7.8. Establish and implement management controls to ensure AE subcontractors comply with paragraphs C1.7.1. through C1.7.7. of this section.

C1.8. SITE AND CONSTRUCTION PLANS

C1.8.1. Contractors shall maintain a current site plan that demonstrates compliance with QD requirements for all AE locations within their facility. In addition, contractors shall prepare and submit site and construction plans for all new construction or major modification of facilities for AE activities and for any facilities potentially exposed to AE hazards if improperly located. Contractors shall provide copies of any of these documents to the Department of Defense upon request. For DoD facilities, site plans are required per paragraph C5.4.1. of Reference (c).

C1.8.2. When the place of performance of the contract is at DoD-owned/contractor-operated facilities, site and construction plans shall be prepared and processed via the ACO and/or PCO through the explosives safety office of the Military Service that owns the facilities for review and approval in accordance with Reference (c) and the Military Service requirements.

C1.8.3. For contractor-owned, contractor-operated (COCO) facilities, the contractor shall submit, through the ACO to the PCO, site and construction plans for all new construction or major modification of facilities for AE activities and for the facilities that may be exposed to AE hazards if improperly located. The contractor shall provide sufficient copies for the review process. The contractor shall not begin construction or modification of proposed facilities until receiving site and construction plan approval from the PCO through the ACO.

C1.8.4. Minor new construction, changes, and modifications of existing COCO AE facilities involving hazard division (HD) or changes that add or remove small portable operating buildings and magazines may not require formal site plan submission. "Minor" applies to all changes that involve only 1.4S HD materials. "Minor" also applies to changes of other HD materials that do not increase the existing net explosive weight for quantity distance (NEWQD) or maximum credible event (MCE) for an AE facility and that do not extend any QD arcs beyond existing inhabited building and public traffic route distance (PTRD) arcs. The contractor shall notify the ACO of a potential minor modification or change and request a determination.

C1.8.5. Site plans shall comply with the following:

C1.8.5.1. Plans shall include maps and drawings which are legible, accurate, and of a scale that permits easy determination of essential details. For general layout of buildings, this is normally a scale of 1 inch to 400 ft (or metric equivalent) or less. Site plans may require other-scaled drawings, which provide details of construction, structure relationships within the project area, barricades, or other unique details. Plans may also include pictures to illustrate details and videotapes of MCE testing data.

C1.8.5.2. Maps and drawings shall identify distances between all potential explosion sites (PESs), all exposed sites (ESs) within the facility, the facility boundary, any additional property under contractor control, ESs on adjacent property when applicable, public railways and highways, power transmission lines, and other utilities.

C1.8.5.3. Plans shall identify and briefly describe all PESs and all ESs within any applicable inhabited building distance (IBD) of a PES. Site plans for major new construction or modification shall also identify and briefly describe all PESs whose IBD arc includes the proposed new or modified site. Fragmentation distances shall be included for IBD arcs, when applicable. Plans shall identify and briefly describe all PESs and all ESs out to 110 percent of IBD of a PES.

C1.8.5.4. Plans shall include the maximum net explosive weight(s) (NEW(s)) and the HD of all PESs and, when applicable, shall include MCE information and maximum NEW for each room or bay. Plans shall also include engineering or test data when substituting construction or shielding for distance to protect from fragmentation or overpressure.

C1.8.5.5. Personnel in buildings are provided a high degree of protection; however, glass breakage and building debris may cause some injuries to personnel. New or modified facilities, located within the IBD arc of any PES, that will include glass panels and will contain personnel shall have a glass breakage personnel hazards risk assessment conducted. Elimination of glass surfaces is the best control. If determined to be necessary, reducing the use of glass or the size of any glass surfaces and the use of blast resistant glass will provide some relief. For new construction, building design characteristics, to include consideration of how any required glass surfaces are oriented and use of blast resistant glass can reduce glass breakage and structural damage.

C1.8.5.6. Plans shall include a topographical map in sufficient detail to permit evaluation when the contractor uses natural terrain for barricading to reduce fragment distance.

C1.8.6. Construction plans for proposed facilities shall contain the information required in subparagraphs C1.8.5.1. through C1.8.5.5. as well as construction details of dividing walls, venting surfaces, firewalls, roofs, operational shields, barricades, exits, ventilation systems and equipment, AE waste disposal systems, lightning protection systems, grounding systems, processing equipment auxiliary support structures, and general materials of construction, as applicable.

C2. CHAPTER 2

ACCIDENT INVESTIGATION AND REPORTING

C2.1. <u>GENERAL</u>. This section contains requirements for investigating and reporting accidents involving AE. Nothing in the reporting requirements contained in this Manual relieves the contractor from notifying Federal, State, or local agencies.

C2.2. <u>REPORTING CRITERIA</u>. Per Reference (c) and DoDI 6055.7 (Reference (e)), the contractor shall investigate and report all AE accidents that result in one or more of the below listed outcomes to the ACO and the cognizant DCMA contract safety specialist. The ACO/DCMA contract safety specialist shall notify the Service and the Service shall notify the DDESB.

C2.2.1. One or more fatalities.

C2.2.2. One or more lost-work day cases with days away from work as defined by part 1904 of title 29, CFR (Reference (f)).

C2.2.3. Five or more non-fatal injuries (with or without lost workdays).

C2.2.4. Damage to government property exceeding $20,000.

C2.2.5. Delay in delivery schedule exceeding 24 hours. (This requirement does not constitute a waiver or amendment of any delivery schedule required by the contract.)

C2.2.6. Contractually required notifications of accidents other than in paragraphs C2.2.1. through C2.2.5.

C2.2.7. Any accident that may degrade operational or production capability or is likely to arouse media interest.

C2.3. <u>ACCIDENT INVESTIGATION REQUIREMENTS</u>. The contractor is contractually responsible for investigating and reporting AE accidents; however, the Government retains the right to conduct an independent DoD investigation when circumstances warrant. DCMA safety representatives will monitor contractor on-site accident investigations but will not formally participate. Contractors experiencing an AE accident shall take those actions necessary to protect life and health, limit property damage, and preserve evidence at the accident scene. In the initial telephonic and written accident reports (See sections C2.4 and C2.5) the contractor shall advise the contracting officer and the DCMA safety representative of the incident. Based on initial reports, the contracting officer may require an additional, more comprehensive technical investigation by the contractor or by an independent DoD investigation team.

C2.4. <u>TELEPHONE REPORT</u>. The contractor shall report any accident described in section C2.2. by telephone, with e-mail confirmation to the ACO and cognizant DCMA contract safety specialist as soon as practicable but not later than 3 hours after the accident. The telephone report with e-mail confirmation should use the report format outlined in section C2.5. and provide all preliminary accident information available.

C2.5. <u>WRITTEN REPORT</u>

C2.5.1. The contractor shall submit a written report by the end of the second business day after accident occurrence to the ACO and the cognizant DCMA contract safety specialist who shall route to the Service. The Service shall route to the DDESB. This report may be provided electronically or in hard copy. The report shall include:

C2.5.1.1. Contractor's name and location.

C2.5.1.2. Date, local time, plant or facility location of the accident.

C2.5.1.3. Type of accident (explosion, fire, loss, other).

C2.5.1.4. Contract, subcontract, or purchase order.

C2.5.1.5. Item nomenclature, hazard classification, lot number.

C2.5.1.6. Accident narrative.

C2.5.1.7. Number of fatalities, injuries, degree of injuries.

C2.5.1.8. Description of property damage and actual or estimated cost.

C2.5.1.9. Quantity of energetic material involved (weight, units, rounds).

C2.5.1.10. Probable cause(s).

C2.5.1.11. Corrective action taken or planned.

C2.5.1.12. Summary of Lessons Learned and Recommendations.

C2.5.1.13. Effect on production.

C2.5.1.14. Name, title or position, and phone number of person submitting the report.

C2.5.1.15. Remarks.

C2.5.2. The contractor shall provide to the ACO, DCMA contract safety specialist, and, through the Service, to DDESB supplemental information to the initial report within 30 days of the accident occurrence and at 30-day intervals until the investigation is complete.

C2.6. <u>TECHNICAL ACCIDENT INVESTIGATION AND REPORT</u>. Based upon the seriousness of the accident and criticality of the munitions or explosives involved, the PCO may require an additional, more comprehensive technical investigation by the contractor or by an independent DoD investigation team. Upon determination by the PCO that a DoD investigation is required, the PCO will immediately advise the contractor. The technical investigation report shall include details such as missile fragmentation maps, photographs, detailed description of accident, event time line, chemistry, effects on adjacent operations, structural and equipment damage, QD drawings, findings, and conclusions. If the contractor performs the special technical accident investigation, the contractor shall forward the report through the ACO to the PCO within 60 days unless otherwise directed by the PCO. Any of these investigations and studies reports shall also be submitted through the Service to the DDESB.

C3. CHAPTER 3

GENERAL SAFETY REQUIREMENTS

C3.1. GENERAL. This chapter provides general safety requirements for all AE operations addressed in this Manual. When these practices exceed or differ from local or national codes or requirements, the more restrictive shall apply.

C3.2. PERSONNEL AND MATERIAL LIMITS

C3.2.1. The cardinal principle of AE safety is to limit exposure to a minimum number of personnel, for a minimum amount of time, to the minimum amount of the hazardous material consistent with safe and efficient operations. To implement this principle, contractors shall establish AE and personnel limits at all AE operations. Contractors shall examine all operations and devise methods for reducing the number of people exposed, the time of exposure, and the quantity of material subject to a single incident.

C3.2.2. Determination of AE limits requires a careful analysis of all facts including normal operation times, intraplant transportation methods, net explosive weight, and the chemical and physical characteristics of the AE. More sensitive and more energetic hazardous materials require lower limits. Contractors shall base limits on safe and efficient operational requirements and not on the maximum quantity of explosives allowed by QD requirements. Contractors may express limits either in units of weight or in the number of each item (tray, box, rack, or other unit) that operators can more easily observe and control.

C3.2.3. Determination of personnel limits requires separation of unrelated jobs and controlled limited access of unrelated personnel from a particular hazardous operation. Hazard analysis shall determine the need for dividing walls, firewalls, or operational shields to protect operators at frequent, consecutive operations in the same room or building. Personnel limits shall include a maximum number of operators and a maximum number of transients including supervisors, workers, and visitors.

C3.2.4. Military Services may have documentation which requires contractors to use special procedures for developing standard operating procedures (SOPs). Therefore, before starting operations involving AE, qualified personnel shall develop, review, and approve written procedures in accordance with the Military Services guidelines or the instructions below.

C3.3. SOPs. Clearly written procedures are essential to avoid operator errors and ensure process control. Therefore, before starting operations involving AE, qualified personnel shall develop, review, and approve written procedures.

C3.3.1. <u>Preparation</u>. Contractors shall examine all aspects of an AE operation and shall determine a safe and orderly course of action for accomplishing the work. Certain AE operations may require controlled tests to validate the safety of procedural steps in the SOP. At a minimum, SOPs shall include:

C3.3.1.1. The specific hazards associated with the process.

C3.3.1.2. Indicators for identifying abnormal process conditions.

C3.3.1.3. Emergency procedures. (SOP may include a separate emergency procedure SOP by reference.)

C3.3.1.4. Personal protective clothing and equipment required for process personnel.

C3.3.1.5. Personnel and AE limits.

C3.3.1.6. Specific equipment, tools, and expendable supplies permitted for use by the process operator.

C3.3.1.7. The location and sequence of job steps the operator is to follow in performing the work.

C3.3.1.8. Instructions for spill cleanup and disposal of any scrap and waste AE.

C3.3.2. <u>Dissemination and Posting</u>. The supervisors shall be responsible for explaining duties prescribed by the SOP to all personnel involved in an AE operation. Written operating procedures need not be posted, but shall be available at the workstation to personnel involved in AE processes and operations or AE equipment maintenance.

C3.3.3. <u>Training</u>. Personnel shall receive appropriate training before performing work that involves exposure to AE. The training shall include specific safety and health hazards, emergency procedures including shutdown, and safe work practices applicable to the employee's job tasks. The contractor shall ensure that each employee involved in an AE process has received and understood the training and receives appropriate refresher training. The contractor shall prepare a record that contains the identity of the employee, the date of training, and the means used to verify that the employee understood the training.

C3.3.4. <u>Emergency Procedures</u>. The contractor shall instruct employees on procedures to follow in the event of electrical storms, utility or mechanical failures, equipment failures, process abnormalities, and other emergencies occurring during AE operations.

CHAPTER 3

C3.3.5. <u>Control and Monitoring</u>. The contractor shall establish and maintain written procedures that define methods for controlling and monitoring outside subcontractors who perform work on the contractor's premises that may affect AE operations. The procedures shall also include: the method used by the contractor to determine that subcontractors are qualified to perform the work safely; and the steps that will be followed by the contractor to limit the subcontractors' exposure to AE operations.

C3.3.6. <u>Revalidation</u>. The managing authority shall ensure that qualified personnel review and update SOPs as often as necessary to reflect improved methods, equipment substitutions, facility modifications, or process changes.

C3.4. <u>STORAGE IN OPERATING BUILDINGS</u>

C3.4.1. The contractor may store limited quantities of hazardous materials in Classes 2 through 9, as defined by part 173 of title 49, CFR (Reference (g)), which are essential for current operations in an operating building.

C3.4.2. The contractor shall store AE materials that exceed the minimum quantity necessary for sustained operations in a service magazine located no closer than intraline distance (ILD) (based on the quantity in the magazine) from the operating building or area. If ILD is not available for a separate service magazine, the contractor may designate storage locations closer than the ILD or within the operating building. The NEW of AE in any designated outside storage location at less than ILD shall be added to the NEW in the operating building and shall be considered as part of the operating building when measuring QD separation distances to other ESs. Designated storage locations must be located at distances to prevent immediate propagation of the stored AE in the event of an explosion in the operating area. The quantity of AE material in the designated storage location shall not exceed that needed for one half of a work shift. The contractor should consider personnel exposure, structural containment afforded, and the venting ability of the proposed storage location when determining where to locate a designated storage location. When storage containers are designed to completely contain all fragments, debris, and overpressure, AE material may be stored without regard to QD requirements listed in paragraph C5.1.2. In-process AE materials and subassemblies awaiting subsequent steps in the manufacturing process are not considered storage and are not subject to the half of a work shift limitation.

C3.4.3. At the end of the workday, personnel should remove all AE material from processing equipment and store it in an appropriate magazine or designated storage location. If operationally required, personnel may store in-process AE materials in the building during non-operating hours provided the physical characteristics and stability of the AE materials are not degraded and the AE material would not compromise the safety of the process equipment or personnel when the process is restarted.

C3.4.4. The contractor may use a separate enclosed room or bay in an operating building specifically adapted for the interim storage of production items awaiting the results of testing before final pack-out. The NEW of the interim storage facility shall be added to the total NEW of the operating building for QD determination. The room or bay must afford the equivalent of service magazine distance protection to other parts of the building. Such a room or bay is limited to its defined and designed function and items, but is not subject to the one half of a work shift limitation for the building or the ultimate pack-out operation.

C3.5. HOUSEKEEPING IN HAZARDOUS AREAS

C3.5.1. Contractors shall keep structures containing AE clean and orderly.

C3.5.2. Contractors shall establish a regular cleaning program to maintain safe conditions. Personnel shall not perform general cleaning concurrently with hazardous operations.

C3.5.3. Explosives and explosive dusts shall not be allowed to accumulate on structural members, radiators, heating coils, steam, gas, air or water supply pipes, or electrical fixtures.

C3.5.4. Contractors shall use proper design of equipment, training of employees, and catch or splash pans to prevent spillage of explosives and other hazardous materials. Operators shall promptly remove spillage of explosives and hazardous materials following proper procedures established per section C8.4.

C3.5.5. Personnel shall use cleaning methods, such as hot water, steam, etc., that do not create ignition hazards for cleaning floors in buildings containing explosives. When these methods are impractical, personnel may use nonabrasive sweeping compounds that are compatible with the explosives involved. Flammable compounds shall not be used. Combustible sweeping compounds (closed cup flash point less than 230°F) are acceptable for use. Personnel shall not use sweeping compounds containing wax on conductive floors if the wax can reduce conductivity. Personnel shall not use cleaning agents containing alkalis in areas with nitrated organic explosives, since these materials are incompatible and can form sensitive explosive compounds.

C3.5.6. Cleaning methods may use nonferrous wire brushes to clean explosives-processing equipment only when other methods of cleaning are ineffective. A thorough inspection should follow such cleaning to ensure that no wire bristles remain in the equipment. This also applies to cleaning magnesium ingot or other metal molds used in explosives processing. Cleaning methods should substitute fiber brushes for hairbrushes to reduce generation of static.

C3.5.7. Contractors shall dispose of all loose explosives swept up from floors of operating buildings. Responsible personnel shall thoroughly inspect and determine disposition of explosives recovered from sources other than ammunition breakdown operations and equipment.

C3.6. EXPLOSIVES WASTE IN OPERATING AREAS

C3.6.1. Explosives safety shall not be compromised while meeting environmental considerations.

C3.6.2. All waste material generated in an explosives area shall require analysis to determine appropriate methods for safe handling and disposition. All explosives waste and contaminated materials shall be kept in covered containers marked to indicate their contents, preferably located in isolated bays or outside the buildings.

C3.6.3. Containers for scrap black powder shall contain water. Waste pyrotechnic, tracer, flare, and similar compositions shall be totally immersed in water, mineral oil, or fuel oil in the waste containers, unless a hazard analysis indicates that it is unnecessary. Waste-initiating explosives shall be kept to a minimum, usually under water or other desensitizing media, and shall be handled with great care. Explosives waste materials should not be left in operating buildings overnight during normal periods of shutdown or over weekends and holidays.

C3.6.4. Workers shall transport explosives wastes in designated vehicles (see section C3.16., paragraph C8.3.12., and subparagraph C15.8.3.1.) to storage locations specifically assigned for that purpose. Explosives waste shall not be stored with serviceable explosives. A minimum of magazine distance shall be maintained between locations where explosives wastes are stored and locations used for serviceable AE.

C3.7. PROCEDURE BEFORE ELECTRICAL STORMS

C3.7.1. A system for monitoring the approach of electrical storms shall be established that provides for the timely shut down of operations and evacuation of personnel from PESs where lightning could initiate explosives. When an electrical storm approaches, all personnel shall evacuate to at least PTRD, or a shelter providing equivalent protection, from:

C3.7.1.1. Operating buildings or facilities containing explosives or explosives-loaded ammunition not equipped with lightning protection systems.

C3.7.1.2. Buildings containing explosives dust or vapors, whether or not equipped with lightning protection systems.

C3.7.1.3. Magazines, open storage sites, or loading docks not equipped with lightning protection systems.

C3.7.1.4. Locations, with or without lightning protection, where operations involving unprotected electro-explosive devices (EEDs) or circuitry are being performed.

C3.7.2. Contractors shall prepare an SOP for electrical storms that defines distances from lightning strikes that trigger an evacuation and provide adequate time for employees to shut down AE operations. The SOP shall establish instructions for notification of affected employees and shall identify safe locations at PTRD (or equivalent protection) to which employees retreat when notified of electrical storm evacuation. Explosives processes requiring constant attention should not be started when an electrical storm threatens.

C3.7.3. During evacuation of explosives buildings due to approaching electrical storms, some operations may still require constant attention. The minimum number of personnel, consistent with safety requirements, shall work these operations until the process reaches a condition that allows personnel to safely evacuate the building. Explosives processes requiring constant attention should not be started when an electrical storm threatens.

C3.8. PRECAUTIONS FOR MAINTENANCE AND REPAIRS TO AE EQUIPMENT AND BUILDINGS

C3.8.1. Before maintenance or repairs can proceed in areas or on equipment previously exposed to explosives; operators shall decontaminate the AE areas and equipment to the degree necessary to perform the work safely and shall place a decontamination tag, signed by the supervisor, on the equipment. The tag shall certify the removal of all explosives from the equipment. When complete removal of explosives is not possible, the tag shall identify areas and parts of the equipment that operators could not clean and shall provide maintenance personnel with specific instructions for safe handling. Prior to maintenance or repair operations, the immediate vicinity shall be inspected to assure no explosives remain.

C3.8.2. Contractors shall establish written procedures that require responsible personnel to clean and decontaminate all AE areas where accumulated AE residue may pose a hazard (i.e., equipment, crevices, vents, ducts, wall cavities, pipes, and fittings) before performing maintenance or repair operations. The decontamination procedures shall apply to tooling and equipment previously exposed to AE, whether removed from or remaining in the AE area for maintenance and repair.

C3.8.3. The contractor shall examine and test all new or repaired AE processing equipment prior to placing the equipment in service in order to ensure that it is safe to operate.

C3.8.4. After repairing, maintaining, or adjusting machines and equipment, an inspection shall be made to assure all tools used for the work are removed. Before work resumes, operators should check their own equipment to ensure its safe operating condition.

C3.8.5. Electricians shall not wear conductive shoes while working on electrical equipment. Exposed explosives and other static-sensitive hazardous material shall be removed before work begins.

C3.8.6. Safe practices specified elsewhere in this Manual shall also apply to maintenance employees.

C3.8.7. Maintenance and tool rooms in an operating line should be separated from explosives by ILD. When ILD is not available, a suitable barrier or shield shall provide equivalent protection. Protective construction designs require DDESB approval for facilities on DoD property. (See paragraph C5.1.2.)

C3.9. SAFETY HAND-TOOLS

C3.9.1. Unless a hazard analysis indicates otherwise, only hand tools constructed of wood or non-sparking metals such as bronze, lead, and "K" Monel shall be used for work in locations and on equipment that contain exposed explosives or hazardous concentrations of flammable dusts, gases, or vapors that are susceptible to mechanical spark. Hand tools shall be cleaned and inspected prior to use. Be aware that nonferrous metals used in so-called non-sparking tools may produce sparks. If the use of ferrous metal tools is required because of their strength and wear characteristics, the contractor's safety office shall approve their use.

C3.9.2. If their strength makes the use of ferrous metal hand tools necessary during maintenance and repair operations, exposed explosives and other highly flammable and combustible materials shall be removed from the area. In addition, explosives operations in the immediate vicinity shall be discontinued to guard against accidental ignition of materials by flying sparks, and potential contact surfaces should be oiled or covered to reduce the likelihood of sparks.

C3.10. OPERATIONAL SHIELDS

C3.10.1. The purpose of operational shields is to prevent propagation of AE material from one AE operation or location to another, protect facilities and equipment, and provide personnel protection. Shields used for these purposes require an evaluation to determine their suitability for their intended purpose (paragraph C5.1.2.). All AE operations and processes require a hazard assessment prior to work performance to determine the type of hazard involved, the level of risk associated with the AE material or item, and the corresponding level of protection required.

C3.10.2. The primary hazards that accompany explosions and deflagrations are blast overpressure, fragmentation (primary and secondary), and thermal effects. The hazard assessment shall consider these hazards and the quantity of AE materials, initiation sensitivity, heat output, burn rate, potential ignition and initiation sources, protection capabilities of shields, various types of protective clothing, fire protection systems, and the acute and chronic health hazards of vapors and combustion products on exposed personnel.

C3.10.3. When the hazard assessment indicates an unacceptable probability of explosion or deflagration, operations or processes shall be conducted remotely. When an analysis of the hazard assessment indicates the hazards associated with an explosion or deflagration are controllable by using operational shields, the contractor shall design, install, and use shields that effectively protect personnel from the hazards. Shields complying with MIL-STD-398 (Reference (h)) are acceptable protection.

C3.10.4. The contractor shall test operational shields under conditions that simulate the operational environment. AE materials or items used in the test shall correspond to those involved in an MCE, plus 25 percent. The contractor shall maintain records of the tests that demonstrate the shields will function as planned. Analysis rather than testing of shields may be acceptable on a case-by-case basis.

C3.10.5. When the doors of AE processing equipment function as operational shields, interlocking devices shall prevent the operator from opening the door while the equipment is in operation or operating the equipment when the door is open.

C3.11. PROTECTIVE CLOTHING

C3.11.1. All AE operations require a hazard assessment to determine the need for protective clothing and personal protective equipment. The assessment shall include an evaluation of all hazards and factors contained in paragraph C3.11.2.

C3.11.2. The contractor shall provide a changing area for employees who must remove their street clothes to wear protective clothing, such as explosive plant clothing, anti-contamination clothing, or impervious clothing. To minimize the risk of exposure to unrelated personnel, AE operators shall not remove contaminated clothing from the AE areas. Employees shall not wear any static-producing clothing in areas where electrostatic discharge (ESD) is a hazard.

C3.11.3. Explosives plant clothing, generally referred to as powder uniforms, shall have nonmetallic fasteners and be easily removable.

C3.11.4. When sending explosives-contaminated clothing to an off-plant laundry facility, the contractor is responsible for informing the laundry of the hazards associated with the contaminants and any special laundering or disposal requirements.

C3.12. MATERIAL HANDLING EQUIPMENT

C3.12.1. The contractor shall not refuel gasoline, diesel, or liquefied petroleum gas (LPG) powered equipment inside buildings containing AE. Personnel shall locate refueling vehicles and refueling operations at least 100 ft [30.48m] (50 ft [15.24] from non-combustible structures) from structures or sites containing AE. This distance is called the fire protection distance. Doors and windows through which vapors may enter the building shall be closed during refueling.

CHAPTER 3

C3.12.2. The contractor shall store gasoline-, diesel-, and LPG-powered equipment at the appropriate fire protection distance from buildings, loading docks, or piers containing AE.

C3.12.3. Gasoline-, diesel-, and LPG-powered equipment shall have spark arrestors. The contractor shall perform and document inspections of the exhaust and electrical systems of the equipment, as necessary, to ensure that the systems are functioning within the manufacturer's specifications. The contractor shall maintain documentation of the two most recent inspections.

C3.13. IGNITION SOURCES IN HAZARDOUS AREAS

C3.13.1. Personnel shall not carry matches, cigarette lighters, or other flame-producing devices into AE areas.

C3.13.2. Smoking in AE operating areas shall be permitted in approved locations only.

C3.14. OPERATIONAL EXPLOSIVES CONTAINERS

C3.14.1. Containers used for intraplant transportation or temporary storage of process explosives and energetic materials shall be designed to prevent leakage. These containers shall be equipped with covers (lids) and should be constructed of (in order of precedence):

C3.14.1.1. Conductive rubber or conductive plastic;

C3.14.1.2. Nonferrous metal-lined boxes without seams or rivet heads under which explosive dusts could accumulate;

C3.14.1.3. Paper-lined wooden boxes; or

C3.14.1.4. Fiber drums.

C3.14.2. These containers shall be marked with the name, hazard division, and quantity of the explosive involved.

C3.14.3. Because of their fragility and potential for fragmentation, glass containers shall not be used for explosives.

C3.15. INTRAPLANT RAIL TRANSPORTATION

C3.15.1. Written Procedures. The contractor shall develop written procedures to ensure safe and efficient rail movement of AE. These procedures shall include, as a minimum, the following information:

C3.15.1.1. The contractor shall maintain all rolling stock used for intraplant rail transportation of AE in a safe and good working condition.

C3.15.1.2. Before moving cars containing A&E, air hoses shall be coupled, air brakes shall be cut-in and in proper working order, and the car doors shall be closed. Cars should remain coupled while in motion. Safety precautions shall be observed when breaking air hose connections.

C3.15.1.3. When single explosives-loaded cars are spotted, the hand brakes shall be set and the wheels shall be properly chocked. When more than one car is spotted and its engine detached, the hand brakes shall be set on enough cars to ensure sufficient braking. Hand brakes shall be set on the downgrade end of the cut of rail cars. Automatic air brakes should not be relied on to hold spotted cars.

C3.15.1.4. A person should be stationed at the hand brake of a car mover when the car mover is in use.

C3.15.1.5. During transfer movements within establishments, full or partial loads of AE in rail cars shall be blocked and braced so they cannot shift position. Movements within classification yards are switch movements and do not require blocking and bracing.

C3.15.1.6. Empty rail cars shall remain at warehouses, magazines, buildings, or loading docks until all warning placards have been removed or reversed, as appropriate.

C3.15.1.7. Special care shall be taken to avoid rough handling of cars containing AE. These cars shall not be "sent off" while in motion and shall be carefully coupled to avoid unnecessary shocks. Other cars shall not be "cut off" and allowed to strike a car containing explosives.

C3.15.1.8. A buffer car should separate rail cars containing explosives and the switching engine when in motion.

C3.15.1.9. Flags or signals at both ends of a rail car or cut of cars shall protect personnel working in, on, or under the cars. During these periods, cars shall not be coupled or moved.

C3.15.1.10. Portable transmitters and railroad locomotives equipped with two-way radios shall not transmit when passing explosives-operating buildings where EEDs are present. The contractor shall determine minimum safe distances based on radio frequency and power output of the transmitter.

C3.15.2. Pre-loading Rail Car Inspections

C3.15.2.1. Qualified personnel shall inspect empty rail cars intended to transport AE upon arrival, verifying that the carrier has complied with Department of Transportation (DOT) requirements.

C3.15.2.2. Before loading, the brakes shall be set on cars spotted for loading, and bridge plates equipped with side boards and stops shall be provided.

C3.15.3. Loaded Incoming Rail Car Inspections

C3.15.3.1. Incoming railroad cars loaded with AE should be inspected upon arrival at remote sites. If no problems are found, rail cars may be opened for interior inspection or moved to the designated unloading point. Only operations addressed in paragraph C5.18.9. are allowed without application of QD.

C3.15.3.2. Railcars loaded with AE that are suspected of being in a hazardous condition shall be moved to a suspect car site that is separated from other PESs or ESs by the applicable QD criteria (paragraph C5.18.12.).

C3.15.3.3. Cars should be inspected after unloading AE to ensure that they are clean and free from loose explosives and flammable materials and that placards and car certificates have been removed. Explosives swept from the floors shall be disposed of properly.

C3.16. INTRAPLANT MOTOR VEHICLE TRANSPORTATION OF AE

C3.16.1. Written Procedures. The contractor shall develop written procedures to ensure safe and efficient transportation of AE in motor vehicles. These procedures shall include, as a minimum:

C3.16.1.1. Brakes shall be set and the wheels chocked when the possibility exists that the vehicle could move during loading or unloading.

C3.16.1.2. AE shall not be loaded or unloaded when a motor vehicle's engine is running, unless the engine is providing power to accessories used in the loading and unloading, such as mechanical handling equipment. If the engine is diesel powered, it may continue to run during loading or unloading of explosives except when exposed explosives are involved.

C3.16.1.3. Vehicles, including partly or completely loaded flatbeds, shall have the load blocked and braced to prevent shifting during transit.

C3.16.1.4. The operator shall not transport AE material in the passenger compartment of the vehicle.

C3.16.1.5. Motor vehicles transporting AE within the establishment but outside the explosives area shall bear at least two appropriate placards identifying the hazard division of the AE. These placards should be removed or covered whenever the vehicle is not loaded. Reflectorized placards are preferred.

C3.16.1.6. The vehicle operator shall be trained in emergency procedures to be followed in the event of a vehicle fire, breakdown, accident, damaged or leaking containers, and spilled AE material.

C3.16.2. <u>Pre-loading Motor Vehicle Inspections</u>. All motor vehicles used to transport AE shall be inspected daily before loading to verify:

C3.16.2.1. Vehicles are in a safe operating condition.

C3.16.2.2. Batteries and wiring are not in contact with containers of AE.

C3.16.2.3. Exposed ferrous metal in the interior of the vehicle body is covered with non-sparking material when scrap and bulk explosives are being transported in containers that could be damaged or when explosives could otherwise become exposed.

C3.16.2.4. A serviceable portable fire extinguisher of the appropriate class is carried on the motor vehicle.

C3.16.2.5. Motor vehicles or equipment with internal combustion engines that are used near explosives scrap, waste, or items contaminated with explosives are equipped with exhaust system spark arresters and carburetor flame arresters (authorized air cleaners). These vehicles and equipment should be inspected and cleaned to prevent accumulation of carbon.

C3.16.3. <u>Loaded Incoming Motor Vehicle Inspections</u>

C3.16.3.1. Vehicles loaded with AE should be inspected upon arrival at remote sites. If no problems are found, vehicles may be opened for interior inspection or moved to the designated unloading location. (See paragraph C5.18.9.)

C3.16.3.2. Motor vehicles loaded with AE that are suspected of being in a hazardous condition shall be moved to a suspect truck site that is separated from other PESs or ESs by the applicable QD criteria. (See paragraph C5.18.12.)

C3.16.3.3. Vehicles should be inspected after unloading AE to ensure that they are clean and free from loose explosives and flammable materials and that placards and vehicle certificates have been removed. Explosives waste cleaned and removed from the floors shall be disposed of properly.

C3.17. <u>INSPECTION OF AE MIXING EQUIPMENT</u>. For all AE mixing equipment, the contractor shall establish a preventive maintenance program that includes an initial inspection prior to use and periodic inspections throughout their operating life.

C3.17.1. The initial inspection shall, as a minimum, include radiographic and dye penetrant inspection of the blades and blade-to-shaft areas, blade-to-bowl clearances, allowable tolerances, testing for proper function of operating systems such as bowl lifting and positioning mechanisms, safety interlocks, fire detection and prevention, and test of computer controller software self-check.

C3.17.2. Periodic inspection shall be performed during the operating life of the mixer. The inspection program shall be based on manufacturer's recommendations, operating history of like mixers, and any items identified in hazards analysis of the particular mixer and its operation. The inspection program shall include:

C3.17.2.1. Tests and visual inspection prior to each use of the mixer, associated equipment, and hardware that might come loose and fall into the mixer.

C3.17.2.2. Periodic inspections of clearances between mixer blades and between mixer blades and all mix bowls at sufficient points to detect any distortion of the mixer blades or bowl. Clearances between blades and between blades and mixer bowls shall be established consistent with quality and process requirements, and should provide for deflection of shafts and wear in journal and bearing areas. These clearances shall be checked at regular intervals based on operating time and experience to assure the clearance is adequate. A record of clearance checks, mixer blade adjustments, and any damage to the mixer blades and bowls shall be maintained.

C3.17.2.3. Inspection and test for drive system wear, bearings condition, and gear alignment while under load to establish operation within tolerances when applicable.

C3.17.2.4. Inspection and test of proper function of operating subsystems such as bowl handling and lifting mechanism, safety and fire control, and computer software self-check.

C3.17.3. Recommend that large (over 80 gallon) vertical blade mixers in high torque applications have a dye penetrant check of the blades annually or after every 300 hours of operation. Melt-cast kettles are not considered high torque mixers. Also recommend that an inspection of clearances and operating systems be performed after any major maintenance or unusual events such as severe weather exposure, earthquakes, mishandling of bowl or mixer, or long idle period.

C3.17.4. After performing major maintenance of the equipment, the contractor shall run the equipment under load to ensure it is safe to operate.

C3.17.5. A log of the maintenance and inspection shall be maintained. Trend analysis of clearances should be used to detect wear that might become hazardous.

C4. CHAPTER 4

HAZARD CLASSIFICATION AND
STORAGE COMPATIBILITY SYSTEMS

C4.1. HAZARD CLASSIFICATION

C4.1.1. The DoD hazard classification system is based on the system recommended for international use by the United Nations Organization. It consists of nine hazard classes plus a non-regulated category that applies when explosives and hazardous materials are present in an item, but not to the degree that criteria for assignment to one of the nine classes are met. AE is assigned to the class that represents an item's predominant hazard characteristic. Class 1 applies to AE in which the explosive hazard predominates. The six Class 1 divisions and three division 1.2 subdivisions (subdivisions are only applicable for storage applications) that are outlined in subparagraphs C4.1.1.1.- C4.1.1.6. are used to indicate the character and predominance of explosive hazards. In addition, a parenthetical number is used to indicate the minimum separation distance (in hundreds of feet) for protection from debris, fragments, and firebrands, when distance alone is relied on for such protection. This number is placed to the left of the hazard classification designators 1.1 through 1.3, e.g., (18)1.1, (03)1.2.3, or (02)1.3. To simply express an item's hazard classification, this Manual uses the term "Hazard Division (HD)" to avoid repeatedly using the more cumbersome terminology "Subdivision X of Division Y of Class Z." The six Class 1 divisions and three hazard sub-divisions are:

C4.1.1.1. HD 1.1 - Mass-explosion

C4.1.1.2. HD 1.2 - Non-mass explosion, fragment producing

C4.1.1.2.1. HD 1.2.1 - Those items with a NEWQD > 1.60 pounds [0.73 kg] or that exhibit fragmentation characteristics similar to or greater than (higher density, longer distance) 105 mm projectiles, Model M1 regardless of NEWQD.

C4.1.1.2.2. HD 1.2.2 - Those items with a NEWQD $\leq$ 1.60 pounds [0.73 kg] or that, at most, exhibit fragmentation characteristics similar to high-explosive 40 mm ammunition regardless of NEWQD.

C4.1.1.2.3. HD 1.2.3 - AE that does not exhibit any sympathetic detonation response in the stack test and does not exhibit any reaction more severe than burning in the external fire test, bullet impact test, and slow cook-off test.

C4.1.1.3. HD 1.3 - Mass fire, minor blast overpressure or fragment.

C4.1.1.4. HD 1.4 - Moderate fire, no significant blast or fragment.

C4.1.1.5. HD 1.5 - Very insensitive explosive substance (with mass explosion hazard).

C4.1.1.6. HD 1.6 - Explosive article, extremely insensitive.

C4.1.2. These classifications pertain to AE in packaged configuration for transportation and storage and may not be valid when applied to in-process hazards associated with handling, manufacturing, or loading operations. Contractors shall analyze AE items and materials on a case-by-case basis to determine in-process hazards. Contractors may use DoD Explosives Hazard Classification Procedures (TB 700-2/NAVSEAINST 8020.8B/TO 11A-1-47) (Reference (i)) or similar sources for guidance to conduct this analysis and may request assistance from Military Service research and development organizations through contract channels. Unless analysis indicates otherwise, unpackaged HD 1.2 materials in process shall be treated as HD 1.1.

C4.2. STORAGE COMPATIBILITY

C4.2.1. Storage of AE is based on the DoD hazard classification and compatibility requirements of this chapter.

C4.2.2. Compatibility groups (CGs) and hazard classification for DoD AE items and materials are listed in the Joint Hazard Classification System (JHCS). (See Reference (i).) The JHCS is available on the World Wide Web at the U. S. Army Defense Ammunition Center website. Additional information may be available from the procuring activity in the form of Hazardous Component Safety Data Statements for intermediate materials and items. When the solicitation or contract lacks such information, it may be requested through contract channels.

C4.2.3. Compatibility and hazard classification information relating to other hazardous materials (including AE) not contained within the JHCS can be derived from references such as:

C4.2.3.1. Parts 100-199 of Reference (g)

C4.2.3.2. NFPA Manual 491M.5 (Reference (j))

C4.2.3.3. Data sheets developed by the National Safety Council

C4.2.3.4. Data sheets developed by the Chemical Manufacturers Association

C4.2.4. Storage and compatibility principles are:

C4.2.4.1. The highest degree of safety in AE storage could be assured if each item or division were stored separately. However, such ideal storage is not generally feasible. A proper balance of safety and other factors frequently requires mixing of several types of AE in storage.

C4.2.4.2. AE shall not be stored with dissimilar materials or items that present hazards to the munitions. Examples are mixed storage of AE with flammable or combustible materials, acids, or corrosives. Non-regulated AE and AE assigned to Classes 2 through 9 may have a CG assigned. When so assigned, the AE may be stored in an explosives magazine in accordance with the CG. The explosive weight of non-regulated AE and AE assigned to Classes 2 through 9 is not considered for QD purposes.

C4.2.4.3. Different types of AE may be mixed in storage, without regard to hazard classification, provided they are compatible. AE are assigned to a CG when they can be stored together without significantly increasing either the probability of an accident or, for a given quantity, the magnitude of the effects of such an accident.

C4.2.4.4. AE may be mixed in storage only when such mixing will facilitate safe operations and promote overall storage efficiency.

C4.2.4.5. As used in these requirements, the term "with its own means of initiation" indicates that the ammunition has its normal initiating device assembled to it and this device has less than two effective protective features. The term "without its own means of initiation" indicates that the ammunition does not have its normal initiating device present or, if present, the initiating device has two or more effective protective features.

C4.2.4.6. AE compatibility considerations are:

C4.2.4.6.1. Different kinds of AE within one compatibility group are compatible and may be stored together, except for some items in CG K and L. (See Table C4.T1.)

C4.2.4.6.2. AE in substandard or damaged packaging, in a suspect condition, or with characteristics that increase the risk in storage are not compatible with other AE and shall be stored separately.

C4.2.4.7. AE are assigned to one of 13 CGs, designated A through H, J, K, L, N, and S. The CGs are categorized as:

C4.2.4.7.1. Group A. Initiating (primary) explosives. Bulk initiating explosives that have the necessary sensitivity to heat, friction, or percussion to make them suitable for use as initiating elements in an explosive train. Examples include: bulk lead azide, lead styphnate, mercury fulminate, tetracene, dry cyclotrimethylenetrinitramine (RDX) (also known as cyclonite, hexogen, or Royal Demolition Explosive), and dry pentaerythritol tetranitrate (PETN).

C4.2.4.7.2. Group B. Detonators and similar initiating devices not containing two or more effective protective features. Items containing initiating (primary) explosives that are designed to initiate or continue the functioning of an explosive train. Examples include detonators, blasting caps, small arms primers, and fuses.

C4.2.4.7.3. <u>Group C</u>. Bulk propellants, propelling charges, and devices containing propellant with or without their own means of ignition. Items that upon initiation will normally deflagrate. Examples are single-, double-, triple-base, and composite propellants, rocket motors (solid propellant), and ammunition with inert projectiles. Liquid propellants are not included.

C4.2.4.7.4. <u>Group D</u>. Bulk black powder; bulk high explosives (HEs) (secondary explosives); and AE without a propelling charge, but containing HE (secondary explosives) without its own means of initiation, i.e., no initiating device is present or the device has two or more effective protective features. Examples include bulk trinitrotoluene (TNT), Composition B, and black powder; bulk wet RDX or PETN; and bombs, projectiles, cluster bomb units, depth charges, and torpedo warheads.

C4.2.4.7.5. <u>Group E</u>. AE containing HE (secondary explosives) without its own means of initiation and with solid propelling charge. Examples include artillery ammunition, rockets, and guided missiles.

C4.2.4.7.6. <u>Group F</u>. AE containing HE (secondary explosives) with its own means of initiation and with or without solid propelling charge. HE ammunition or devices (fused), with or without solid propelling charges. Examples include grenades, sounding devices, and similar items having an in-line explosive train in the initiator.

C4.2.4.7.7. <u>Group G</u>. Fireworks; illuminating, incendiary, smoke (including hexachlorethane), or tear-producing munitions other than those munitions that are water-activated or contain white phosphorus or flammable liquid or gel. Examples include flares and signal and pyrotechnic substances.

C4.2.4.7.8. <u>Group H</u>. AE containing both explosives and white phosphorus (WP) or other pyrophoric material. AE in this group contains fillers that are spontaneously flammable when exposed to the atmosphere. Examples include WP and plasticized white phosphorus.

C4.2.4.7.9. <u>Group J</u>. AE containing flammable liquids or gels other than those that are spontaneously flammable when exposed to water or the atmosphere. Examples are liquid-filled or gel-filled incendiary ammunition; fuel-air-explosives devices; flammable, liquid-fueled missiles; and torpedoes.

C4.2.4.7.10. <u>Group K</u>. AE containing both explosives and toxic chemical agents. AE in this group contains chemicals specifically designed for incapacitating effects more severe than lachrymation (tear producing). Examples are artillery or mortar ammunition (fused or unfused), grenades, and rockets or bombs filled with a lethal or incapacitating chemical agent. (See Note 8 of Table C4.T1.)

C4.2.4.7.11. <u>Group L</u>. AE not included in other compatibility groups, having characteristics with special risks that do not permit storage with other types of AE, other kinds of explosives, or dissimilar AE of this group. Examples include water-activated devices, prepackaged hypergolic liquid-fueled rocket engines, triethyl aluminum (TEA), thickened TEA, and damaged or suspect ammunition of any group. NOTE: Different types of AE in CG L presenting similar hazards (that is, oxidizers with oxidizers, fuels with fuels, etc.) may be stored together.

C4.2.4.7.12. <u>Group N</u>. AE containing only extremely insensitive detonating substances (EIDS). An example is HD 1.6 AE.

C4.2.4.7.13. <u>Group S</u>. AE presenting no significant hazard. AE packaged or designed so that any hazardous effects from functioning are limited to the extent that they do not significantly hinder firefighting. Examples are thermal batteries, explosive switches or valves, and small arms ammunition.

C4.2.4.8. For the purpose of storage where substantial dividing walls are utilized to reduce MCE, each HD 1.1 and HD 1.2 AE item is designated, based on its physical attributes, into one of five sensitivity groups (SGs). Directed energy weapons are further identified by assigning the suffix "D" following the SG designation, e.g., SG2D. The SG assigned to an HD 1.1 and HD 1.2 AE item is found in the JHCS.

C4.2.4.8.1. The five SGs, in relative order from least sensitive to most sensitive, are:

C4.2.4.8.1.1. <u>SG 2</u>: Non-robust or thin-skinned AE. (See glossary.)

C4.2.4.8.1.2. <u>SG 1</u>: Robust or thick-skinned AE. An SG 1 item meets any two of the criteria listed:

C4.2.4.8.1.2.1. Ratio of explosive weight to empty case weight is < 1.

C4.2.4.8.1.2.2. Minimum case thickness is > 0.4 inches (1 cm).

C4.2.4.8.1.2.3. Ratio of case thickness to $NEWQD^{1/3}$ is > 0.05 in/lb$^{1/3}$ [0.165 cm/kg$^{1/3}$].

C4.2.4.8.1.3. <u>SG 3</u>: Fragmenting AE. These items, which are typically air-to-air missiles, have warhead cases designed for specific fragmentation, e.g., pre-formed fragment warhead, scored cases, continuous rod warheads.

C4.2.4.8.1.4. <u>SG 4</u>: Cluster bombs and dispenser munitions.

C4.2.4.8.1.5. <u>SG 5</u>: Other AE (items for which high performance magazine (HPM) non-propagation walls are not effective). Items are assigned to SG 5 because they are either very sensitive to propagation or their sensitivity has not been determined.

C4.2.4.8.2. Item-specific testing or analyses can be used to change an item's SG.

C4.2.4.9. Mixed Storage

C4.2.4.9.1. Mixing of CGs is permitted as indicated in Table C4.T1. For purposes of mixing, all items shall be packaged in approved storage containers. Outer containers may be opened in storage locations for inventory and for magazines storing only HD 1.4 items for unpackaging, inspection, and repackaging of the HD 1.4 AE. NOTE: Before storage of mixed items in Group K, PCO approval shall be obtained.

C4.2.4.9.2. Items from CGs C, D, E, F, G, J, and S may be combined in storage, provided the net quantity of explosives in the items or in bulk does not exceed 1000 pounds per storage site.

C4.2.4.9.3. In addition to subparagraph C4.2.4.9.1., items assigned to HD 1.4, CG C, G, or S, may be combined in storage without regard to explosives quantity limitations; however, siting is still required.

Table C4.T1. <u>Storage Compatibility Mixing Chart</u>

Group	A	B	C	D	E	F	G	H	J	K	L	N	S
A	X	Z											
B	Z	X	Z	Z	Z	Z	Z					X	X
C		Z	X	X	X	Z	Z					X	X
D		Z	X	X	X	Z	Z					X	X
E		Z	X	X	X	Z	Z					X	X
F		Z	Z	Z	Z	X	Z					Z	X
G		Z	Z	Z	Z	Z	X					Z	X
H								X					X
J									X				X
K										Z			
L													
N		X	X	X	X	Z	Z					X	X
S		X	X	X	X	X	X	X	X			X	X

CHAPTER 4

Notes:

1. The marking "X" at an intersection indicates that these groups may be combined in storage. Otherwise, mixing is either prohibited or restricted according to Note 2.

2. The marking "Z" at an intersection indicates that, when warranted by operational considerations or magazine non-availability and when safety is not sacrificed, logical mixed storage of limited quantities of some items of different groups may be approved. These relaxations involving mixed storage shall be approved by the DoD Component and are not considered waivers. Combinations that violate the principles of paragraph C4.2.4. require justification by a waiver or exemption in accordance with section C1.4. Items from Group B or Group F shall be segregated from articles of other compatibility groups by means that prevent propagation of fire or detonation.

   Examples of acceptable combinations are:

   a. HD 1.1, Group A (initiating explosives) with HD 1.1, Group B (fuses not containing two or more independent safety features).

   b. HD 1.3, Group C (bulk propellants or bagged propelling charges) with HD 1.3, Group G (pyrotechnics without their own means of initiation).

3. Equal numbers of separately packaged components of complete rounds of any single type of ammunition may be stored together. When so stored, compatibility is that of the assembled round; that is, WP filler in Group H, HE filler in Groups D, E, or F, as appropriate.

4. Group K requires not only separate storage from other groups, but also may require separate storage within the group. The controlling DoD Component shall determine which items under Group K may be stored together and those that must be stored separately.

5. Ammunition items without explosives that contain substances properly belonging to another U.N. hazard class may be assigned to the same compatibility group as items containing explosives and the same substance, and be stored with them.

6. DoD Components may authorize ammunition designated "Practice" by National Stock Number and nomenclature to be stored with the fully loaded ammunition it simulates

7. In addition to the CG mixing authorized in subparagraph C4.2.4.9.2., DoD Components may authorize the mixing of CGs B, H, and N in limited quantities (generally 1000 lbs or less).

8. For purposes of mixing, all items must be packaged in approved storage or shipping containers. Items shall not be opened for purposes of issuing unpackaged munitions in storage locations. Outer containers may be opened in storage locations for purposes of inventorying; for removing munitions still inside an approved inner package in limited amounts; and for magazines storing only HD 1.4 items, unpacking inspecting, and repacking the HD 1.4 ammunition.

9. When using the "Z" mixing authorized by Note 2, articles of either compatibility Group B or F, each shall be segregated in storage from articles of other compatibility groups by means that prevent the propagation of Group B or F articles to articles of other compatibility groups.

10. If dissimilar HD 1.6 are mixed together and have not been tested to assure non-propagation; the mixed munitions are considered to be HD 1.2, Compatibility Group D for purposes of transportation and storage. When mixing Group N munitions with Groups B through G, see Chapter 5, paragraph C5.3.2. about changing QD hazard divisions.

CHAPTER 4

C5. CHAPTER 5

QD PRINCIPLES, CRITERIA, AND SITING REQUIREMENTS

C5.1. GENERAL

C5.1.1. Reference (c) establishes minimum QD standards for all DoD AE operations. QD tables are not presented in this chapter but are incorporated in Appendix 2 and cross referenced to Reference (c) QD tables in the appendix. Distances determined by formulae and presented in the tables are based on the probability of injury and damage and do not provide absolute protection. Greater distances than those shown in the tables should be used when practicable.

C5.1.2. Distances required in Reference (c) QD tables may be reduced if structural or engineering data demonstrate that explosion effects will be reduced or eliminated through containment, direction or suppression shields, or building volume. The rationale or test results justifying the proposed distance reduction shall become part of the AE facility site plan and shall accompany AE site and general construction plans submitted through the ACO to the PCO for approval, or through the DoD Component for DDESB approval.

C5.1.3. This chapter sets forth:

C5.1.3.1. QD principles.

C5.1.3.2. Rules for determining NEWQD.

C5.1.3.3. General QD rules.

C5.1.3.4. Types of QD.

C5.1.3.5. Explosion effects, expected consequences, and exposure controls.

C5.1.3.6. Permissible exposures at specific scaled distances.

C5.1.3.7. Siting requirements for specific facilities.

C5.2. QD PRINCIPLES

C5.2.1. QD is a relationship between a specific quantity of AE at a PES and the expected effects of an accidental or planned explosion on an ES at scaled distances. The primary potential hazards of an explosion are blast (overpressure), fragmentation, and thermal, and their effects can result in serious personnel injury and property damage. QDs have been developed to provide separation distances from a PES that minimize the risk of propagation between PESs, serious injury to personnel, and property damage dependent upon the type of ES.

C5.2.2. The basis for determining required QD separation distances are the hazard classification(s) and NEWQD of AE present in a PES; the type of PES; the ability of the PES to suppress blast overpressure and fragments (primary and secondary); the type of ES; and the ability of the ES to resist explosion effects.

C5.2.3. QDs are determined by establishing a NEWQD at a point and measuring from that point to an exposure. The source of a QD measurement is called a potential explosion site, or PES. For QD purposes, one considers the total NEWQD that will be involved in an accidental explosion at the PES. A PES may be a round of ammunition, a vehicle, a building, or simply a location where explosives are stacked.

C5.2.4. Any building, vehicle, location, or ammunition that is to be protected from an accidental explosion at another source is called an ES. An ES may contain explosives requiring protection from a second explosive source located a distance away. An ES may also be a home, stadium, high-rise apartment, public highway, the facility boundary, or any other location requiring protection from an accidental explosion.

C5.2.5. The QD tables in Reference (c) and the associated formulae are used to provide minimum distances from PESs. Those tables are duplicated in Appendix 2 of this Manual with the numbers for the associated QD tables from Reference (c) included in the Appendix. The hazard classification of the AE and the NEWQD of explosives involved are primary characteristics governing the use of QD tables. The definitions and methods for determining hazard classifications are presented in Chapter 4.

C5.2.6. The minimum distance for protection from hazardous fragments shall be based on primary and secondary fragments from the PES and the population or traffic density of the ES. This is the distance when the density of hazardous fragments become 1 per 600 ft^2 [55.7 m^2]. However, this distance is not the maximum fragment range. DDESB approved analyses and/or approved tests may be used to determine minimum distances for both primary and secondary fragments. DDESB TP No. 13 (Reference (k)) is an example of a method to determine minimal distances for building debris, while DDESB TP No. 16 (Reference (l)) provides similar information to determine minimal distances for primary fragments.

C5.3. DETERMINING NEWQD

C5.3.1. NEWQD Determination Methods. NEWQD is usually equal to the NEW unless hazard classification testing has shown that a lower weight is appropriate for QD purposes. If the NEWQD is less than the NEW, the reason is usually that propellant or other substances do not contribute as much to the blast effect as the same amount of high explosives would. For items that have been hazard classified, use the NEWQD given in the JHCS. For items that have not been hazard classified, use the following methods for determining the NEWQD:

C5.3.1.1. HD 1.1. The NEWQD is the total high explosives weight (HEW) plus the total net propellant weight (NPW). For HD 1.1, NEWQD equals the NEW.

C5.3.1.2. <u>HD 1.2.</u>

C5.3.1.2.1. <u>HD 1.2.1</u>. The NEWQD is the HEW plus the NPW in all HD 1.2.1 items. In certain situations, the MCE, as outlined in paragraph C5.12.3., shall be used as the basis for determining applicable QD.

C5.3.1.2.2. <u>HD 1.2.2</u>. The NEWQD is the HEW plus the NPW in all HD 1.2.2 items.

C5.3.1.2.3. <u>HD 1.2.3</u>. The NEWQD is the HEW plus the NPW in all HD 1.2.3 items. This material is treated as HD 1.3; however, a minimum IBD shall apply, as outlined in paragraph C5.12.12.

C5.3.1.3. <u>HD 1.3</u>. The NEWQD is the HEW plus the NPW plus the total weight of pyrotechnics in all HD 1.3 items.

C5.3.1.4. <u>HD 1.4</u>. The NEWQD is the HEW plus the NPW plus the total weight of pyrotechnics in all HD 1.4 items.

C5.3.1.5. <u>HD 1.5</u>. The NEWQD is the HEW plus the NPW in all HD 1.5 items. For HD 1.5, NEWQD equals the NEW.

C5.3.1.6. <u>HD 1.6</u>. The NEWQD is the total weight of EIDS in all HD 1.6 items. However, the weight of EIDS in a single HD 1.6 item shall also be considered (as specified in Table AP2.T16.) for determining QD.

NOTE: The JHCS provides explosives weights for all DoD hazard classified AE.

C5.3.2. <u>Determining NEWQD for Mixed HD</u>

C5.3.2.1. <u>General</u>

C5.3.2.1.1. The presence of HD 1.4 does not affect the NEWQD of mixed HD. However, for QD determinations, HD 1.4 criteria shall be considered.

C5.3.2.1.2. When HD 1.1 is mixed with any other HD; treat the mixture as HD 1.1 except as noted in subparagraph C5.3.2.2.

C5.3.2.1.3. HD 1.5 is always treated as HD 1.1.

C5.3.2.1.4. When dissimilar HD 1.6 are mixed and have not been tested to ensure non-propagation, the mixed HD 1.6 AE shall be individually considered to be HD 1.2.1 or HD 1.2.2, based on their individual NEWQD or overriding fragmentation characteristics.

C5.3.2.2. <u>HD 1.1 with HD 1.2 (HD 1.2.1, HD 1.2.2, and HD 1.2.3)</u>. (Use whichever generates the largest QD.)

C5.3.2.2.1. Sum the NEWQD for HD 1.1 and NEWQD for HD 1.2 and treat the mixture as HD 1.1.

C5.3.2.2.2. The NEWQD of the mixture is the NEWQD of the HD 1.2 subdivision requiring the largest QD.

C5.3.2.3. <u>HD 1.1 with HD 1.3</u>. Sum the NEWQD for HD 1.1 and the NEWQD for HD 1.3 and treat the mixture as HD 1.1.

C5.3.2.4. <u>HD 1.1 with HD 1.6</u>. Sum the NEWQD for HD 1.1 and the NEWQD for HD 1.6 and treat the mixture as HD 1.1.

C5.3.2.5. <u>HD 1.2.1 with HD 1.2.2</u>. The NEWQD for the mixture is the NEWQD of the subdivision requiring the largest QD.

C5.3.2.6. <u>HD 1.2.1 with HD 1.2.3</u>. The NEWQD for the mixture is the NEWQD of the subdivision requiring the largest QD.

C5.3.2.7. <u>HD 1.2.2 with HD 1.2.3</u>. The NEWQD for the mixture is the NEWQD of the subdivision requiring the largest QD.

C5.3.2.8. <u>HD 1.2.1 with HD 1.2.2 with HD 1.2.3</u>. The NEWQD for the mixture is the NEWQD of the subdivision requiring the largest QD.

C5.3.2.9. <u>HD 1.2 (HD 1.2.1, HD 1.2.2, and HD 1.2.3) with HD 1.3</u>. The NEWQD for the mixture is the NEWQD of the HD requiring the largest QD.

C5.3.2.10. <u>HD 1.2 (HD 1.2.1, HD 1.2.2, and HD 1.2.3) with HD 1.6</u>. Treat the HD 1.6 as HD 1.2.3 and determine NEWQD in accordance with subparagraphs C5.3.2.6. through C5.3.2.8., as applicable.

C5.3.2.11. <u>HD 1.3 with HD 1.6</u>. Sum the NEWQD for the HD 1.6 and the NEWQD for the HD 1.3 and treat the mixture as HD 1.3.

C5.4. <u>GENERAL QD RULES</u>

C5.4.1. The NEWQD of explosives in a magazine, operating building, or other explosives site shall be the NEWQD of all the explosives contained therein. QD shall be based on the total NEWQD, unless the NEW is subdivided by walls or shields to reduce the NEWQD.

C5.4.2. Contractors can justify reductions in required QD separation distances from a PES when the NEWQD at the PES is subdivided and adequately separated by distance or barrier to prevent simultaneous detonation or initiation. The basis for subdividing a quantity of AE into smaller units for the purpose of QD reduction is:

C5.4.2.1. <u>Separation by Time (Distance)</u>. Blast waves coalesce when two or more proximate stacks of mass-detonating explosives (HD 1.1) detonate within short time intervals (that is, when the time in milliseconds is less than 4 times the cube root of the NEW in pounds ($4.0W^{1/3}$ [$5.21Q^{1/3}$]) for lateral target positions and less than 5.6 times the cube root of the NEW in pounds $5.6W^{1/3}$ [$7.29Q^{1/3}$] for axial target positions). The resultant shock wave, after coalescence, is that of a single detonation of a charge equal to the sum of the several stacks. When the two or more stacks of HD 1.1 (NEWQD) at the PES are adequately separated by distance or barrier to prevent simultaneous detonation within the short time interval, coalescence does not occur and the MCE for the stacks is equal to the NEWQD for one stack.

C5.4.2.2. <u>Separation by Barriers</u>. Barriers designed per the principles of DDESB TP No. 15 (Reference (m)) will ensure no propagation between AE stacks. Barriers designed and constructed in accordance with TM 5-1300/AFM 88-22/NAVFAC P-397 (Reference (n)) also satisfy this requirement. When barriers are constructed per this guidance or when supported by test data, the MCE is equal to the NEWQD of the AE stack with the largest QD requirement. Otherwise, QD computations must be based upon the summation of NEWQD for all of the AE stacks. Barrier design shall include adequate standoff distances and take into account acceptor AE sensitivity.

C5.4.3. The QD criteria for a PES-ES pair (when both contain AE) are determined by considering each location, in turn, as a PES and an ES. The quantity of AE to be permitted in each PES shall be the amount permitted by the distance specified in the appropriate QD tables. The separation distance required for the pair is the greater of the two separation distances. An exception is permitted for service magazines supporting an AE operation (see subparagraphs C5.7.1.1.6. and C5.7.1.2.6.).

C5.4.4. Flight ranges for units (e.g., rockets, missile motors, and cartridge or propellant actuated devices in a propulsive state) shall be disregarded because it is impractical to specify QD separations that allow for their designed flight range. However, the distance required to afford protection from fragments in credible accident situations shall be established in accordance with the hazardous fragment criteria in section C5.8.

C5.4.5. Separation distances are measured along straight lines from the nearest wall of the PES or, when the NEWQD at the PES is subdivided, from the exterior of the nearest intervening wall of the controlling AE stack, to the nearest part of an ES. For large intervening topographical features such as hills, measure over or around the feature, using whichever is the shorter distance.

CHAPTER 5

C5.4.6. When an AE conveyance (e.g., railroad car or motor vehicle) containing AE is not separated from a PES in such a manner as to prevent mass detonation, then the conveyance and PES shall be considered as a unit and their NEWQD shall be summed. The separation distance shall be measured from the nearest outside wall of the PES or conveyance, as appropriate, to an ES.

C5.4.7. Throughout these requirements, NEWQD is used to calculate QD by means of formulae. The formula for calculating the blast overpressure hazard of HD 1.1, 1.5, and 1.6 is $D = KW^{1/3}$ [D (m) = $K_m \bullet Q^{1/3}$], where D [D_m] is the distance in feet [meters], K [K_m] is a factor that is dependent upon the risk assumed or permitted, and W[Q] is the NEWQD in pounds [kilograms]. Distance requirements determined by the formula using English units are sometimes expressed by the value of K, such as K9, K11, and K18 to signify K = 9, K = 11, K = 18, respectively. The formulae for HD 1.2 subdivisions and HD 1.3 are based on equations with exponent and natural logarithm functions and do not include a K factor. QD tables and their formulae and notes are incorporated into this chapter by reference to Appendix 2. The formulae specified in the QD tables may be used to calculate exact QD distances.

C5.5. TYPES OF QDs

C5.5.1 IBD is the required separation distance between a PES and exposures unrelated to the AE mission. (See subparagraph C5.7.1.5.) For HD 1.1, IBD is determined based either on the blast overpressure hazard or the fragment hazard (whichever requires the greatest distance) associated with the quantity of AE considered. Table AP2.T1. combines the HD 1.1 overpressure and fragment hazards into a single table. For PESs other than earth-covered magazines (ECMs), at an NEWQD < 30,000 lbs [13,608 kg], the distance is controlled by fragments and debris. When fragments and debris are absent, or the range to a hazardous fragment density < 1/600 ft^2 is less than the blast overpressure hazard range, as determined by test or analysis, or the hazardous fragment distance is specifically exempted (see subparagraph C5.8.1.5.2.), then the blast overpressure criteria may be used.

C5.5.2. PTRD is the required separation distance between a PES and any public street, road, highway, navigable stream, or passenger railroad used routinely by the general public; parking lots for private vehicles in administrative areas; certain open-air recreation facilities; and remote controlled operations. (See subparagraphs C5.7.1.3. and C5.7.1.4.). For HD 1.1, PTRD (like IBD) is determined based either on the blast overpressure hazard or the fragment hazard; whichever requires the greater distance. In either case, for HD 1.1, PTRD is 60 percent of the applicable IBD. Table AP2.T1. combines the HD 1.1 overpressure and fragment hazards into a single table. For PESs other than ECMs, at an NEWQD < 30,000 lbs [13,608 kg] the distance is controlled by fragments and debris. When fragments and debris are absent, or the range to a hazardous fragment density < 1/600 ft^2 is less than the blast overpressure hazard range (as determined by test or analysis) or the hazardous fragment distance is specifically exempted (see subparagraph C5.8.1.5.2.), then the blast overpressure criteria may be used. For HD 1.3 and 1.4, PTRD and IBD are the same distance.

CHAPTER 5

C5.5.3. ILD is the required separation distance between a PES and other facilities related to the explosives mission. ILD prevents propagation between two explosives locations and provides minimal protection to adjacent facilities and personnel. For the exposures identified in subparagraph C5.7.1.1., ILD for HD 1.1 can be reduced by placing appropriately constructed barricades between a PES and exposed facilities. The HD 1.1 barricaded ILD is one half of the unbarricaded ILD. ILD for HD 1.1, 1.3, and 1.4 does not consider fragment hazards.

C5.5.4. Intermagazine distance (IMD) is the required separation distance between PESs to prevent one PES from simultaneously detonating an adjacent PES. IMD does not prevent the possible delayed propagation from one PES to another; it only prevents simultaneous detonation. The exception is between ECMs where IMD will provide virtually complete protection of AE against the propagation effects of an explosion; however, AE in adjacent ECMs may be damaged.

C5.6. EXPLOSION EFFECTS, EXPECTED CONSEQUENCES, EXPOSURE CONTROLS

C5.6.1. <u>HD 1.1 Effects</u>. Facility damage and personnel injury from HD 1.1 AE principally depend on blast overpressure and impulse, although for limited quantities and certain types of PESs or ESs, fragment hazards may determine QD. For general purposes, peak incident overpressure is the blast parameter defining maximum permissible levels of exposure. However, in specific instances the physical characteristics of exposed structures (such as mass, stiffness, ductility, and so forth) can make blast impulse the principal damage-causing factor.

C5.6.1.1. Separation distances for ECMs provide virtually complete protection against propagation of explosions among ECMs by blast, fragments, or fire. However, structural damage ranging from cracks in concrete, damage to doors and ventilators, to complete structural failure may occur.

C5.6.1.2. Aboveground magazine (AGM) distances provide considerable protection against propagation of explosions among AGMs by blast. Depending on explosive type, however, there is a risk of delayed propagation by fragments or of fire spreading from one magazine to another. Properly designed and placed barricades reduce the risk of communicating explosion through high-velocity, low-angle fragments. Without barricades, this risk is high.

C5.6.2. <u>HD 1.1 Expected Consequences and Exposure Controls</u>

C5.6.2.1. Barricaded AGM is $6W^{1/3}$ ft [$2.38Q^{1/3}$ m], which yields or equates to an overpressure of 27 pounds per square inch (psi) [186.1 kilopascal (kPa)]. At this distance:

C5.6.2.1.1. Unstrengthened buildings will be destroyed.

C5.6.2.1.2. Personnel will be killed by blast, by being struck by debris, or by impact against hard surfaces.

C5.6.2.1.3. Transport vehicles will be overturned and crushed by the blast.

C5.6.2.1.4. Explosives-loaded vessels will be damaged severely, with propagation of explosion likely.

C5.6.2.1.5. Aircraft will be destroyed by blast, thermal, and debris effects.

C5.6.2.1.6. Barricades are effective in preventing immediate propagation of explosion by high velocity low angle fragments. However, they provide only limited protection against any delayed propagation of explosives caused by a fire resulting from high angle firebrands.

C5.6.2.2. Barricaded ILD is $9W^{1/3}$ ft [$3.57Q^{1/3}$ m], which yields or equates to an overpressure of 12 psi [82.7 kPa]. At this distance:

C5.6.2.2.1. Unstrengthened buildings will suffer severe structural damage approaching total destruction.

C5.6.2.2.2. Personnel will be subject to severe injuries or death from direct blast, building collapse, or translation.

C5.6.2.2.3. Aircraft will be damaged beyond economical repair both by blast and fragments. NOTE: If the aircraft are loaded with explosives, delayed explosions are likely to result from subsequent fires.

C5.6.2.2.4. Transport vehicles will be damaged heavily, probably to the extent of total loss.

C5.6.2.2.5. Improperly designed barricades or structures may increase the hazard from flying debris, or may collapse in such a manner as to increase the risk to personnel and equipment.

C5.6.2.2.6. Barricading is required. Direct propagation of explosion between two explosive locations is unlikely when barricades are placed between them to intercept high-velocity, low-angle fragments. Exposed structures containing high value, mission-critical equipment or personnel may require hardening.

C5.6.2.3. Unbarricaded AGM distance is $11W^{1/3}$ ft [$4.36Q^{1/3}$ m], which yields or equates to an overpressure of 8 psi [55.3 kPa]. At this distance:

C5.6.2.3.1. Unstrengthened buildings will suffer damage approaching total destruction.

C5.6.2.3.2. Personnel are likely to be injured seriously due to blast, fragments, debris, and displacement.

C5.6.2.3.3. There is a 15 percent risk of eardrum rupture.

CHAPTER 5

C5.6.2.3.4. Explosives-loaded vessels are likely to be damaged extensively and delayed propagation of explosion may occur.

C5.6.2.3.5. Aircraft will be damaged heavily by blast and fragments; destruction by resulting fire is likely.

C5.6.2.3.6. Transport vehicles will sustain severe body damage, minor engine damage, and total glass breakage.

C5.6.2.3.7. Barricading will significantly reduce the risk of propagation of explosion and injury of personnel by high velocity low angle fragments.

C5.6.2.4. Unbarricaded ILD is $18W^{1/3}$ ft [$7.14Q^{1/3}$ m], which yields or equates to an overpressure of 3.5 psi [24 kPa]. At this distance:

C5.6.2.4.1. Direct propagation of explosion is not expected.

C5.6.2.4.2. Delayed propagation of an explosion may occur at the ES, as either a direct result of a fire or as a result of equipment failure.

C5.6.2.4.3. Damage to unstrengthened buildings may approximate 50 percent or more of the total replacement cost.

C5.6.2.4.4. There is a 2 percent chance of eardrum damage to personnel.

C5.6.2.4.5. Personnel may suffer serious injuries from fragments, debris, firebrands, or other objects.

C5.6.2.4.6. Aircraft can be expected to suffer considerable structural damage from blast. Fragments and debris are likely to cause severe damage to aircraft at distances calculated from the formula $18W^{1/3}$ [$7.14Q^{1/3}$] when small quantities of explosives are involved.

C5.6.2.4.7. Transport vehicles will incur extensive (but not severe) body and glass damage consisting mainly of dishing of body panels and cracks in shatter-resistant window glass.

C5.6.2.4.8. Suitably designed suppressive construction at PESs or protective construction at ESs may be practical for some situations. Such construction is encouraged when there is insufficient distance to provide the required protection.

C5.6.2.5. PTRD for under 100,000 lbs of high explosives is $24W^{1/3}$ ft [$9.52Q^{1/3}$ m], which yields or equates to an overpressure of 2.3 psi [15.8 kPa]. At this distance:

C5.6.2.5.1. Unstrengthened buildings can be expected to sustain damage that may approximate 20 percent of the replacement cost.

C5.6.2.5.2. Occupants of exposed structures may suffer temporary hearing loss or injury from blast effects, building debris, and displacement.

C5.6.2.5.3. Although personnel in the open are not expected to be killed or seriously injured by blast effects, fragments and debris may cause some injuries. The extent of these injuries depends largely upon the PES structure and the amount and fragmentation characteristics of the AE involved.

C5.6.2.5.4. Vehicles on the road should suffer little damage, unless they are hit by a fragment or the blast causes a momentary loss of control.

C5.6.2.5.5. Aircraft may suffer some damage to the fuselage from blast and possible fragment penetration, but should be operational with minor repair.

C5.6.2.5.6. Barricading can reduce the risk of injury or damage due to fragments for limited quantities of AE at a PES. When practical, suitably designed suppressive construction at the PES or protective construction at the ES may also provide some protection.

C5.6.2.6. PTRD for over 250,000 lbs HE is $30W^{1/3}$ ft [$11.9Q^{1/3}$ m], which yields or equates to an overpressure of 1.7 psi [11.7 kPa]. At this distance:

C5.6.2.6.1. Unstrengthened buildings can be expected to sustain damage that may approximate 10 percent of their replacement cost.

C5.6.2.6.2. Occupants of exposed, unstrengthened structures may be injured by secondary blast effects such as falling building debris.

C5.6.2.6.3. Pilots of aircraft that are landing or taking off may lose control and crash.

C5.6.2.6.4. Parked military and commercial aircraft will likely sustain minor damage due to blast, but should remain airworthy.

C5.6.2.6.5. Although personnel in the open are not expected to be killed or seriously injured by blast effects, fragments and debris may cause some injuries. The extent of these injuries will largely depend upon the PES structure, the NEW, and the fragmentation characteristics of the AE involved.

C5.6.2.6.6. Barricading or the application of minimum fragmentation distance requirements may reduce the risk of injury or damage due to fragments for limited quantities of AE at a PES.

C5.6.2.7. IBD varies from $40W^{1/3}$ ft to $50W^{1/3}$ ft [$15.87Q^{1/3}$ - $19.8Q^{1/3}$ m], which yields or equates to an overpressure between 1.2 psi and 0.90 psi [8.3 kPa - 6.2 kPa]. See Note 4 of AP2.T1. for more detail. At this distance:

C5.6.2.7.1. Unstrengthened buildings can be expected to sustain damage that approximates 5 percent of their replacement cost.

C5.6.2.7.2. Personnel in buildings are provided a high degree of protection from death or serious injury; however, glass breakage and building debris may still cause some injuries.

C5.6.2.7.3. Personnel in the open are not expected to be injured seriously by blast effects. Fragments and debris may cause some injuries. The extent of injuries will depend upon the PES structure and the NEW and fragmentation characteristics of the AE involved.

C5.6.2.7.4. Elimination of glass surfaces is the best control. If determined to be necessary, reducing the use of glass or the size of any glass surfaces and the use of blast resistant glass will provide some relief. For new construction, building design characteristics -- to include consideration of how any required glass surfaces are oriented and use of blast resistant glass -- can reduce glass breakage and structural damage.

C5.6.3. <u>Hazard Division 1.2 Effects</u>. Facility damage and personnel injury from HD 1.2 AE principally depend on fragmentation. Fragmentation may include primary fragments from AE casings or secondary fragments from containers and structures. HD 1.2, when not stored with HD 1.1 or HD 1.5, is not expected to mass detonate. An incident involving HD 1.2 by itself or when stored with HD 1.3, HD 1.4, or HD 1.6 AE can be expected to both explode sporadically and burn over a prolonged period of time. The progressive nature of an HD 1.2 event minimizes the thermal hazard by allowing personnel time to evacuate and fire suppression systems to extinguish fires in their early stages. Airblast, fragment, and thermal hazards to buildings, parked aircraft, and vehicles cannot be predicted reliably because the effects will depend on the MCE.

C5.6.4. <u>HD 1.3 Effects</u>. In an HD 1.3 event, heat flux presents the greatest hazard to personnel and assets. HD 1.3 substances include both fuel components and oxidizers. Burning these materials emits fuel-rich flammable gases, fine particles, or both. This unburned material may ignite when it comes in contact with air and cause a large fireball. This fireball will expand radially from the ignition site and could wrap around obstacles, even those designed to provide line-of-sight protection from HD 1.1 events. Under certain circumstances of minimal venting and extreme structural containment, HD 1.3 material can transfer from a deflagration to a detonation. Internal gas pressures may produce fragments that are generally large and have low velocity. Firebrands can be thrown more than 50 ft [15 m] from the incident site and present a severe fire-spread hazard. Exposed personnel may receive severe burns from fireballs or flash burning. Buildings, vehicles, and aircraft may be ignited by radiant heat, sparks, or firebrands or may be damaged by heat (searing, buckling, etc.).

C5.6.5. <u>HD 1.4 Effects</u>. HD 1.4 presents no blast hazard, no fragment hazard with appreciable energy, and only a moderate fire hazard. A fireball or jet of flame may extend 3 ft [1 m] beyond the location of the HD 1.4 event. A burning time of less than 330 seconds [5.5 minutes] for 220 lbs [100 kg] of the HD 1.4 AE is expected.

CHAPTER 5

C5.6.6. <u>HD 1.5 Effects</u>. HD 1.5 effects are similar to those produced by HD 1.1, without the fragmentation effects.

C5.6.7. <u>HD 1.6 Effects</u>. HD 1.6 effects are similar to those produced by HD 1.3.

C5.7. <u>PERMISSIBLE EXPOSURES</u>

C5.7.1. <u>HD 1.1 Blast Overpressure</u>

C5.7.1.1. At sites exposed to potential blast overpressure of 12 psi [82.7 kPa] occurring at $9W^{1/3}$ [$3.57Q^{1/3}$] (see Table AP2.T4. and Table AP2.T5.), with a barricade meeting the requirements of paragraph C5.18.17., these facilities or operations are permitted:

C5.7.1.1.1. Buildings housing successive steps of a single production, renovation, or maintenance operation.

C5.7.1.1.2. Breakrooms and change houses that are both part of an operating line and used exclusively by personnel operating the line. An exception is when the breakroom is integral to the PES and used only by personnel from that PES. For this situation, no QD applies.

C5.7.1.1.3. Dunnage preparation or similar non-AE operations, if used only by personnel employed at the PES.

C5.7.1.1.4. Temporary holding areas for AE conveyances servicing production or maintenance facilities.

C5.7.1.1.5. AE related operations in magazine areas, when performing minor maintenance, preservation, packaging, or surveillance inspection.

C5.7.1.1.6. Barricaded service magazines that are part of an operating line. Separation distances shall be based on the NEWQD and the HD of the AE in the magazine and not that of the operating line.

C5.7.1.1.7. Exceptions:

C5.7.1.1.7.1. Unmanned auxiliary utility facilities (e.g., transformer stations, water treatment and pollution abatement facilities) that serve, but are not an integral function in, the PES and would not create an immediate secondary hazard if lost. Such unmanned facilities need not be barricaded. See subparagraph C5.18.1.2. for situations in which auxiliary facilities serving only one PES or AE operation are permitted to be separated from the facility or operation they support based on fire separation distance only.

C5.7.1.1.7.2. Unmanned auxiliary power generation or conversion facilities that exclusively supply power to an AE storage area or security fence lighting may be located at fire protection distance (50 ft [15.2 m] for non-combustible structures, 100 ft [30.5 m] for combustible structures) from AE facilities.

CHAPTER 5

C5.7.1.2. At sites exposed to potential blast overpressure of 3.5 psi [24 kPa] occurring at $18W^{1/3}$ [$7.14Q^{1/3}$] (see Tables AP2.T4. and AP2.T5.), these facilities or operations are permitted:

C5.7.1.2.1. Labor-intensive AE operations (e.g., surveillance, maintenance, inspection) closely related to the PES.

C5.7.1.2.2. Buildings, excluding magazine-area loading docks, for comfort, safety, or convenience (e.g., lunchrooms, motor pools, area offices, auxiliary fire stations, transportation dispatch points, and shipping and receiving buildings) that are used exclusively in support of the PES.

C5.7.1.2.3. Parallel operating lines, whether or not barricaded, provided the AE involved in each operating line present similar hazards. For purposes of this Manual only, "similar hazards" are defined as similar sensitivities to initiation. NOTE: The criticality or survivability of one or more of the operating lines may require that each line be given IBD-level protection.

C5.7.1.2.4. Operational support buildings (day rooms, operation offices, training and similar functional facilities) used and attended only by personnel operating the PES.

C5.7.1.2.5. Auxiliary power plants; compressor stations; electric power transformers; tool rooms; and buildings housing materials handling equipment service, battery charging, and minor repair.

C5.7.1.2.6. Unbarricaded service magazines that are part of operating lines. Separation distances shall be based on the NEWQD and the HD of the AE in the magazine and not that of the operating line.

C5.7.1.2.7. Container stuffing and unstuffing operations that provide routine support to a PES. This subparagraph only applies to main support functions set aside for support of manufacturing operations. Container stuffing and unstuffing in magazine areas are permitted at IMD (Tables AP2.T6, AP2.T7A., AP2.T7B., and AP2.T8.). Loading and unloading of a conveyance at a magazine may be permitted without regard to QD between the magazine and the operation if the requirements of paragraph C5.18.4. are met.

C5.7.1.2.8. Parking lots for privately owned automobiles belonging to personnel employed at or stationed at multiple PESs. When a parking lot supports a single PES, it may be separated at less than ILD only from its associated PES facility. A minimum distance of 100 ft [30.5 m] is required to the associated PES facility to protect it from vehicle fires. Access for emergency vehicles shall be provided.

C5.7.1.2.9. Exposures indicated in this section that are provided blast suppression and structure hardening so that comparable protection levels for personnel and equipment as provided by $18W^{1/3}$ [$7.14Q^{1/3}$] may be sited at $9W^{1/3}$ [$3.57Q^{1/3}$].

C5.7.1.3. At sites exposed to potential blast overpressure of 2.3 psi [15.86 kPa] occurring at $24W^{1/3}$ [$9.52Q^{1/3}$] (see Table AP2.T1.), personnel exposed to remotely controlled operations are permitted. NOTE: Personnel at remote operations shall also be protected from fragment and thermal hazards. Personnel at control stations less than $24W^{1/3}$ from the PES shall be protected from fragments to energies of less than 58 ft-lbs [79 joules], thermal fluxes to 0.3 calories per square centimeter per second [12.56 kwatts/m^2], and shall not be exposed to overpressure greater than 2.3 psi [15.86 kPa].

C5.7.1.4. At sites exposed to potential blast overpressure of 2.3-1.7 psi [15.8-11.7 kPa] occurring at $24\text{-}30W^{1/3}$ [$9.52\text{-}11.9Q^{1/3}$] (see Table AP2.T1.), these facilities or operations are permitted:

C5.7.1.4.1. Public traffic routes with medium and low traffic density as described in subparagraph C5.8.1.7.5.

C5.7.1.4.2. Open-air recreation facilities such as baseball diamonds, golf courses, and volleyball courts used by personnel assigned to the plant, where structures are not involved.

C5.7.1.4.3. Parking lots for administrative areas. NOTE: Minimum fragment distances apply.

C5.7.1.4.4. Inert storage located in the open (no structures involved) when not directly related to the explosives mission and when accessed by personnel not directly related to the explosives mission. (See subparagraph C5.7.1.5.8. if located within a structure.)

C5.7.1.5. At sites exposed to potential blast overpressure of 1.2 - 0.90 psi [8.3 – 6.2 kPa] occurring at $40 \text{ - } 50W^{1/3}$ [$15.87 \text{ - } 19.84Q^{1/3}$] (see Table AP2.T1.), these facilities or operations are permitted:

C5.7.1.5.1. Inhabited buildings; administrative and housing areas.

C5.7.1.5.2. Plant boundaries. The IBD blast overpressure (K40 – 50) distance may extend onto uninhabited areas (such as wildlife preserve, desert, prairie, swamp, forest, agricultural land, or government land not open to the public) adjacent to contractor facilities but not within control of the contractor when access is restricted or controlled either naturally or by some other means. When IBD QD arcs extend past the plant boundary the contractor shall certify in his site plan that IBD protection is not required for the encumbered area and shall establish procedures to monitor the area for any change in status.

C5.7.1.5.3. Recreation facilities (e.g., ball diamonds, golf courses, and volleyball courts) that contain structures.

C5.7.1.5.4. Utilities providing vital utilities to a major portion of a DoD contractor plant.

C5.7.1.5.5. Storehouses and shops having strategically or intrinsically valuable contents that shall not be jeopardized.

C5.7.1.5.6. Functions that, if momentarily out of action, would cause an immediate secondary hazard by reason of their failure to function.

C5.7.1.5.7. Public traffic routes with high traffic density as described in subparagraph C5.8.1.7.5.

C5.7.1.5.8. Inert storage located in a structure when not directly related to the explosives mission and when accessed by personnel not directly related to the explosives mission. (See subparagraph C5.7.1.4.4. if no structure is involved.)

C5.7.2. HD 1.2, HD 1.3, HD 1.4, and HD 1.6 Hazards

C5.7.2.1. ILD. The exposures listed in subparagraphs C5.7.1.1. and C5.7.1.2. are permissible at the ILDs specified in applicable tables in Appendix 2 for HD 1.2, HD 1.3, HD 1.4, and HD 1.6. Barricades are insignificant on the ILDs in these tables without specific analysis.

C5.7.2.2. PTRD. The exposures listed in subparagraph C5.7.1.4. are permissible at the PTRDs specified in applicable tables in Appendix 2 for HD 1.2, HD 1.3, HD 1.4, and HD 1.6.

C5.7.2.3. IBD. The exposures listed in subparagraph C5.7.1.5. are permissible at the IBDs specified in applicable tables in Appendix 2 for HD 1.2, HD 1.3, HD 1.4, and HD 1.6.

C5.8. HAZARDOUS FRAGMENT DISTANCE (HFD)

C5.8.1. An important consideration in the analysis of the hazards associated with an explosion is the effect of any fragments produced. Although the predominant hazard for HD 1.1 is blast overpressure, an incident involving this HD may project hazardous fragments greater distances than the blast overpressure. Depending on their origin, fragments are referred to as "primary" or "secondary" fragments.

C5.8.1.1. Primary fragments result from the shattering of a container (e.g., shell casings, kettles, hoppers, and other containers used in the manufacture of explosives and rocket engine housings) in direct contact with the explosive. These fragments usually are small, initially travel at thousands of feet per second, and may be lethal at long distances from an explosion.

C5.8.1.2. Secondary fragments are debris from structures and other items in close proximity to the explosion. These fragments, which are somewhat larger in size than primary fragments and initially travel at hundreds of feet per second, do not normally travel as far as primary fragments.

C5.8.1.3. The minimum HFD for protection from hazardous fragments shall be based on primary and secondary fragments from the PES and the population or traffic density of the ES. "Minimum HFD" is defined as the distance at which the density of hazardous fragments becomes one (1) hazardous fragment per 600 ft^2 [55.7 m^2]. A hazardous fragment is one having an impact energy of 58 ft-lb [79 joules] or greater. The test protocol for determining the HFD is described in Reference (i).

C5.8.1.4. HFDs do not indicate the maximum range to which fragments may be projected, and therefore do not provide complete protection from fragments.

C5.8.1.5. QD criteria recognize the operational need for some personnel and facilities to be in the proximity of explosives and the risk of these exposures to fragment hazards is unavoidable. Therefore, HFD does not apply to all exposures.

C5.8.1.5.1. Minimum HD 1.1 HFDs apply to:

C5.8.1.5.1.1. Plant boundaries. The minimum HFD distance may extend onto uninhabited areas (such as wildlife preserve, desert, prairie, swamp, forest, agricultural land, or government land not open to the public) adjacent to contractor facilities but not within control of the contractor when access is restricted or controlled either naturally or by some other means. When HFD QD arcs extend past the plant boundary, the contractor's site plan shall certify that HFD protection is not required for the encumbered area and shall establish procedures to monitor the area for any change in status.

C5.8.1.5.1.2. Administration and housing areas.

C5.8.1.5.1.3. Recreation facilities, e.g., ball diamonds, golf courses, and volleyball courts. (See subparagraph C5.8.1.5.2.1. for situations where minimum fragment distances do not apply to recreational facilities.)

C5.8.1.5.1.4. Flight-line passenger service functions, e.g., terminal buildings.

C5.8.1.5.1.5. Utilities that provide vital utilities to a major portion of a DoD contractor plant.

C5.8.1.5.1.6. Inert storage and shops that, by reason of their vital strategic nature or high intrinsic value of their contents, should not be placed at risk.

C5.8.1.5.1.7. Functions that, if momentarily put out of action, would cause an immediate secondary hazard by reason of their failure to function.

C5.8.1.5.1.8. Private vehicles parked in administrative areas.

C5.8.1.5.2. Examples where minimum HD 1.1 HFDs do not apply:

C5.8.1.5.2.1. Recreation or training facilities when such facilities are located near AE support operations and are used solely by DoD contractor personnel who directly support these AE operations.

C5.8.1.5.2.2. AE related and support facilities and functions for which IMD and ILD would normally apply.

C5.8.1.5.2.3. Between a PES and inert storage, whether in a facility or in the open.

C5.8.1.5.2.4. Between facilities in an operating line; between operating lines; and between operating lines and storage locations.

C5.8.1.5.2.5. From PESs when engineering analysis, computer modeling, or testing demonstrate that fragments from the MCE are contained within the PES and the PES does not produce secondary fragments, or that the HFD is less than the minimum fragment distance specified in applicable QD tables in Appendix 2. Examples of potential fragment reduction methods include protective structures, suppressive shields, blast mats and curtains, equipment design and location, and barricades or terrain capable of stopping low angle, high velocity fragments. The demonstrated and documented reduced range becomes the minimum HFD.

C5.8.1.6. Selected AE items have been evaluated for minimum HFD and are listed in Table AP2.T3. Other AE items, through testing, have been hazard classified with a specific HFD presented in the format HD (xx) 1.1 or 1.3. The HFD for these items is specified in hundreds of feet (in parenthesis), and they may not be listed in Table AP2.T3. The distances for these two categories of select items apply only to items in the open. When in facilities, secondary debris as well as primary fragments must be considered.

C5.8.1.7. For exposures requiring HFD (see subparagraph C5.8.1.5.1.) and when HFD has not been established or is not known, the minimum default HFD shall apply (HFD for public traffic route (PTR) is 60 percent of the specified HFD for IBD):

C5.8.1.7.1. For all types of HD 1.1 in quantities $\leq$ 450 lbs NEWQD [204 kg], the HFD shall be determined as:

C5.8.1.7.1.1. For HD 1.1 in a 7-Bar or a 3-Bar ECM, use "Earth-Covered Magazine" distances shown in Table AP2.T1. as discussed in section C5.9.

C5.8.1.7.1.2. For HD 1.1 in an undefined ECM, where the loading density = NEWQD (lbs)/internal volume (ft^3) is $\leq$ 0.028 lbs/ft^3 [0.449 kg/m^3], use "Earth-Covered Magazine" distances shown in Table AP2.T1., as discussed in section C5.9.

CHAPTER 5

C5.8.1.7.1.3. For HD 1.1 in an undefined ECM where the loading density is > 0.028 lbs/ft^3 [0.449 kg/m^3], use "Earth-Covered Magazine - side and rear" distances of Table AP2.T1. For front exposure, apply the greater of "Earth-Covered Magazine – front" IBD distance of Table AP2.T1. or the HFD from the "STRUCTURE" column of Table AP2.T2. for the NEW in the ECM.

C5.8.1.7.1.4. Where ECMs, regardless of structural designation, have been designed, analyzed, or tested to have a reduced IBD and have been approved by the PCO for COCO and DDESB for government-owned, contractor-operated (GOCO) facilities, use the approved IBD.

C5.8.1.7.1.5. For HD 1.1 in a structure (excluding ECMs) capable of stopping primary fragments, but which can contribute to the debris hazard, use hazardous debris and PTRD distances found in Table AP2.T11. Structures that are capable of stopping primary fragments include all heavy wall (H) and heavy wall/roof (H/R) aboveground structure/site (AGS), as defined in the legend for Table AP2.T9. Doors and other openings through which primary fragments could exit must be capable of stopping primary fragments from exiting the facility or shall be barricaded in accordance with (IAW) paragraph C5.18.17. in order to trap primary fragments that could exit the facility.

C5.8.1.7.1.6. For HD 1.1 in the open or in a structure incapable of stopping primary fragments, use HFD listed in the "OPEN" column of Table AP2.T2. Structures (other than ECMs) that are capable of stopping primary fragments include all H and H/R AGSs, as defined in the legend for Table AP2.T9. All other structures (other than ECMs) are considered incapable of stopping primary fragments.

C5.8.1.7.1.7. The HFD for selected AE items that have established minimum HFDs (i.e., those listed in Table AP2.T3. and those with a numerical figure in parentheses in their HD designators) apply only to these items in the open. When AE is stored in operating facilities, secondary debris as well as primary fragments must be considered. If in a facility designed to contain primary fragments, apply criteria of subparagraphs C5.8.1.7.1.1. through C5.8.1.7.1.5. If the AE is in a facility that was not designed to stop primary fragments, compare the HFD from Table AP2.T3. for the item being considered, or the HFD associated with the (xx)(1.1) item, to the HFD in the "OPEN" column of Table AP2.T2. and use the greater distance for determining the applicable HFD.

C5.8.1.7.1.8. For bare explosives in the open, distance is computed by the formula d=40W$^{1/3}$ [15.87Q$^{1/3}$] .

C5.8.1.7.2. For HD 1.1 NEWQDs in the range 451 to 30,000 lbs [205 to 13,608 kg], HFD shall be determined according to the criteria indicated:

CHAPTER 5

C5.8.1.7.2.1. The minimum HFD shall be 1250 ft [381 m] as shown in Table AP2.T1. Lesser distances are permitted if supported by a structural analysis. Facilities sited at 1,235 ft [376 m] or 1,245 ft [380 m] per past standards shall be considered to be in compliance with the 1,250 ft [381 m] minimum requirement.

C5.8.1.7.2.2. For HD 1.1 in a 7-Bar or a 3-Bar ECM, use "Earth-Covered Magazine" distances shown in Table AP2.T1., as discussed in section C5.9.

C5.8.1.7.2.3. For HD 1.1 in an undefined ECM, where the loading density is $\leq$ 0.028 lbs/ft^3 [0.449 kg/m^3], use "Earth-Covered Magazine" distances of Table AP2.T1. as discussed in section C5.9.

C5.8.1.7.2.4. For HD 1.1 in an undefined ECM with minimum internal dimensions of 26 ft [7.92 m] wide and 60 ft [18.29 m] long, use "Earth-Covered Magazine - side and rear" distances of Table AP2.T1. and "Other PES" distance of Table AP2.T1. for the front exposure.

C5.8.1.7.2.5. For HD 1.1 in an undefined ECM where the loading density is > 0.028 lbs/ft3 [0.449 kg/m^3] and internal dimensions are less than 26 ft [7.92 m] wide and 60 ft [18.29 m] long, use "Other PES" distances of Table AP2.T1. for front, side, and rear exposures.

C5.8.1.7.2.6. The HFD for selected AE items that have established minimum fragment distances (i.e., those listed in Table AP2.T3. and those with a numerical figure in parentheses in their HD designators) apply only to these items in the open. When these items are placed in a facility, apply the criteria of subparagraphs C5.8.1.7.2.1. through C5.8.1.7.2.5., as appropriate.

C5.8.1.7.2.7. For bare explosives in the open, distance is computed by the formula d=40W$^{1/3}$ [15.87Q$^{1/3}$].

C5.8.1.7.3. For HD 1.1 NEWQDs > 30,000 lbs [13,608 kg], HFD will be in accordance with Table AP2.T1. Subparagraphs C5.8.1.7.3.1. through C5.8.1.7.3.4. apply to use of the reduced "Earth-Covered Magazine" distances shown in Table AP2.T1., for the NEW range between 30,000 lbs [13,608 kg] and 250,000 lbs [113,398 kg]:

C5.8.1.7.3.1. For HD 1.1 in a 7-Bar or a 3-Bar ECM, where internal dimensions are a minimum of 26 ft [7.92 m] wide and 60 ft [18.29 m] long, use "Earth-Covered Magazine" distances shown in Table AP2.T1.

C5.8.1.7.3.2. For HD 1.1 in a 7-Bar or a 3-Bar ECM, where internal dimensions are less than 26 ft [7.92 m] wide and 60 ft [18.29 m] long, use "Other PES" distances of Table AP2.T1. for front, side, and rear exposures.

C5.8.1.7.3.3. For HD 1.1 in an undefined ECM, where internal dimensions are a minimum of 26 ft [7.92 m] wide and 60 ft [18.29 m] long, use "Earth-Covered Magazine - side and rear" distances of AP2.T1. and "Other PES" distances of Table AP2.T1. for the front exposure.

C5.8.1.7.3.4. For HD 1.1 in an undefined ECM, where internal dimensions are less than 26 ft [7.92 m] wide and 60 ft [18.29 m] long, use "Other PES" distances of Table AP2.T1. for front, side, and rear exposures.

C5.8.1.7.4. For sparsely populated locations, the minimum 1,250 ft [381 m] fragment distance may be reduced to 900 ft [274 m] if the NEWQD of the PES does not exceed 11,400 lbs [5,171 kg]. For this purpose, "sparsely populated" is defined as no more than 25 persons located in any sector bounded by the sides of a 45 degree angle, with the vertex at the PES and the 900 ft [274 m] and 1,250 ft [381 m] arcs from the PES.

C5.8.1.7.5. For PTRs, the minimum HFD for HD 1.1 AE shall be based on the traffic density considered at three levels: high, medium, and low traffic density. The traffic density shall be averaged over a normal (non-holiday) week in terms of number of passengers during a 24-hour period. Minimum fragment distance reductions based on sparse population considerations addressed in subparagraph C5.8.1.7.4. do not apply to PTRs. In applying criteria other than the default values given in subparagraphs C5.8.1.7.5.1. through C5.8.1.7.5.4. (which are based on car (and rail) speed of 50 mph [80 kph], and a ship speed of 10 mph [16 kph]), considerations such as speed of vehicles, number of passengers per vehicle, protection afforded by the vehicle, variation in daily traffic levels in relation to AE activities, and seasonal traffic trends shall be taken into account to establish exposure levels. The default value of two passengers per car may be used to estimate traffic density.

C5.8.1.7.5.1. High Traffic Density. If routes have 10,000 or more car or rail passengers per day, or 2,000 or more ship passengers per day, then HFD criteria apply.

C5.8.1.7.5.2. Medium Traffic Density. If routes have between 400 and 10,000 car or rail passengers per day, or between 80 and 2,000 ship passengers per day, then 60 percent of the specified minimum HFD for IBD applies. As a minimum, these criteria apply to any recreational activity that is extensive and occurs on a regular basis.

C5.8.1.7.5.3. Low Traffic Density. If routes have fewer than 400 car or rail passengers per day, or fewer than 80 ship passengers per day, then no minimum fragment distance is required. Minimum distance shall be based on blast criteria ($24W^{1/3}/30W^{1/3}$ [$9.52Q^{1/3}/11.9Q^{1/3}$]).

C5.8.1.7.5.4. Miscellaneous. For other exposures that are permitted at PTRD, fragment distance minima for HD 1.1 AE shall be at least 60 percent of the specified minimum HFD for IBD.

CHAPTER 5

C5.9. IBD and PTRD

C5.9.1. Subparagraph C5.8.1.7. specifies the required separation distances to inhabited buildings and public traffic routes for ECMs and other types of PESs containing HD 1.1. Permissible exposures at these distances are listed in subparagraphs C5.7.1.4. and C5.7.1.5.

C5.9.2. Specified separations from ECMs consider reductions in blast overpressure attributable to the earth cover of ECMs, when the earth cover has a minimum thickness of 2 ft [0.61 m]. See subparagraph C5.8.1.7. for application of "Earth-Covered Magazine" distances of Table AP2.T1. to 7-Bar, 3-Bar, and undefined ECMs. The definitions for "front," "side," and "rear" for ECMs are illustrated in Figure AP3.F1. and are:

C5.9.2.1. The forward sector or "front" of an ECM is that area 60 degrees on either side of the ECM's centerline (120 degrees combined angle), with the vertex of the angle placed so that the sides of the angle pass through the intersection of the headwall and sidewalls.

C5.9.2.2. The rear sector or "rear" of an ECM is that area 45 degrees on either side of the magazine centerline (90 degrees combined angle), with the vertex of the angle placed so that the sides of the angle pass through the intersection of the rear and side walls.

C5.9.2.3. All other orientations are considered "side" sectors.

C5.10. ILD

C5.10.1. Separation Distances. Separation distances required between AE and non-AE buildings and sites within an AE operating line are listed for various quantities of HD 1.1 AE in Table AP2.T5. Permissible exposures at ILD are listed in subparagraphs C5.7.1.1. (barricaded ILD) and C5.7.1.2. (unbarricaded ILD). In order to apply barricaded ILD, barricades must comply with paragraph C5.18.17. NOTE: The separation distance between an operating building and its service magazine shall be based on the NEWQD and the HD of the AE in the magazine and not that of the operating line.

C5.10.2. ILD From ECMs. Testing has shown that some attenuation of airblast overpressure relative to an unconfined surface burst occurs out the sides and rear of an ECM and a slight increase occurs out the front of an ECM. The equivalent $9W^{1/3}$ [$3.57Q^{1/3}$] (12 psi [82.7 kPa] (barricaded)) and $18W^{1/3}$ [$7.14 Q^{1/3}$] (3.5 psi [24 kPa] (unbarricaded)) ILD from an ECM, when accounting for this attenuation, are given in Table AP2.T4. NOTE: Airblast forms the basis for the equations given in the Notes in this table. Paragraph C5.11.3. provides criteria for the application of barricaded ILD from ECMs.

CHAPTER 5

C5.11. <u>IMD</u>

Magazines for HD 1.1 shall be separated one from another per Tables AP2.T6., AP2.T7., and AP2.T8. (NOTE: Table AP2.T6. provides orientation relationships for ECMs; Tables AP2.T7. and AP2.T8. provide the actual separation distances.)

C5.11.1. For examples of siting rules for various magazine orientations, see Figures AP3.F1. through AP3.F7.

C5.11.2. Other factors limiting ECM storage include:

C5.11.2.1. Quantities above 500,000 lbs [226,795 kg] NEWQD in one ECM are not authorized, except for energetic liquids.

C5.11.2.2. The 7-foot separation distance given in Table AP2.T7. for 100 lbs [45.4 kg] NEWQD constitutes the minimum side-to-side magazine separation distance.

C5.11.3. Application of barricaded ILD and barricaded IMD from an ECM. Figure AP3.F7. illustrates the IMD relationships that can exist between an ECM and AGM and the ILD relationships that can exist between an ECM and facilities permitted to be at ILD or barricaded ILD from an ECM, when each contain HD 1.1 AE. Permissible exposures at ILD are listed in subparagraphs C5.7.1.1. (barricaded ILD) and C5.7.1.2. (unbarricaded ILD). Siting criteria for AGMs are provided in Table AP2.T6. These criteria shall apply to the use of barricaded IMD for AGMs and for use of barricaded ILD:

C5.11.3.1. <u>Front Sector of an ECM</u>. Use of barricaded ILD or barricaded IMD, as applicable, between an ECM and a facility located within the ECM's front sector requires that a properly constructed, intervening barricade be located between the ES and the PES. This barricade must meet the construction and location criteria of section C5.18.17. If it does not meet these criteria, then unbarricaded IMD or unbarricaded ILD, as applicable, shall be used for siting purposes.

C5.11.3.2. <u>Side and Rear Sectors of an ECM</u>. If an ECM's earth cover meets all construction criteria of subparagraph C5.18.17.2., it will qualify as a barricade. Use of barricaded ILD or barricaded IMD, as applicable, from the sides or rear of the ECM is permissible. Failure of the ECM's earth cover to meet these criteria shall require use of unbarricaded IMD or unbarricaded ILD, as applicable, for siting purposes.

C5.11.4. These IMD standards apply only to storage of HD 1.1 AE. Existing ECMs, regardless of orientation, that meet the construction and barricading requirements of C5.18.17. and are sited one from another for a minimum of 100 lbs [45.4 kg] NEWQD of HD 1.1 may be used to their physical storage capacity for HD 1.2, HD 1.3, and HD 1.4 AE; provided distances to other exposures comply with applicable QD requirements.

CHAPTER 5

C5.12. HD 1.2

C5.12.1. HD 1.2 are items configured for storage and transportation that do not mass detonate when a single item or package in a stack is initiated. Explosions involving the items result in their burning and exploding progressively with no more than a few at a time reacting. These reactions will project fragments, firebrands, and unexploded items from the explosion site. Blast effects are limited to the immediate vicinity and are not the primary hazard.

C5.12.2. Small quantities of HD 1.2.1 ($\leq$ 450 lbs NEWQD [204 kg],), in certain packaging configurations, will react in a manner more typical of an HD 1.1 event. When located in structures that stop primary fragments, but which generate a secondary debris hazard (e.g., certain ECMs and hardened structures), the structural damage and debris hazards produced from these events are more characteristic of an HD 1.1 explosion rather than the progressive nature of an HD 1.2.1 event as described above. When the NEWQD and the MCE of the packaged HD 1.2.1 items fall within the ranges specified in the equation {NEWQD $\leq$ MCE $\leq$ 450 lbs [204 kg]}, the HD 1.2.1 shall be treated as HD 1.1 and the criteria of subparagraph C5.8.1.7.1., as applicable, shall be used. If they fall outside the ranges of the equation, then the criteria of Table AP2.T9. shall be applied.

C5.12.3. The NEW of an HD 1.2 item (used for transportation) is the sum of the weight of the HD 1.1 and HD 1.3 material contained within the item. The NEWQD for an item is equal to NEW (NEWQD = NEW) unless testing has been conducted. Based on testing, the NEWQD may include a reduced contribution ($\leq$ 100 percent) from the HD 1.3 material as a result of the HD 1.1 material being functioned. The NEWQD should be determined by the Single Package Test (United Nations (UN) Test 6 (a) or its equivalent), not the Bonfire Test (UN Test 6 (c)) (Reference (i)). The NEWQD for a specific item may be obtained from the JHCS. The effects produced by the functioning of HD 1.2 items vary with the size and weight of the item. HD 1.2 AE is separated into two subdivisions in order to account for the differences in magnitude of these effects for purposes of setting QD criteria. The more hazardous items are referred to as HD 1.2.1 items. The less hazardous items are referred to as HD 1.2.2. NOTE: It is important not to exaggerate the significance of the value of 1.60 lbs [0.73 kg] used to differentiate HD 1.2.1 from HD 1.2.2. This value is based on a break point in the database supporting the QD relationships and tables and the NEWQD of the rounds tested. If comprehensive data are available for a particular item, then the item may be placed in that category of HD 1.2 supported by the data and allocated the relevant QDs:

C5.12.3.1. HD 1.2.1: NEWQD > 1.60 lbs [0.73 kg]

C5.12.3.2. HD 1.2.2: NEWQD $\leq$ 1.60 lbs [0.73 kg]

C5.12.4. The MCE for HD 1.2.1 is the NEWQD of an item times the number of items in three unpalletized, outer shipping packages, unless testing or analogy demonstrates a different MCE. The authorized MCE for a specific HD 1.2.1 item is listed in the JHCS.

C5.12.5. The QD specified for HD 1.2 AE achieve the desired degree of protection against immediate hazards from an incident. Events involving HD 1.2 items lob large amounts of unexploded rounds, components, and subassemblies that will remain hazardous after impact. Such items are likely to be more hazardous than their original state because of possible damage by heat and impact to fuse, safety device, energetic, or other features. Many types of AE containing submunitions, such as cluster bombs, can be expected to be projected out to distances as great as the relevant inhabited building distances. Furthermore, it is impractical to specify QDs, which allow for the maximum possible flight ranges of propulsive items.

C5.12.6. Table AP2.T9. provides a summary matrix of all the appropriate IBD, PTRD, and ILD separations for HD 1.2.1 and HD 1.2.2 AE, for the various combinations of ESs and PESs. When HD 1.2.1 items are stored in structures that may contribute to the debris hazard, the IBD is determined by using the larger of two distances: either that given in Table AP2.T10. for the appropriate explosive weight (number of items times NEWQD) or that given in Table AP2.T11. for the appropriate MCE. NOTE: Hazardous debris distance (HDD) specified in Table AP2.T11. equates to IBD.

C5.12.7. IMD is dependent upon the types of structures acting as both the PES and the ES.

C5.12.8. PTRDs given in Tables AP2.T9. through AP2.T12. give consideration to the transient nature of the exposure in the same manner as for HD 1.1. PTRD is computed as 60 percent of the IBD for items in this HD, with minimum distances specified in Table AP2.T9.

C5.12.9. ILDs given in Tables AP2.T9. through AP2.T12. take into account the progressive nature of explosions involving these items (normally resulting from fire spread), up to the magnitude of the MCE, and the ability to evacuate personnel from endangered areas before the progression involves large numbers of items. Exposed structures may be extensively damaged by projections and delayed propagation of explosions may occur due to the ignition of combustibles by projections. ILD is computed as 36 percent of the IBD for items of this HD, with a minimum distance equal to the IMD given in Table AP2.T9. for the applicable PES-ES combination.

C5.12.10. When storing mixed subdivisions of HD 1.2 AE (HD 1.2.1 and HD 1.2.2), consider each subdivision separately and apply the greater of the two distances. The general mixing rules for HD 1.2 AE are given in Table AP2.T13.

C5.12.11. For reasons of operational necessity, limited quantities of HD 1.2.2 items may be stored in facilities such as hangars, troop buildings, and manufacturing or operating buildings without regard to QD. Fragmentation shielding shall be provided.

C5.12.12. HD 1.2.3 is a special storage subdivision for AE (see subparagraph C4.1.1.2.3.).

C5.12.13. The IBD for HD 1.2.3 is determined using Table AP2.T14. (HD 1.3 QD) for the NEWQD of the HD 1.2.3 item multiplied by the number of rounds present, but with a minimum IBD determined by:

CHAPTER 5

C5.12.13.1. If the AE are located in a structure that can interrupt primary fragments and can contribute debris, the minimum IBD is the hazardous debris distance given in Table AP2.T11. for an MCE equal to the NEWQD of a single round.

C5.12.13.2. If the AE are in the open or in a light structure that will not interrupt primary fragments, the minimum IBD is the HFD based on the HD 1.1 hazardous fragment areal number density criteria applied to a single HD 1.2.3 item. The HFD applicable to AE in the open is specified in hundreds of feet in parentheses as "(xx) HD 1.2.3."

C5.12.13.3. As an alternative to the preceding HD 1.2.3 QD criteria, when an increase in the allowable quantity or a reduction in the required distance will result, HD 1.2.3 AE may be treated as indicated:

C5.12.13.3.1. If the single-round NEWQD is > 1.6 lbs [0.73 kg]; consider the items as HD 1.2.1. Use the total NEWQD present, with an MCE equal to the NEWQD of one round to determine the maximum QD.

C5.12.13.3.2. If the single-round NEWQD is ≤ 1.6 lbs [0.73 kg], consider the items as HD 1.2.2, based on the total NEWQD present.

C5.12.14. For storage of mixed HD 1.2.3 AE, multiply the NEWQD for the HD 1.2.3 items by the corresponding number of HD 1.2.3 rounds and use Table AP2.T14. to determine the HFD for the mixture based on the largest HFD for the HD 1.2.3 AE in storage. When HD 1.2.3 AE is located with any other HD 1.2 subdivision, use the distances given in Table AP2.T13. When HD 1.2.3 AE is located with any other HD AE, the HD 1.2.3 AE is considered HD 1.2 (HD 1.2.1 or HD 1.2.2, according to NEWQD) for QD purposes. The mixing rules in paragraph C5.3.2. then apply to the combination of the HD.

C5.12.15. HD 1.2 AE in the current inventory, with IBD given in hundreds of feet and presented in parentheses in the format HD (xx) 1.2, need not use the QD criteria specified in paragraph C5.12.5. Instead, constant value QD criteria for these items may be specified as:

C5.12.15.1. IBD is the distance specified in hundreds of feet (in parentheses).

C5.12.15.2. PTR is computed as 60 percent of IBD.

C5.12.15.3. ILD is computed as 36 percent of IBD, with a minimum distance equal to the IMD given in Table AP2.T9. (Appendix 2).

C5.13. <u>HD 1.3</u>

HD 1.3 includes items that burn vigorously with little or no possibility of extinguishment in storage situations. Explosions normally will be confined to pressure ruptures of containers and will not produce propagating shock waves or damaging blast overpressure beyond the magazine distance specified in Table AP2.T14. A severe hazard of spread of fire may result from tossing about of burning container materials, propellant, or other flaming debris.

C5.14. <u>HD 1.4</u>

C5.14.1. HD 1.4 AE presents a fire hazard with minimal blast, fragmentation, or toxic hazards. Separate facilities for storage and handling of these AE shall be located IAW Table AP2.T15.

C5.14.2. In mixed storage, the NEWQD of HD 1.4 is not additive (see subparagraph C5.3.2.1.1.). However, QD criteria for each HD present, including HD 1.4, must be determined and the largest value shall be used.

C5.14.3. HD 1.4S AE may be stored (including associated handling) without regard to the QD criteria in Table AP2.T15.

C5.15. <u>HD 1.6</u>

QD separations for HD 1.6 AE shall be based on the storage location and configuration. This information is detailed in Table AP2.T16. and its footnotes. A maximum of 500,000 lbs [226,795 kg] NEWQD shall be permitted at any one location. Any special storage configuration and siting approved for HD 1.1 AE may be used for storage of like explosive weights of HD 1.6 AE.

C5.16. <u>HD 6.1</u>

C5.16.1. HD 6.1 includes items that contain only toxic chemical or riot control agents. AE containing both explosives and toxic chemical or riot control agents may be hazard classified as HD 1.1 through HD 1.4, based on testing IAW Reference (i).

C5.16.2. Hazard zones for toxic chemical agents are determined by the relative toxicity of the agents, the amount released to the atmosphere, and the rate at which they are released (that is, evaporation, pressure, or explosive dispersal), terrain features, and meteorological conditions. Hazard zone calculations are based on MCE, using DDESB TP No. 10, (Reference (o)). DoD criteria for toxic chemical munitions and agents are provided in Chapter 11 of Reference (c).

C5.16.3. When siting AE containing toxic chemical agents, both the explosives and toxic chemical agent hazards shall be evaluated with the greatest QD criteria governing siting.

C5.17. ENERGETIC LIQUIDS

C5.17.1. Scope and Application

C5.17.1.1. This section applies to the storage of energetic liquids listed in Table AP2.T17. in all types of containers, including rocket and missile tankage. Laboratory quantities shall be stored and handled as determined by the DoD contractor. NOTE: The QD requirements are based on only the energetic liquids' energetic reaction (blast overpressure and container fragmentation). These QD requirements do not consider the toxicity or potential down-wind hazard. Therefore, QD may not be the only factor that needs to be considered when selecting a location for storage of and operations involving energetic liquids.

C5.17.1.2. These requirements DO NOT govern the storage or handling of energetic liquids for uses other than in space launch vehicles, rockets, missiles, associated static test apparatus, and AE.

C5.17.2. Concept

C5.17.2.1. These QD standards were developed on the premise that the DoD contractor shall ensure that the materials of construction are compatible with the energetic liquids, facilities are of appropriate design, fire protection and drainage control techniques are employed, and other specialized controls (e.g., nitrogen padding, blanketing, and tank cooling) are used, when required.

C5.17.2.2. When additional hazards associated with AE are involved; the safety distances prescribed in other sections of this standard shall be applied, as required.

C5.17.2.3. These standards are based upon the estimated credible damage resulting from an incident, without considering probabilities or frequency of occurrence.

C5.17.3. Determination of Energetic Liquids Quantity

C5.17.3.1. The total quantity of energetic liquids in a tank, drum, cylinder, or other container shall be the net weight of the energetic liquids contained therein. Quantity of energetic liquids in the associated piping must be included to the points that positive means are provided for interrupting the flow through the pipe, or interrupting a reaction in the pipe in the event of an incident.

C5.17.3.2. When the quantities of energetic liquids are given in gallons [liters], the conversion factors given in Table AP2.T18. may be used to determine the quantity in pounds [kg].

CHAPTER 5

C5.17.4. Measurement of Separation Distances

C5.17.4.1. Measure from the closest controlling hazard source, e.g., containers, buildings, segment, or positive cutoff point in piping.

C5.17.4.2. Measure from the nearest container or controlling subdivision when buildings containing a small number of cylinders or drums are present or when quantities of energetic liquids are subdivided effectively.

C5.17.5. Hazard Classification of Energetic Liquids

C5.17.5.1. The main UN hazard classification designators for energetic liquids are (the original liquid propellant Hazard Groups I - IV and CG A - F are no longer used):

C5.17.5.1.1. Class 1: Explosives.

C5.17.5.1.2. Class 2: Compressed or Liquefied Gases.

C5.17.5.1.3. Class 3: Flammable Liquids.

C5.17.5.1.4. Class 4: Flammable Solids and Self-Reactive Materials.

C5.17.5.1.5. Class 5: Oxidizers.

C5.17.5.1.6. Class 6: Toxic and Infectious Substances.

C5.17.5.1.7. Class 8: Corrosive.

C5.17.5.1.8. Class 9: Miscellaneous.

C5.17.5.2. Because two energetic liquids might each be compatible with certain explosive AE stores, but incompatible with each other, a two-part compatibility group designation is assigned to an energetic liquid. NOTE: The design and logistics of modern weapons sometimes require that consideration be given to permitting storage or operations involving energetic liquids in a storage structure containing solid explosives. For example, it may be necessary to store hydrocarbon-fueled cruise missiles having high explosive warheads with fueled configurations not containing explosive warheads. Another example is the storage of liquid gun propellant with explosive AE components.

C5.17.5.2.1. The first element is the standard storage and transportation CG designation. The alpha designations are the same as the CG designations for UN Class 1 as given in Chapter 4 of this Manual. However, for storage and handling on DoD facilities, a CG may also be assigned to an energetic liquid in a Class other than Class 1. The absence of a CG indicates incompatibility with solid explosives.

C5.17.5.2.2. The second element is a new Energetic Liquid Compatibility Group (ELCG) designation. The ELCG applies to mixed storage of energetic liquids or AE containing energetic liquids. The ELCG is specified in parentheses as the last element of the hazard classification. The ELCG designations and definitions are:

C5.17.5.2.2.1. <u>LA</u>: Energetic liquids that are strong oxidizers, mainly of acidic character. These materials may cause or contribute to the combustion of other material, possibly resulting in serious flare fires or explosions. Includes, but is not limited to, nitrogen tetroxide and mixed oxides of nitrogen (MON), inhibited red fuming nitric acid (IRFNA), liquid oxygen (LO$_2$), hydrogen peroxide (H$_2$O$_2$), and gels, slurries, or their emulsions.

C5.17.5.2.2.2. <u>LB</u>: Energetic liquids that are readily combustible when exposed to or ignited in the presence of an oxidizing agent, but that are not strong reducing agents. Some may be hypergolic with group LA materials. Includes, but is not limited to, hydrocarbons such as kerosenes and strained ring ramjet fuels; liquid hydrogen (LH$_2$); and gels, slurries, or their emulsions.

C5.17.5.2.2.3. <u>LC</u>: Energetic liquids that are readily combustible when exposed to, or ignited in the presence of an oxidizing agent, and are also strong reducing agents. These will likely be hypergolic with group LA substances. Includes, but is not limited to, hydrazines and other amines; and gels, slurries, or their emulsions.

C5.17.5.2.2.4. <u>LD</u>: Energetic liquids that act mainly as combustible fuels, similar to groups LB and LC, when exposed to or ignited in the presence of oxidizing agents, but that may act as oxidizers in some combinations. They may be a monopropellant with the right catalyst, or may be pyrophoric and ignite upon release to the atmosphere. Examples are ethylene and propylene oxides and boranes.

C5.17.5.2.2.5. <u>LE</u>: Energetic liquids having characteristics that do not permit storage with any other energetic liquid. They may react adversely with either fuels (reducing agents) or oxidizers. Examples are nitromethane, nitrate ester-based formulations such as Otto Fuel II, liquid monopropellants containing hydroxyl ammonium nitrate (HAN), halogen fluorides (C$_I$F$_3$ and C$_I$F$_5$) and fluorine, and gels, slurries, or their emulsions.

C5.17.5.2.3. <u>Mixing of Energetic Liquids</u>

C5.17.5.2.3.1. Different energetic liquids in the same ELCG may be stored together.

C5.17.5.2.3.2. ELCG-LE may not be mixed with other ELCG or dissimilar ELCG-LE.

C5.17.5.2.3.3. Mixed storage is prohibited between energetic liquids of different ELCG designations with one exception. ELCG-LB and ELCG-LC usually should not be stored together, particularly when the majority of the material stored is ELCG-LB; however, mixed storage of ELCG-LB and ELCG-LC is permitted when operationally necessary.

C5.17.5.2.4. As an example of mixing of energetic liquids, consider the HD 1.3C (LE) hazard classification for HAN-based liquid gun propellant XM-46:

C5.17.5.2.4.1. "C" indicates the propellant can be stored in the same magazine with CG-C solid propellants. Because CG-C and CG-D can be mixed, CG-D high explosive projectiles could also be stored with the energetic liquid gun propellant.

C5.17.5.2.4.2. "LE" indicates that hydrocarbon fuels (e.g., JP-10) that are an ELCG-LB would not be permitted in this storage scenario, because its ELCG-LB indicates incompatibility with ELCG-LE.

C5.17.5.3. Complete DoD hazard classification assignments for current energetic liquids are shown in Table AP2.T17. NOTE: Conversions for gallons of energetic liquids to pounds is provided in Table AP2.T18.

C5.17.5.4. Each new energetic liquid, or new non-bulk packaging configuration of an energetic liquid, developed by a DoD Component or adopted for DoD use must be examined and assigned a hazard classification per Reference (i).

C5.17.5.5. A different minimum distance may be assigned during the hazard classification process when the hazards of a particular new packaging configuration are not adequately addressed. This distance shall be indicated parenthetically, in hundreds of feet, as the first element of the hazard classification. For example, if a new liquid oxidizer pressure vessel configuration is hazard classified as HD (04)2.2(LA), then a minimum distance of 400 ft [122 m] would apply for IBD and PTRD; otherwise the prescribed liquid oxidizer QD criteria would apply.

C5.17.5.6. The predominant hazard of the individual energetic liquids can vary depending upon the location of the energetic liquid storage and the operations involved. These locations are listed in the order of decreasing hazards.

C5.17.5.6.1. <u>Launch Pads</u>. Operations at these facilities are very hazardous because of the proximity of fuel and oxidizer to each other, the frequency of launchings, lack of restraint of the vehicle after liftoff, and the possibility of fallback with resultant dynamic mixing on impact. To compute the explosive equivalent for the launch pad, use Table AP2.T19. with the combined energetic liquids weight in the launch vehicle tanks and any energetic liquids in piping that are subject to mixing, except as indicated in subparagraph C5.17.5.8.

C5.17.5.6.2. <u>Static Test Stands</u>. Operations at these facilities are less hazardous because test items are restrained and subject to better control than launch vehicles. As with launch pads, the proximity of fuel and oxidizer presents a significant hazard. To reduce this hazard, tankage should be separated and remotely located from the static test stand. Explosive equivalents of Table AP2.T19. shall be used, with the combined energetic liquids weight subject to mixing as determined by hazard analysis. The amount of energetic liquids held in run tanks can be excluded from consideration if the test stand meets the criteria provided in subparagraphs C5.17.5.6.2.1. through C5.17.5.6.2.4., if applicable:

C5.17.5.6.2.1. All tanks are American Society of Mechanical Engineers (ASME) certified and maintained per ASME Code, section VIII, Division 1 or Division 2 (Reference (p)).

C5.17.5.6.2.2. For cryogenic propellants, all tanks are constructed with double wall jacketing.

C5.17.5.6.2.3. Run tankage is protected from fragments produced by an engine malfunction.

C5.17.5.6.2.4. Both the fuel and oxidizer lines contain two (redundant), remotely operated valves to shut off flow in the event of a malfunction.

C5.17.5.7. Ready storage is relatively close to the launch and static test stands; normally it is not involved directly in feeding the engine as in the case with run tankage, which is an integral part of all launch and test stand operations. The explosive equivalents of Table AP2.T19. shall be used with the combined energetic liquids weight subject to mixing if the facility design does not guarantee against fuel and oxidizer mixing and against detonation propagation to, or initiation at, the ready storage facility when a mishap occurs at the test stand, on the ground at the launch pad, or at the ready storage areas. Otherwise, fire and fragment hazards shall govern (see Tables AP2.T17., AP2.T20., AP2.T21., AP2.T22., and AP2.T23.).

C5.17.5.8. Fire and fragment hazards govern cold-flow test operations (Tables AP2.T17., AP2.T20., AP2.T21., AP2.T22., and AP2.T23.) if the design is such that the system is closed except for approved venting; is completely airtight; fuel and oxidizer never are employed concurrently; each has a completely separate, isolated system and fitting types to preclude intermixing; and the energetic liquids are of required purity. Otherwise, explosive equivalents (Table AP2.T19.) shall be used with the combined energetic liquids weight.

C5.17.5.9. Bulk storage requires the most remote storage with respect to launch and test operations. It consists of the area, tanks, and other containers therein, used to hold energetic liquids for supplying ready storage and, indirectly, run tankage where no ready storage is available. Fire and fragment hazards govern (Tables AP2.T17., AP2.T20., AP2.T21., AP2.T22., and AP2.T23.) except in special cases as indicated in Tables AP2.T17. and AP2.T19.

CHAPTER 5

C5.17.5.10. Rest storage is a temporary type of storage and most closely resembles bulk storage. It is a temporary parking location for barges, trailers, tank cars, and portable hold tanks used for topping operations when these units actually are not engaged in the operation; and for such vehicles when they are unable to empty their cargo promptly into the intended storage container. Fire and fragment hazards govern (Tables AP2.T17., AP2.T20., AP2.T21., AP2.T22., and AP2.T23.) except in special cases as indicated in Tables AP2 T17. and AP2.T19. The transporter becomes a part of that storage to which it is connected during energetic liquids transfer.

C5.17.5.11. Run or operating tankage consists of the tank and other containers and associated piping used to hold the energetic liquids for direct feeding into the engine or device during operation. The contents of properly separated "run tanks" (operating tankage) and piping are normally considered on the basis of the pertinent hazards for the materials involved, except for quantities of incompatible materials that are or can be in a position to become mixed. Explosive equivalents shall be used (Table AP2.T19.) for quantities of such materials subject to mixing unless provisions of subparagraphs C5.17.5.6.2.1. through C5.17.5.6.2.4. are satisfied.

C5.17.5.12. A 25-ft [7.6 m] clear zone to inhabited buildings shall be maintained, as a minimum, on each side of pipelines used for energetic liquids (excluding flammable or combustible liquids that exhibit normal fire hazards such as RP-1, JP-10, and Otto Fuel II). Tables AP2.T17., AP2.T21., AP2.T22., and AP2.T23. apply, as appropriate.

C5.17.6. <u>QD Standards</u>. Since many energetic liquids are not classified as UN Class 1 explosives, conventional QD storage criteria do not generally apply to these materials. At the same time, the (non-Class 1) UN transportation hazard classifications for many energetic liquids appear to be inappropriate or inadequate for application to storage safety (based on available accident and test data). For example, hydrazine has a UN hazard classification of 8 (corrosive), while it also is subject to dangerous fire and explosive behavior. Thus, the implementation of QD criteria for energetic liquids is based on an independent determination of the predominant hazard presented by the material in the storage environment. Standards applicable to energetic liquids used for propulsion or operation of missiles, rockets, and other related devices are:

C5.17.6.1. Tables AP2.T17., AP2.T20., AP2.T21., AP2.T22., and AP2.T23. provide minimum distance requirements for storage of bulk quantities and, in some cases, pressure vessels and other commercial packagings of energetic liquids. In general when two or more storage locations contain different energetic liquids, compute the separation distance for each of the materials using Tables AP2.T17., AP2.T20., AP2.T21., AP2.T22., and AP2.T23.; the greater distance shall be the minimum distance for separating storage of the different energetic liquids. In addition, positive measures shall be taken to control the flow of energetic liquids in the event of a leak or spill, in order to prevent possible fire propagation or accumulation of flammable liquids near other storage, and to prevent mixing of incompatible energetic liquids (except for specific hazardous locations as identified in subparagraph C5.17.5.6.). Explosives equivalence applies for some materials as indicated in Tables AP2.T17. and AP2.T19. Fragment hazards

CHAPTER 5

govern for some materials in certain packaging configurations. For the more conventional fuels and oxidizers, and also where minimum blast or fragment criteria are not required due to low confinement packaging, QD standards are adopted from OSHA and NFPA guidelines to account for normal fire protection principles.

C5.17.6.2. For specific hazardous locations as defined in subparagraph C5.17.5.6., explosives equivalency may apply. If so, consult Tables AP2.T17. and AP2.T19. with the combined energetic liquids weight subject to mixing and use distances found in Table AP2.T1. or AP2.T5. Enter weight of explosives equivalent in Table AP2.T1. or AP2.T5. QD standards for other conditions and explosive equivalents for any combination not contained in Table AP2.T17. or AP2.T19. shall be determined by the DoD contractor.

C5.17.7. Contaminated Energetic Liquids

C5.17.7.1. Caution shall be exercised in the storage and handling of contaminated energetic liquids. Such contamination may increase the degree of hazard associated with the energetic liquids.

C5.17.7.2. Energetic liquids known to be contaminated or in a suspect condition shall be isolated and provided separate storage from all other energetic liquids pending laboratory analysis for verification of contamination and disposition requirements, if any.

C5.18. FACILITIES SITING CRITERIA

This section provides specific criteria for siting AE and non-AE facilities with respect to PESs.

C5.18.1. Administration and Industrial Areas and Auxiliary Facilities

C5.18.1.1. Administration and industrial areas shall be separated from PESs by IBD.

C5.18.1.2. Auxiliary facilities (e.g., heating plants, line offices, break areas, briefing rooms for daily work schedules or site safety matters, joiner shops, security posts, and similar functions) located at or near AE operations and servicing only one building or operation may be located at fire protection distance (50 ft [15.2 m] for non-combustible structures, 100 ft [30.5 m] for combustible structures) from the building or operation they support.

C5.18.2. Temporary Construction or Maintenance Operations. Construction and maintenance personnel who are temporarily near a PES to perform their job shall be provided the maximum practicable protection from the effects of an explosion if one occurs at a PES. The contractor shall determine the minimum practicable separation distance from the PES for such personnel and shall control operations at the PES to minimize exposure of these personnel to hazards from an explosion. Documentation of the rationale for the control measures taken shall be maintained until construction or maintenance operations are completed.

C5.18.3. <u>Detached Loading Docks</u>. Detached loading docks that normally service multiple facilities shall be sited on the basis of use.

C5.18.3.1. When servicing magazines, they must be separated from magazines by IMD.

C5.18.3.2. When servicing operating buildings, they must be separated from the operating buildings by ILD.

C5.18.4. <u>Conveyance Loading and Unloading at a Magazine</u>. A conveyance (e.g., truck, trailer, railcar, International Organization for Standardization [ISO] or Military-owned demountable [MILVAN] container) loading and unloading operation is permitted at a magazine without regard to QD between the magazine and the operation. "At a magazine" means loading and unloading operations at a loading dock attached to the magazine, on the pad/apron in front of the magazine, or within the established boundaries of an AGM. Detached ramps or loading docks that normally service multiple facilities will be sited IAW subparagraph C5.18.3.

C5.18.5. <u>Areas for Burning AE</u>

C5.18.5.1. Use QD formula $D = K24W^{1/3}$ [$9.52Q^{1/3}$] to determine the minimum safe distance for either personnel burning AE or those conducting unrelated AE operations.

C5.18.5.2. Use QD formula $D = K40W^{1/3}$ [$15.87Q^{1/3}$] to determine the safe distance for persons not performing AE operations. However, if the NEWQD of burn material is more than 450 lbs [204 kg], the minimum safe distance shall be at least 1,250 ft [381 m]. If the NEWQD of burn material is ≤ 450 lbs [204 kg], use the minimum HFD given in Table AP2.T2.

C5.18.5.3. Locate burning grounds at ILD from other PESs.

C5.18.6. <u>Areas Used for Intentional Detonations</u>

C5.18.6.1. Protective structures for personnel or measures to suppress blast or fragment effects may be used to reduce the required withdrawal distances in subparagraphs C5.18.6.2 and C5.18.6.3.

C5.18.6.2. Control sites for intentional detonations for AE disposal shall be located at ILD from other PESs, based on the PES NEWQD.

C5.18.6.3. The minimum separation distances between areas used for intentional detonation (excluding hands-on training) and non-essential personnel are determined by application of the appropriate criteria:

C5.18.6.3.1. For non-fragmenting AE, use $D = 328W^{1/3}$ but not less than 1,250 ft [$D = 130.1Q^{1/3}$, but not less than 381 m]. If known, maximum debris throw distance, with a safety factor determined by the DoD contractor, may be used to replace the 1,250 ft [381 m] minimum distance.

C5.18.6.3.2. For fragmenting AE, use the larger of the two distances:

C5.18.6.3.2.1. Either the distance determined from the equation $D = 328W^{1/3}$

C5.18.6.3.2.2. Or not less than 1,250 ft. [$D = 130.1Q^{1/3}$ but not less than 381 m].

C5.18.6.3.3. The distances given in Table AP2.T24, based on the diameter of the AE being destroyed. A calculated or measured maximum fragment throw distance (including the interaction effects for stacks of items or single items, whichever applies), with a safety factor determined by the DoD contractor, may be used to replace these distances. Calculated case fragment maximum throw distances for selected munitions are given in Table AP2.T25.

C5.18.6.3.3.1. The calculated case fragment throw distances in Tables AP2.T24. and AP2.T25. are for individual items. These throw distances do not consider "rogue" fragments that are produced by sections of nose plugs, base plates, or lugs, and they do not directly apply to stacks of munitions. In addition, shaped charge jets or slugs from directed energy munitions can travel significantly greater distances than case fragments; therefore, these munitions require specific analysis.

C5.18.6.3.3.2. "Rogue" fragments can travel significantly greater distances (> 10,000 ft [3,048 m]) than those shown in Tables AP2.T24. and AP2.T25. Care must be taken either to properly orient the munitions (e.g., lugs or strongbacks and nose or tail plate sections oriented away from personnel locations) or to minimize or eliminate the hazard of rogue fragments, e.g., sand bagging the munitions prior to detonation.

C5.18.6.3.4. For multiple munitions detonation, the preferred approach is:

C5.18.6.3.4.1. Place the munitions in a single layer with their sides touching such that their axis is horizontal.

C5.18.6.3.4.2. Place the munitions so that the nose of each munition is pointing in the same direction.

C5.18.6.3.4.3. Orient the munitions so that lugs or strongbacks and nose or tail plate sections are facing away from areas to be protected.

C5.18.6.3.4.4. Initiate the stack detonation so that all munitions detonate simultaneously.

C5.18.6.3.4.5. When the procedures outlined in subparagraphs C5.18.6.3.3.1. through C5.18.6.3.3.4. cannot be met, use:

C5.18.6.3.4.5.1. If the orientation of the potential rogue fragments can be controlled, then the ranges given in Tables AP2.T24. and AP2.T25. shall be increased by 20 percent to account for the interaction effects.

C5.18.6.3.4.5.2. If the orientation of potential rogue fragments cannot be controlled; fragment ranges must be evaluated on a case-by-case basis.

C5.18.6.3.4.5.3. If detonations involve stacks of mixed munitions; evaluate the distance for each munition separately using the procedures in subparagraph C5.18.6.3.2.2. and select the largest distance.

C5.18.6.4. The databases associated with Reference (l) may be used to determine maximum fragment projection distance.

C5.18.7. Spacing for Movement of AE Within Operating Lines. Items or groups of items of AE that are transported from one operating building to another, or from bay to bay within an operating building, shall be separated to preclude the establishment of a path for the propagation of an explosion or fire between the buildings or bays. For this purpose, the minimum spacing between AE items or groups of items during transport shall be ILD unless hazard analysis or testing justifies reduced distances.

C5.18.8. Classification Yard

C5.18.8.1. For protection of the classification yard from a PES, separation distances shall be at least the applicable IMD.

C5.18.8.2. Specific QD separation is not required from the classification yard to ES when the classification yard is used exclusively for:

C5.18.8.2.1. Receiving, dispatching, classifying, and switching of cars.

C5.18.8.2.2. Interchanging of trucks, trailers, or railcars between the common carrier and the contractor.

C5.18.8.2.3. Conducting external inspection of motor vehicles or railcars, or opening of free rolling doors of railcars for the purpose of removing documents and making a visual inspection of the cargo.

C5.18.8.3. A classification yard used for any other purpose shall comply with applicable QD criteria.

C5.18.9. Inspection Stations for Railcars and Trucks Containing AE

C5.18.9.1. Inspection stations for railcars and trucks containing AE that are used exclusively for the activities described in subparagraphs C5.18.9.1.1. through C5.18.9.1.3. are not subject to QD criteria. However, these stations should be located as far as practical from other hazards or populated areas.

C5.18.9.1.1. External visual inspection of the railcars or motor vehicles.

C5.18.9.1.2. Visual inspection of the external condition of the cargo packaging in vehicles that have passed the external inspection indicated in subparagraph C5.18.9.1.1.

C5.18.9.1.3. Interchange of trucks, trailers, or railcars between the common carrier and the contractor.

C5.18.9.2. Inspection stations used for any other purpose shall comply with applicable QD criteria.

C5.18.10. Interchange Yards

C5.18.10.1. Truck, trailer, or railcar interchange yards are not subject to QD requirements, when used exclusively:

C5.18.10.1.1. For the interchange of vehicles or railcars containing AE between the commercial carrier and the establishment.

C5.18.10.1.2. To conduct external inspection of the trucks, trailers, or railcars containing AE.

C5.18.10.1.3. To conduct visual inspection of the external condition of the cargo in vehicles (e.g., trucks, trailers, and railcars) that passed the external inspection.

C5.18.10.2. Truck, trailer, or railcar interchange used, at any time, for any purpose other than those given in subparagraphs C5.18.10.1.1. through C5.18.10.1.3. are subject to applicable QD tables. (See paragraph C5.4.6.)

C5.18.11. Holding Yards for Railcars and Trucks Containing AE

C5.18.11.1. Railcar-groups containing AE shall be separated from each other by AGM distance in a rail holding yard. For example:

C5.18.11.1.1. If the railcar holding yard is formed by two parallel ladder tracks connected by diagonal spurs, the parallel tracks and the diagonal spurs shall be separated by AGM distance for the quantities of AE involved.

C5.18.11.1.2. If the railcar holding yard is a "Christmas tree" arrangement, consisting of a ladder track with diagonal dead-end spurs projecting from each side at alternate intervals, the spurs shall be separated by AGM distance for the quantities of AE involved.

C5.18.11.2. Truck-groups containing AE in holding yards shall be separated from each other by AGM distance.

C5.18.11.3. Both railcar and truck holding yards containing AE shall be separated from other facilities by the applicable IBD, PTRD, ILD, or IMD.

C5.18.11.4. In addition to the temporary parking of railcars, trucks, or trailers containing AE, holding yards may also be used to interchange trucks, trailers, or railcars between the commercial carrier and the establishment and to conduct visual inspections.

C5.18.12. <u>Holding Areas for Suspect Railcars or Trucks Containing AE</u>. Railcars or trucks that are suspected of being in a hazardous condition shall be separated (isolated) from other PESs or ESs by the applicable QD before any other action.

C5.18.13. <u>Storage Tanks for Hazardous Materials</u>

C5.18.13.1. Unprotected, aboveground bulk storage tanks shall be separated from PESs by IBD per Table AP2.T1. A dike system satisfying NFPA 30 (Reference (q)) is required. Aboveground storage tanks that are provided protection against rupture or collapse from blast and fragment hazards may be sited at distances less than Table AP2.T1. when supported by testing or analysis.

C5.18.13.2. For installation of smaller bulk storage tanks, weigh the cost of distance or protective construction against the strategic value of the stored material, the ease of replacement in the event of an accident, and the potential environmental impact. Reduced distances may be approved if:

C5.18.13.2.1. The losses are accepted by the contractor. For GOCO facilities, the losses must also be acceptable to the owning Military Service.

C5.18.13.2.2. The tanks are sited.

C5.18.13.2.3. Spill containment is provided so other exposures are not endangered.

C5.18.13.3. Unprotected service tanks solely supporting AE storage, or operating complexes that are supplied by a pipe system designed to resist blast and fragments, may be sited at IBD based on only blast with a minimum distance of 400 ft [121.9 m] if:

C5.18.13.3.1. A dike system meeting the requirements of Reference (q) is provided.

C5.18.13.3.2. The contractor accepts the possible loss of the tanks and any collateral damage that a fire might cause as a result of the tanks being punctured by fragments. For GOCO facilities, the losses must also be acceptable to the owning Military Service.

C5.18.13.4. A service tank supporting a single PES shall be separated from that PES by the applicable NFPA fire protection distance. The distance from this service tank to any other PES shall be the larger of the required distance between the two PESs or the applicable NFPA fire protection distance.

C5.18.13.5. Buried tanks and buried pipelines should be separated from all PESs containing HD 1.2, HD 1.3, HD 1.4, or HD 1.6 AE by at least 80 ft [24.4 m]. The required separation distance for HD 1.1 or HD 1.5 AE is K3 [$K_m1.19$] with a minimum of 80 ft [24.4 m]. If the PES is designed to contain the effects of an explosion, then no QD is required.

C5.18.13.6. Small quantities of petroleum, oils, and lubricants(POL) or other hazardous materials used for operational purposes require no specific separation distance for explosives safety; however, operating procedures shall be implemented to limit adverse environmental impacts in the event of an accidental explosion.

C5.18.14. Storage Tanks for Water. QD criteria do not apply to water storage tanks and associated components if loss is acceptable to the contractor. For GOCO facilities, the losses must also be acceptable to the owning Military Service. When the loss is unacceptable, water storage tanks should be separated by IBD per Table AP2.T1.

C5.18.15. Underground Tanks or Pipelines for Non-Hazardous Materials. (See subparagraph C5.18.13.5.)

C5.18.16. Inert Storage. The DoD contractor shall determine acceptable locations for contractor-owned, inert material storage that is directly related to the explosives mission and for contractor-owned, inert material storage that is not directly related but where control of and access to such inert storage is restricted only to personnel directly related to the explosives mission. The DoD contractor shall determine what constitutes "directly related."

C5.18.16.1. Locations for inert storage shall be determined only after consideration of personnel exposure, the importance of the materiel in relation to the explosives mission, the operational conditions, and the availability of space.

C5.18.16.2. Inert storage that will be accessed by personnel not related to the explosives mission shall be sited per subparagraphs C5.7.1.4.4. and C5.7.1.5.8. (based on only blast). Minimum fragment distances do not apply (see subparagraph C5.8.1.5.2.3.).

C5.18.17. Barricades and ECM Design Requirements

C5.18.17.1. General. Testing has shown that earth cover over storage magazines can attenuate airblast overpressure and reduce the hazardous fragment range out the sides and rear of the magazine. In addition, properly constructed barricades and undisturbed natural earth can protect ammunition and explosives, structures, and operations against high-velocity, low-angle fragments and can reduce shock overpressure loads very near the barricade. However, barricades provide no protection against high-angle fragments or lobbed AE and are ineffective in reducing the blast overpressure in the far field (inhabited building or PTRD). If the barricade is destroyed in the process of providing protection, then secondary fragments from the destroyed barricade must also be considered as part of a hazard analysis.

CHAPTER 5

C5.18.17.2. <u>Earth Cover for ECMs and Barricades</u>. Earth cover material for ECMs and barricades shall be relatively cohesive (solid or wet clay and similar types of soil are too cohesive and shall not be used) and free from unsanitary organic matter, trash, debris, and stones heavier than 10 pounds or larger than 6 inches in diameter. The larger of acceptable stones shall be limited to the lower center of fill. Compaction and surface preparation shall be provided, as necessary, to maintain structural integrity and avoid erosion. Where cohesive material cannot be used, as in sandy soil, the barricade or the earth cover over magazines should be finished with a suitable material (e.g., geotextiles, gunnite) to ensure structural integrity.

C5.18.17.3. <u>ECM Design Criteria</u>

C5.18.17.3.1. An ECM's primary purpose is to protect AE from the effects of a nearby detonation. To qualify for the default IMD in Table AP2.T6., an ECM, acting as an ES, must not collapse. Although substantial permanent deformation of the ECM may occur, sufficient space should be provided to prevent the deformed structure or its doors from striking the contents.

C5.18.17.3.2. Descriptions and construction details of 7-Bar, 3-Bar, and undefined ECMs can be found in Reference (m). At a minimum, ECMs must be designed to withstand:

C5.18.17.3.2.1. Conventional (e.g., live, dead, snow) loads for the barrel of an arch-shaped ECM.

C5.18.17.3.2.2. Conventional (e.g., live, dead, snow) and blast-induced loads for the roof of a flat-roofed ECM.

C5.18.17.3.2.3. Conventional (e.g., live, dead, snow) loads for the rear wall of an arch-shaped ECM and for the rear and sidewalls of a flat-roofed ECM.

C5.18.17.3.2.4. Expected blast loads as applicable:

C5.18.17.3.2.4.1. On the head wall and door of a 3-Bar ES ECM is a triangular pulse with peak overpressure of 43.5 psi [3 bars, 300 kPa] and impulse of $11.3\ W^{1/3}$ psi-ms [$100Q^{1/3}$ Pa-s].

C5.18.17.3.2.4.2. On the head wall and door of a 7-Bar ES ECM is a triangular pulse with peak overpressure of 101.5 psi [7 bars, 700 kPa] and impulse of $13.9\ W^{1/3}$ psi-ms [$123Q^{1/3}$ Pa-s].

C5.18.17.3.2.4.3. On the roof of a flat-roofed undefined, 3-Bar, or 7-Bar ES ECM is a triangular pulse with peak overpressure of 108 psi [7.5 bars, 745 kPa] and impulse of $19W^{1/3}$ psi-ms [$170Q^{1/3}$ Pa-s].

CHAPTER 5

C5.18.17.3.2.5. The earth fill between or earth cover over an ECM may be either solid or sloped, in accordance with the requirements of other construction features, but a minimum of 2 feet of earth cover over the top of each magazine shall be maintained. NOTE: If the specified thickness and slope of earth on the ECM is not maintained, the ECM shall be sited as an AGM.

C5.18.17.4. Barricade Design Criteria

C5.18.17.4.1. Slope. The slope of an earthen barricade shall be two horizontal to one vertical, unless erosion controls are used. Earthen barricades with slopes no steeper than one and one half horizontal to one vertical that were approved prior to 1976 may continue to be used. However, renovations to these barricades should meet the 2:1 criteria, when feasible. Earth barricades meeting the slope requirements may be modified by substituting a retaining wall, preferably of concrete, for the slope on one side. The other side shall have slope and thickness sufficient to ensure that the width of earth required for the top is held firmly in place.

C5.18.17.4.2. Alternate Barriers. Other barriers, such as earth-filled steel bin barricades, may also be used when analysis or test demonstrate their effectiveness. See Reference (m) for additional barricade details.

C5.18.17.4.3. Barricade Size and Orientation for Protection Against High-Speed, Low-Angle Fragments. The location, height, and length shall be determined by:

C5.18.17.4.3.1. Barricade Location, Size, and Orientation. The distance between the foot of the barricade and the stack of ammunition or explosives or the buildings containing explosives represents a compromise. The shorter the distance, the shorter the height and length required for the barricade. However, it may be necessary to extend the distance to provide access for maintenance and vehicles. If it is impracticable to locate the barricades near the stack of ammunition or explosives or building containing explosives, barricades may be located adjacent to the facility to be protected.

C5.18.17.4.3.2. Location. The barricade may be placed anywhere between the PES and the ES. The location shall determine the barricade's required height and length.

C5.18.17.4.3.3. Height. Establish a reference point at the top of the far edge of one of the two stacks that the barricade is to separate. If the tops of the stacks are at different elevations, this reference point shall be on the lower stack. Draw a line from the reference point to the top of the other stack. Draw a second line from the reference point to form a 2-degree angle above the first line. To limit barricade height, each should be as close as possible to the stack that served as the reference point. (See Figures C5.F1. and C5.F2.)

C5.18.17.4.3.4. Length. The length of the barricade shall be determined as shown in Figure C5.F3.

C5.18.17.4.4. Barricade Size and Orientation for Protection Against Overpressure. General procedures to predict pressure mitigation versus barricade design and location have not been developed. However, based on direct-experimental work, the overpressure loading on a surface area shielded by a barricade is reduced by approximately 50 percent when:

C5.18.17.4.4.1. The barricade's base is within two barricade heights of the protected ES.

C5.18.17.4.4.2. The top of the barricade is at least as high as the top of the protected area.

C5.18.17.4.4.3. The length of the barricade is at least two times the length of the protected ES.

Figure C5.F1. Determination of Barricade Height (Equal Height)

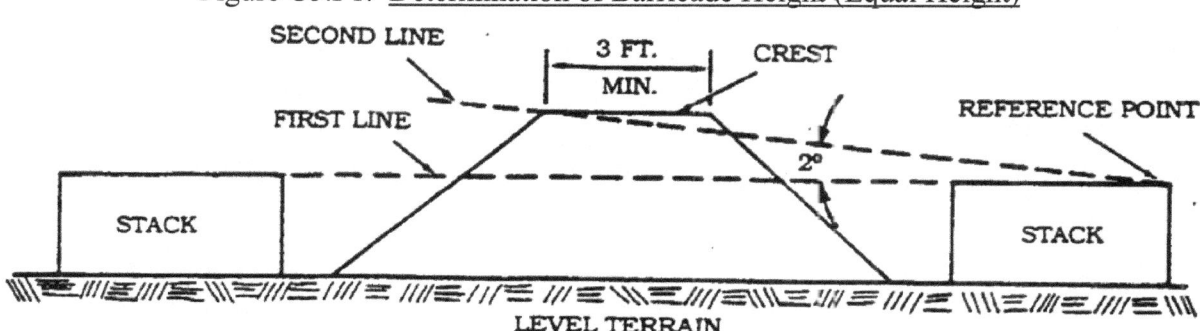

Figure C5.F2. Determination of Barricade Height (Unequal Height)

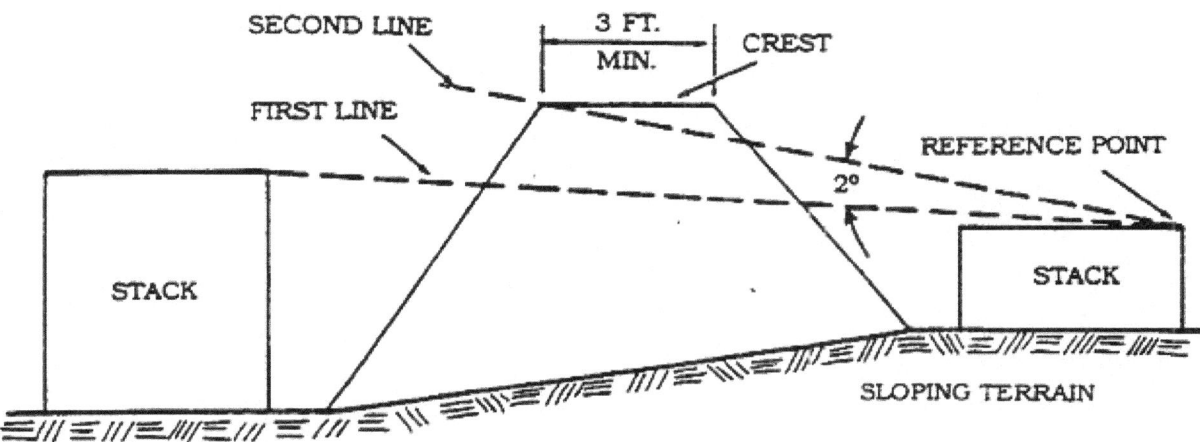

CHAPTER 5

Figure C5.F3. <u>Determination of Barricade Length</u>

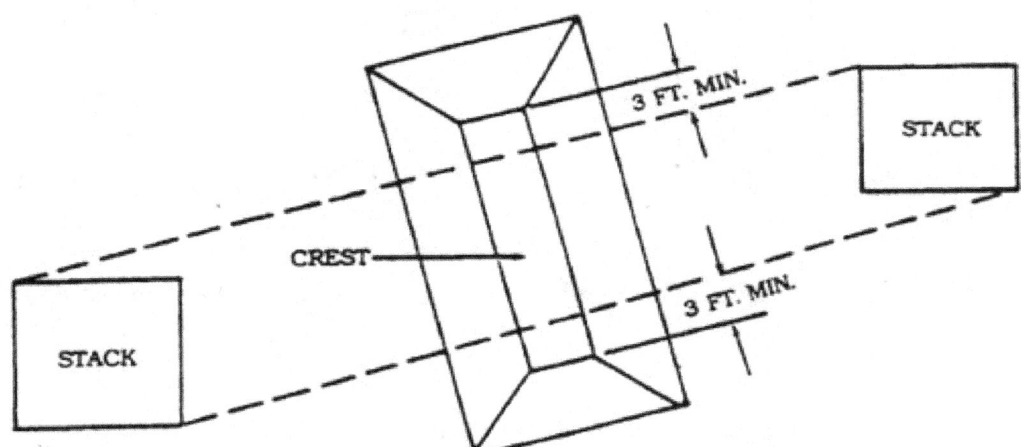

C6. CHAPTER 6

ELECTRICAL SAFETY REQUIREMENTS FOR AE FACILITIES

C6.1. GENERAL

Initiation systems often use the controlled input of electrical energy to initiate explosive mixtures and compounds, which start an explosive train. The uncontrolled release of electrical energy in explosive atmospheres or near explosives and explosive-loaded articles can result in unintended initiation and serious accidents. Electrical energy manifests itself in many forms (e.g., standard electrical installations, lightning, electrostatic discharge, electrical testing) and with various intensities that require special precautions. This chapter contains minimum electrical safety requirements for existing, new, or modified explosives facilities and equipment.

C6.2. ELECTRICAL INSTALLATIONS

C6.2.1. National Fire Protection Association Guidelines. NFPA Standard No. 70 (Reference (r)) and this section contain minimum requirements for areas containing explosives. Reference (r) does not specifically address explosives, but it does establish standards for the design and installation of electrical equipment and wiring in atmospheres containing combustible dusts and flammable vapors and gasses which, in general, are comparably hazardous. Article 500 of Reference (r) defines "hazardous locations" according to the hazard presented by electrical equipment installed in environments where flammable gases or vapors, combustible dusts, or flyings may exist. The presence of AE may or may not result in rating a particular location as a "hazardous location." DoD contractors shall use the exceptions in subparagraphs C6.2.1.1. through C6.2.1.3. when applying the Reference (r) definitions of Class I, Division 1, and Class II, Division 1 hazardous locations:

C6.2.1.1. Classify areas containing explosive dusts or explosive substances that may produce dust capable of suspension in the atmosphere as Class II, Division 1 hazardous locations.

C6.2.1.2. Classify areas where explosive sublimation or condensation may occur as both Class I Division 1 and Class II Division 1 hazardous locations.

C6.2.1.3. Exceptions are extraordinarily hazardous explosive substances such as nitroglycerin (NG) which require special consideration, including physical isolation from electric motors, devices, lighting fixtures, etc.

C6.2.2. Multiple Classifications. In some PESs (e.g., powder blending with solvents), hazards resulting from both dusts and flammable vapors may exist. In these cases, it is necessary for that area to have a dual, or multiple, classification. Use only electrical equipment listed by Underwriters Laboratories (ULs) or other recognized testing laboratories as suitable for use in all classes of hazardous locations.

C6.2.3. <u>Change of Classification</u>. The specific processes performed in operating buildings and magazines dictate the requirements for electrical equipment installation. If functions performed in the facility change, responsible personnel shall inspect, approve, or reclassify the hazardous locations.

C6.2.4. <u>Alternate Power Source</u>. Facilities shall have an alternate power source for special processes and operations requiring a continuous supply of power whenever the loss of power will result in a more hazardous condition.

C6.2.5. <u>Portable Engine-Driven Generators</u>. The exposed, non-current-carrying metallic frame and parts shall be electrically grounded. In addition, observe these requirements when supplying power to magazines or explosives operating facilities:

C6.2.5.1. Place generating units at least 50 ft [15.2 m] from magazines or hazardous (classified) locations.

C6.2.5.2. Keep the ground area between and around the generator and the location (classified hazardous per Reference (r)) clear of debris and other combustible materials.

C6.2.5.3. Ensure the exhaust from the generator does not impinge on grass or any other combustible material.

C6.2.5.4. Position the power cord connecting the generator to the load to prevent trucks or personnel from running over or otherwise damaging the cord.

C6.2.5.5. Do not use cable-to-cable splices within a magazine, explosives operating facility, or other location that is classified hazardous per Reference (r). Use only three-wire, three-prong, approved service type plugs and connectors.

C6.2.5.6. Refer to paragraph C3.12.1. for refueling procedures.

C6.2.6. <u>Electric Supply Systems</u>. Electrical and explosives hazards may mutually exist when PESs are in close proximity to electric supply lines. To protect these hazards from each other, the separation requirements in subparagraphs C6.2.6.1. through C6.2.6.4. shall apply to all new construction. (PTRDs and IBDs specified in subparagraphs C6.2.6.3. and C6.2.6.4. are based on air blast overpressure only; fragment distances do not apply.)

C6.2.6.1. Electric lines serving explosives operating facilities shall be installed underground from a point not less than 50 ft [15.3 m] away from such facilities.

C6.2.6.2. Separate overhead service lines from a PES of combustible construction or a PES in the open by the distance between the poles or towers supporting the lines, unless an effective means is provided to ensure that energized lines cannot contact the facility or its appurtenances if they break. Four acceptable alternatives are cable trays and messenger lines, a ground-fault circuit-interrupter that causes a disconnecting device to open all ungrounded conductors of the faulted circuit, weighted triangle line separators or similar weights that ensure broken lines fall straight down away from PESs, and constructed physical barriers.

C6.2.6.3. Separate the electric distribution lines carrying less than 69 kilovolts (kV), the tower or poles supporting those lines, and unmanned electrical substations from PESs by PTRD.

C6.2.6.4. Separate the electric transmission lines carrying 69 kV or more and the tower or poles supporting them from PESs by:

C6.2.6.4.1. IBD if the line in question is part of a grid system serving a large area off the establishment.

C6.2.6.4.2. PTRD if loss of the line does not create serious social or economic hardships.

C6.2.6.4.3. Distances in accordance with subparagraph C6.2.6.2. when the line(s) in question can be interrupted without loss of power, i.e., other lines or networks exist for rerouting power.

C6.2.7. Electrical Installations in Hazardous Locations. Contractors should avoid locating permanent electric installations in hazardous (classified) locations as defined by Article 500 of Reference (r). When practical operating reasons prevent locating permanent electrical installations outside of hazardous locations, or require the use of portable electrical equipment (e.g., lighting equipment) in hazardous locations, contractors shall install or use only electrical equipment approved for the Reference (r)-defined "hazardous location" and listed by UL or other nationally recognized testing agencies.

C6.2.8. Primary Electric Supply. Contractors should arrange the primary electric supply to an entire explosives area to allow cutting off the supply by remote switches located at one or more central points away from the area.

C6.2.9. Ventilation. Contractors shall equip exhaust fans in hazardous (classified) locations as defined by Reference (r) -- through which combustible dust or flammable vapor pass -- with nonferrous blades or line the casing with nonferrous material. Fan motors shall meet the requirements for the applicable Reference (r) hazardous (classified) locations. Contractors shall bond and ground the entire exhaust system and shall clean and service the system on a regular schedule. (See Chapter 12 for more details.) NFPA Standard No. 91 (Reference (s)) provides guidance for exhaust systems.

C6.3. LIGHTNING PROTECTION

When lightning protection systems are installed, the installation, inspection, and maintenance shall comply with NFPA Standard No. 780 (Reference (t)), at a minimum. Typically, 6-month visual tests and 24-month electrical tests of installed systems are acceptable. Tests should be made as suggested in paragraph B.1.1.3. of Reference (t), which advises staggering inspections so that earth resistance measurements can be made in dry months as well as in rainy months. For DoD-owned facilities, the lightning protection requirements outlined in Chapter 7 of Reference (c) and Reference (t) apply.

C6.4. STATIC ELECTRICITY AND GROUNDING

C6.4.1. Static Electricity. Two unlike materials (at least one of which is non-conductive) produce static electricity due to contact and separation. Contact creates a redistribution of charge across the area of contact and establishes an attractive force. Separation of the materials overcomes these attractive forces and sets up an electrostatic field between the two surfaces. If no conducting path is available to allow the charges to equalize on the surfaces, the voltage difference between the surfaces can easily reach several thousand volts as they separate.

C6.4.2. Static Electricity Hazards. The potential hazard of static electricity arises when an accumulated electrical charge subsequently discharges as a spark in the presence of hazardous atmospheres, flammable vapors, dusts, exposed sensitive explosives, or EEDs. ESD does not present a substantial hazard during the handling of most bulk explosive substances if the explosives are in approved containers. It also does not present a hazard near explosives totally contained and unexposed within loaded articles. It is not possible to prevent the generation of static electricity entirely. Elimination of potential ESD hazards requires proper grounding to dissipate static charges before they accumulate to dangerous levels. The NFPA, UL, and the U.S. Department of Commerce publish detailed discussions of the hazards of static electricity and ways of reducing it. Where electrostatic discharge (spark) may be hazardous, NFPA Standard No. 77 (Reference (u)) shall apply, except as otherwise specified.

C6.4.3. Static Ground System. A basic static ground system consists of one or more electrodes in contact with the earth and a conductor (i.e., metal wire) bonded to the electrode and routed throughout the protected facility. The static ground system may use building structural steel (unless structural steel is used as a lightning protection system down conductor), metallic water pipes, ground cones, buried copper plates, and rods driven into the earth as electrodes. The ground system shall not use gas, steam, or air lines, dry pipe sprinkler systems, or air terminals and down conductors of lightning protection systems as earth electrodes. A static ground system provides a conductive path to earth from conductive floors, conductive work surfaces, and AE equipment. A static ground system also allows any generated static charges to dissipate.

C6.4.4. Testing Equipment Grounds. Trained personnel shall test ground systems after installation, after repairs, and at locally determined intervals and shall keep all records. Remove all exposed explosives or exposed hazardous materials from the room or area before testing. The resistance of the electrode to earth shall not exceed 25 ohms. The electrical resistance from any point on the conductor to the electrode shall not exceed 1 ohm. The ground system design shall provide for interconnecting all ground electrodes of structures equipped with a lightning protection system. (See Reference (t), Annex E for further guidance.)

C6.4.5. <u>Grounding of Equipment</u>. Large ungrounded objects can accumulate and store electrostatic charges that can discharge in the form of a spark when approaching other conductive objects. Therefore, contractors shall perform a static electricity hazards evaluation of facilities housing AE operations to identify any objects (e.g., building structural steel, permanently installed equipment), including personnel, and any materials that could insulate and interfere with proper bonding and grounding. Unless the static electricity hazards evaluation indicates ESD is not a potential ignition source, contractor maintenance personnel shall bond all AE equipment (e.g., mixers, grinding mills, screening and sifting devices, assembly and disassembly machines, conveyors, elevators, steel work tables, presses, and hoppers) to the ground system. The resistance of the AE equipment to the grounding system shall not exceed 1 ohm. Trained personnel shall test this resistance initially at installation and at least annually thereafter, and shall keep all records. Exclude the resistance of conductive belting when testing for resistance of belt-driven machinery to the ground system. Bonding straps shall bridge contact points where oil, paint, or rust could disrupt electrical continuity. Permanent equipment in contact with conductive floors or tabletops does not meet the bonding requirement to the ground system. Maintain compatibility of metallic bonding and grounding cables, straps, or clamps with the explosives involved in the process.

C6.4.6. <u>Conductive Belts</u>. Use conductive belting wherever ESD is an ignition hazard. The resistance of conductive conveyor belts shall not exceed 1,000,000 ohms as measured between two electrodes placed on the belt and as measured between an electrode placed on the conductive conveyor belt and an electrode attached to the ground system. Do not use static combs to drain off static charges generated from belts or pulleys used in hazardous locations.

C6.4.7. <u>Conductive Floors, Tabletops, and Footwear</u>. Contractors shall use conductive tabletops, floors, and shoes for grounding personnel at operations involving exposed explosives with electrostatic sensitivity of 0.1 J or less, e.g., primer, initiator, detonator, igniter, tracer, and incendiary mixtures. Bonding wires or straps shall connect the tabletops and floors to the static ground system. Materials sensitive to initiation by ESD sparks include: lead styphnate, lead azide, mercury fulminate, tetrazene, diazodinitrophenol, potassium chlorate-lead styphanate mixtures, some igniter compositions, grade B magnesium powder, and exposed layers of black powder dust. Air and dust mixtures of ammonium picrate, tetryl, tetrytol, and solid propellants are also sensitive to initiation by ESD. Testing indicates mixtures of air with vapors from many flammable liquids (e.g., ethyl ether, ethyl alcohol, ethyl acetate, acetone, and gasoline) may ignite by ESD from the human body. Therefore, contractors shall equip areas where personnel might contact these kinds of explosives and flammable liquids with conductive floors and tabletops, except when hazard analysis indicates adequate housekeeping, dust collection, ventilation, or solvent recovery methods eliminate the ignition hazard. (Refer to Reference (u) for additional information concerning ESD test data; ESD ignition sensitivity may vary depending on variations within the process.)

C6.4.7.1. <u>Alternate Operational Use</u>. Unless hazard analyses indicate otherwise, conductive tabletops, floors, and shoes shall also protect operations involving:

C6.4.7.1.1. Unpackaged detonators and primers and EEDs.

C6.4.7.1.2. Electrically initiated items, such as rockets, with exposed circuits.

C6.4.7.1.3. Hazardous materials capable of initiation by ESD from the human body.

C6.4.7.2. <u>Conducive Mats or Runners</u>. When a hazard remains localized, the contractor may use conductive mats or runners instead of conductive floors throughout an entire building or room. These mats and runners shall meet all the specifications and test requirements that apply to conductive floors. When justified by hazard analysis, contractors may use conductive wrist straps in place of conductive floors and shoes for grounding personnel at small scale and isolated operations. When using wrist straps, operators shall test wrist straps before each use (whenever removed and re-worn) and record test results. The resistance of the wrist strap while the operator is wearing the strap shall fall within a range of 250,000ohms (minimum) and 1,200,000 ohms (maximum) when measured from opposite hand to ground. Use test equipment capable of testing 1,200,000 ohms + 10 percent. (Operators with dry skin may use special contact creams to decrease the resistance to the required value.)

C6.4.7.3. <u>Conductive Floor and Tabletop Specifications</u>. Conductive floors and tabletops made of or covered with non-sparking materials such as lead, conductive rubber, or conductive compositions shall meet these requirements:

C6.4.7.3.1. Provide a continuous electrical path to the static ground system and the electrical resistance shall not exceed the limits specified in subparagraph C6.4.7.5.1.

C6.4.7.3.2. Provide a reasonably smooth surface that is free from cracks.

C6.4.7.3.3. Maintain compatibility of conductive floor and tabletop materials with the energetic materials present.

C6.4.7.4. <u>Conductive Footwear</u>. Operators shall wear conductive shoes in areas requiring conductive mats, floors, or runners. Personnel visiting such areas shall wear conductive shoes, ankle straps, or similar devices, one on each leg. Prominent markings should identify conductive shoes to help supervisors ensure personnel compliance. Personnel required to work on electrical equipment in areas where conductive floors are installed shall not wear conductive shoes and shall not begin work until operators remove all AE sensitive to ESD.

C6.4.7.5. <u>Testing Conductive Footwear, Floors, and Tabletops</u>

C6.4.7.5.1. <u>Test Criteria</u>. The maximum resistance of a body, plus the resistance of the conductive shoes, plus the resistance of the floor to the ground system shall not exceed 1,000,000 ohms total. That is, if 500,000 ohms is the maximum resistance allowed from the floor to the ground system, then 500,000 ohms is the maximum combined resistance allowed for the person's body plus the resistance of the conductive shoes. The contractor can set the maximum resistance limits for the floor to the ground system and for the combined resistance of a person's body plus the shoes, as long as the total resistance does not exceed 1,000,000 ohms.

C6.4.7.5.2. <u>Minimum Resistance</u>. To protect against electrocution, the minimum resistance of the floor to the ground system and the minimum resistance of the tabletop to the ground system shall exceed 40,000 ohms in areas with 110 volts service and 75,000 ohms in areas with 220 volts service. A ground fault interrupt circuit also meets this requirement.

C6.4.7.5.3. <u>Tabletop Test Criteria</u>. The maximum resistance of conductive tabletops to the ground system shall not exceed 1,000,000 ohms.

C6.4.7.5.4. <u>Conductive Footwear Test Criteria</u>. All personnel shall test conductive footwear daily before use to ensure that the combined resistance of the person's body and the conductive shoes do not exceed the limit specified in subparagraph C6.4.7.5.1. Supervisors shall keep documentation of all test results, including calibration of test equipment. The test voltage of the shoe tester shall not exceed 500 volts. The short circuit current across the shoe tester electrodes (plates) should be limited between 0.5 ma and 2.0 ma. The design of the test instrument shall include built-in safeguards to prevent the test subject from experiencing electric shock. Personnel shall not test shoes in rooms or areas with exposed explosives or flammable gas mixtures. Personnel shall not wear static generating stockings such as silk, wool, and synthetics; and shall not use foot powders, which have a drying action that can increase resistance. Dirt and grit increase resistance of conductive shoes. Personnel should avoid wearing conductive shoes outdoors and shall keep shoes clean.

C6.4.7.5.5. <u>Test Procedure.</u> Trained personnel shall test conductive floors and tabletops upon installation and at least annually thereafter using test equipment specifically designed for this purpose and shall keep records of all test results for at least 5 years. Testing shall proceed only when the room or area is free from exposed explosives and flammable gas mixtures. The test procedure shall measure the resistance of the floor between an electrode attached to the ground system and an electrode placed at any point on the floor or tabletop and also as measured between two electrodes placed 3 ft [1 m] apart at any points on the floor or tabletop. Make both electrode-to-electrode and electrode-to-ground system measurements at five or more locations in each room, with at least two of the test locations in heavily trafficked areas. If the resistance measurement changes appreciably with time, record the resistance at the 5-second interval. To prevent biased measurements, locate the electrodes for both the electrode-to-electrode and electrode-to-ground measurements a minimum of 3 ft [1 m] away from an earth ground or other grounded items such as a door frame, ordnance handling equipment, or any grounded item resting on a conductive floor. Only trained personnel shall operate and maintain test instruments. NOTE: The size of the floor or tabletop may make it impractical to conduct five surface resistance (electrode-to-electrode) or resistance-to-ground measurements and still remain 3 ft [1 m] away from all grounded items. In such cases, take enough measurements to ensure adequate testing of all parts of the conductive surface and document the justification for a reduced number of electrode-to-electrode or electrode-to-ground measurements in the grounding system test plan.

CHAPTER 6

C6.4.8. <u>Handling Low-Energy Initiators</u>. Low-energy initiators are those that initiate when subjected to 0.1 joule of energy or less. The history of accidents involving low-energy initiators and their sensitivity to ESD requires supplemental safety precautions when handling these devices. When manufacturing, processing, using, or testing low-energy initiators, controls implemented are:

C6.4.8.1. Workstations shall have conductive floors or mats and conductive tabletops, unless the initiators are in their original packaging or are part of a finished metallic end item that provides complete protection from electromagnetic or electrostatic energy.

C6.4.8.2. Operators shall wear both conductive shoes and a conductive wrist strap bonded to the ground system. Operators shall test conductive shoes per subparagraph C6.4.7.5.1. and wrist straps per subparagraph C6.4.7.2. Special contact creams may be used to decrease the resistance to the required value.

C6.4.8.3. Operators shall wear non-static generating clothing.

C6.4.8.4. All metal parts of equipment shall be electrically bonded together and grounded.

C6.4.8.5. Glass, acrylic, or polycarbonate materials required for transparent shielding shall be periodically coated with an anti-static material to prevent buildup of static electricity.

C6.4.8.6. When procedures establish a humidity range for operations, the relative humidity and temperature in the work area shall be checked before starting operations and throughout the workday. (See section C6.6. for more information.)

C6.4.8.7. Metal surfaces subjected to rubbing or friction shall not be painted. If a lubricant is necessary, it shall not raise the metal's surface resistance above 25 ohms.

C6.4.8.8. Work shall not be conducted in the vicinity of actual or potential electromagnetic or electrostatic fields. Sources of static electricity and electromagnetic energy include radio transmission, electrical storms, transformer stations, high voltage transmission lines, improperly grounded electric circuitry, rotating equipment, belts, etc. Adequate lightning protection, grounding, and adequate resistances for fixed sources of energy shall be established for locations with low-energy initiator operations. These locations shall be shielded to afford protection against local mobile radio transmission.

C6.4.8.9. Locate electrical equipment out of the range of an operator working with a low-energy initiator. When using soldering irons, recommend obtaining commercially available irons made of anti-static plastic housings that are grounded and equipped with devices capable of limiting short-circuit current below initiating thresholds.

C6.4.8.10. When not part of an end item or end item subassembly, transport initiators only when packed according to the latest DOT requirements or equivalent packaging that protects against initiation by ESD.

C6.4.8.11. Periodically measure any potential static charges at workstations to ensure controls are working. Refer to Reference (u) for additional information.

C6.5. ELECTRICAL TEST EQUIPMENT

C6.5.1. Electrical and electronics test equipment should use the weakest possible power source. Batteries should be used in lieu of 110-volt power sources. Testing should not use a power source capable of initiating the explosives test item. When test specifications require using electrical energy at or above the initiating threshold level of explosive devices, test chambers or shielding capable of containing all hazards shall be used and energy shall be applied remotely. Design of test chambers and shields shall provide safeguards against the possibility of human error.

C6.5.2. Test equipment should not be placed in hazardous atmospheres but, when absolutely necessary, operational shields shall be used to protect personnel unless a hazard analysis indicates otherwise.

C6.6. HUMIDIFICATION AND IONIZATION

C6.6.1. Humidification that maintains relative humidity above 60 percent effectively prevents static electricity accumulations and subsequent discharges. This technique involves pre-operational checks and regular monitoring of the humidity levels throughout the day. Do not use humidification with metallic powders unless hazard analysis indicates the powders are not susceptible to spontaneous ignition in air with 60 percent relative humidity.

C6.6.2. Ionization is electrical neutralization and serves as an effective method of removing static charges from certain processes and operations. Methods of application can be found in Reference (u).

C6.6.3. Contractors may use ionization or humidification to augment their ESD control program but may not use them in lieu of conductive floors and footwear (where required).

C7. CHAPTER 7

MANUFACTURING AND PROCESSING SOLID PROPELLANTS

C7.1. GENERAL

C7.1.1. These requirements apply to solid propellant manufacturing and augment other requirements contained in this Manual.

C7.1.2. The safety precautions for fabrication of solid propellants, propellant-loaded items, gun ammunition, and rocket motors follow the generally accepted principles used for many types of explosives and energetic materials. Solid propellants are divided into four classes: single-base, double-base, triple-base, and composite. Division of the propellants into these classes is on the basis of composition, not use. Single-base compositions are used in cannons, small arms, and grenades. Double-base compositions are used in cannons, small arms, mortars, rockets, and jet propulsion units. Triple-base compositions are used in cannon units. Composite compositions are used primarily in rocket assemblies and jet propulsion units. The choice of a propellant for a specific use is determined by ballistic and physical requirements rather than on the basis of composition. A given propellant composition may be suitable for use in several applications.

C7.1.3. Although processing safety considerations for finished propellant and loaded rocket motors are similar, each propellant type formulation has unique hazardous properties and characteristics that may be exhibited during the processing of raw materials and the formulation of intermediate and final compositions (uncured and cured and during post cure trimming to final configuration). Knowledge of the types of propellants and their hazardous properties is critical to the establishment of proper hazard controls that ensure safety during processing. Understanding the initiation thresholds of propellants to impact, friction, heat, and electrostatic discharge stimuli during specific processes and handling situations is essential to any hazard analysis. Consider the response of the materials in terms of energy input sensitivity and magnitude of energy release when evaluating and applying the guidelines of this chapter. Follow the general requirements for manufacturing and processing of pyrotechnics given in Chapter 8 for safety precautions regarding ignition system fabrication. NOTE: An exception to this requirement is allowed for processing of a propellant grain igniter, which is considered the same as motor propellant until the grain is mated with the initiator assembly.

C7.2. PROPERTIES OF PROPELLANTS. Propellants present a wide range of hazardous properties and characteristics even within the four classes due to variations in particle size of ingredients and energy content of additives, both solid and liquid. Test data are essential for determining the chemical, physical, and explosive properties and hazards of raw materials, intermediate compositions, and solid propellant, both uncured and cured.

C7.2.1. <u>Single Base Propellants</u>. Single base propellants are essentially pure nitrocellulose. They are made by nitrating cellulose, normally cotton or wood pulp. When exposed to elevated temperatures, these propellants decompose giving off nitric oxide and nitrogen dioxide gases that react with the remaining nitrocellulose and accelerate the decomposition process. Stabilizers are added to react with the nitrogen oxides to control the decomposition. Other ingredients are added during the manufacturing process to allow extrusion into strings, tubes, or perforated tubes and forming into sheets, flakes, or spheres.

C7.2.2. <u>Double Base Propellants</u>. Double base propellants contain nitrocellulose and NG (or other liquid nitrate ester) as the two main ingredients. Other ingredients act as a gelatinizer or plasticizer to allow the forming and extrusion of the propellant at elevated temperature without the use of a solvent. Like single-base propellants, they contain a stabilizer. Other ingredients include oxidizers, other plasticizers, and lubricants. These propellants can be extruded/cut or cast into their final shape.

C7.2.3. <u>Triple Base Propellants</u>. Triple base propellants are double base propellants with nitroguanidine added as a major ingredient. The nitroguanidine in the formulation produces a lower flame temperature and a greater amount of gaseous combustion products. The lower flame temperature considerably reduces erosion of gun barrels, and the greater amounts of gas produce a greater force on the projectile. Triple-base propellants also contain a stabilizer and other additives. These propellants can be extruded, cut, or cast into their final shape.

C7.2.4. <u>Composite Propellants</u>. Composite propellants generally consist of a physical mixture of a fuel such as metallic aluminum, a binder that is normally an organic polymer (generally a synthetic rubber which is also a fuel), and an inorganic oxidizing agent such as ammonium perchlorate. Nitrates and other perchlorates are also commonly used as oxidizers. Common binders include: hydroxyl terminated polybutadiene, carboxyl terminated polybutadiene, polybutadiene-acrylonitrile, polyurethane, polybutadieneacrylic acid, and polysulfides. These propellants are typically cast into their final shape.

C7.3. <u>IN-PROCESS HAZARDS</u>

C7.3.1. Prior to propellant operations, the in-process hazard classification for raw ingredients, intermediate compositions, and propellant formulations (uncured and cured) shall be determined by analogy or previous test data, or by conducting appropriate tests for propellant characterization. During scale-up of new propellants from research and development to an established manufacturing process, the chemical, physical, and explosive properties and hazards of raw materials, intermediate compositions, and solid propellant, both uncured and cured, and the in-process hazard classification shall be updated when warranted.

C7.3.2. When testing is required; tests shall be conducted to determine thermal stability, chemical compatibility of ingredients, exothermic reactions, and sensitivity to ignition or detonation from friction, impact, and electrostatic discharge. However, caution must be used when interpreting test results, as small-scale tests may not accurately reflect the in-process hazard classification when quantities are increased or confinement exists. Additional tests such as deflagration-to-detonation, card gap, and dielectric breakdown tests may also provide valuable data. Descriptions of some of these tests may be found in Reference (i).

C7.3.3. Minimum testing may satisfy the in-process hazard classification requirements for several operations. For example:

C7.3.3.1. If reliable data exist that indicate that the propellant mixing operations have a mass explosion or detonation hazard, no testing would be needed to site as HD 1.1.

C7.3.3.2. If testing shows that only uncured propellant (and not cured propellant) will mass explode or detonate, then only the mixing, casting, and curing operations shall be hazard classified as a mass explosion or detonation hazard and sited as HD 1.1.

C7.3.3.3. If tests show that only the cured propellant (and not uncured propellant) will mass explode or detonate, then only curing and subsequent operations shall be hazard classified as a mass explosion or detonation hazard and sited as HD 1.1.

C7.3.4. Ammonium perchlorate (AP) is a common ingredient used as an oxidizer in composite propellants and has unique hazard characteristics. It is manufactured and commercially shipped as an oxidizer, HD 5.1. When used under a DoD contract as an AE ingredient for initiation, propulsion, or detonation, it shall be treated as Hazard Class 1. Unless hazard characterization test data indicate otherwise, the in-process classification for siting of AP shall be determined as:

C7.3.4.1. AP with a particle size over 15 microns in original shipping container or equivalent shall be considered to be HD 1.4 and CG L.

C7.3.4.2. AP with a particle size over 15 microns, not in original shipping container or equivalent, exposed to fire hazards only or exposed to detonation hazards at more than ILDs shall be considered to be HD 1.3 and CG C.

C7.3.4.3. AP with a particle size over 15 microns, not in original shipping container or equivalent, and exposed to detonation hazards at less than ILDs shall be considered to be HD 1.1 and CG D.

C7.3.4.4. AP with a particle size 15 microns or less shall be considered to be HD 1.1 and CG D.

C7.4. SEPARATION OF OPERATIONS AND BUILDINGS

C7.4.1. Propellant and rocket motor manufacturing and processing should be performed in dedicated buildings or areas (i.e., operating buildings and operating lines) separated by the applicable QD criteria. Table C7.T1. provides remote control and personnel protection requirements for certain propellant processing operations.

C7.4.2. Generally, sequential operations on rocket motors in a single operating building should be treated as one process. Multiple missile systems and their components that present similar hazards (subparagraph C5.7.1.2.3.) may be worked concurrently in the same operating building without compromising explosives safety. The criticality of a particular program and the survivability of the production facility may justify the PCO accepting the additional costs and requiring dedicated facilities. The special provision for a dedicated facility must be specifically included in the contract.

C7.4.3. Propellant mixing and associated operations shall be performed in buildings used exclusively for that purpose. Small mixers (50 gallon capacity or less) may be located in buildings containing other operations, provided the mixer is in a separate bay with operational shields that protect all other operations and personnel from the mixing operation.

C7.4.4. The Department of Defense currently uses propellants with mass explosion or detonation and mass fire hazards (according to the stimuli), and reevaluations have resulted in changes to hazard classification. For this reason propellant operating buildings should be sited for both HD 1.1. and HD 1.3. when locating new facilities or updating site plans for current facilities.

C7.5. EQUIPMENT AND FACILITIES

C7.5.1. For facilities housing propellant manufacturing and rocket motor operations, contractors shall bond and ground all AE equipment. Large ungrounded conductive objects can accumulate and store electrostatic charges that can discharge in the form of a spark when approaching other conductive objects. Similarly, personnel can accumulate lesser electrostatic charges that can discharge as a spark when they approach a conductive surface on or near a rocket motor. Therefore, contractors shall perform a static electricity hazards evaluation of facilities housing rocket motors to determine if ESD is a potential ignition source. When ESD is a hazard, the rocket motor, conductive equipment, tooling, building structure, and personnel shall be grounded and tested per the requirements of Chapter 6 of this Manual.

C7.5.1.1. Unless a hazard analysis indicates ESD is not a potential ignition source, the igniter, motor, and personnel shall be bonded and grounded per the requirements of Chapter 6 of this Manual during assembly of igniter components and mating of igniters into rocket motors.

C7.5.1.2. When making a grounding connection, the operator shall attach the ground wire, cable, or strap to the item requiring grounding first, then connect the other end of the ground wire, cable, or strap to the approved facility grounding system. This ensures that, if a spark occurs, it will occur at the connection to the facility grounding system instead of at the item. When a different or new ground is needed for the same item, the operator shall always make the new ground connection first (in the same manner as previously described) before disconnecting the existing ground connection (make-before-break grounding); this ensures that the item will be grounded at all times while transitioning from one ground connection to another.

C7.5.2. Accident history involving rotating blade type mixers shows foreign objects (FO) entering the mix bowl and creating friction between the mixer blades and bowl has caused the majority of mixer fires. Therefore, DoD contractors mixing and manufacturing propellant and other energetic materials shall establish a foreign object elimination (FOE) program with a level of detail commensurate with the complexity of the mixing and manufacturing process and equipment.

C7.5.2.1. As a minimum, the FOE program shall include:

C7.5.2.1.1. A written procedure.

C7.5.2.1.2. Identification of all critical FOE areas and potential FO entry points into the mix bowl or other processing equipment.

C7.5.2.1.3. Elimination of non-essential FO in the mixing and manufacturing process (e.g., jewelry, pens, coins, badges). Pocketless laboratory coats or coveralls should be used.

C7.5.2.1.4. Methods and instructions for securing hardware in FOE-critical areas that could loosen and fall into a mixer.

C7.5.2.1.5. Inventory control of all process tools and equipment (e.g., tool checklists, shadow boards).

C7.5.2.1.6. Inventory control of all process-essential FO entering FOE critical areas.

C7.5.2.1.7. Employee training and records.

C7.5.2.1.8. An audit and inspection plan.

C7.5.2.2. Propellant mix bowls shall be provided with lightweight covers to prevent materials from dropping into the mixer bowl and to prevent sunlight from impinging directly on the materials in the bowl. The cover design shall allow adequate venting in the event of an ignition in the mix bowl.

C7.5.2.3. Nuts, bolts, and other hardware on mixers, monorail systems, or in other locations that could loosen and fall into a mixer shall be effectively secured.

C7.5.3. Non-sparking and non-rusting materials that are chemically compatible with the propellant material shall be used for equipment, tooling, and machinery that will come in contact with propellant or propellant ingredients.

C7.5.4. Certain solid propellant operations involve significant energy input that increases the possibility of ignition. Examples are rolling mills, machining, and drilling operations. In these situations, complete hazard analysis and evaluation shall be conducted prior to starting the operation.

C7.5.5. Heat-conditioning devices used in the propellant manufacturing process shall comply with the design and operating requirements in section C13.4.

C7.5.6. Exposed radiant surfaces in the form of S-shaped smooth pipe or fin-type radiators are easy to clean and should be used for general heating in an AE operating building. Other types of radiators are acceptable, but are less desirable because of cleaning difficulties.

C7.5.7. When mechanical ventilating equipment is used in operations involving potential concentrations of solvent vapors, dusts, and nitro ester vapors, the electric motor and motor controls shall not be located directly in the potentially contaminated air stream and the system shall be provided with a suitable means of collecting condensate.

C7.5.8. Air conditioning and cure oven air-circulating equipment of the closed system type shall be designed to prevent contaminated air from contacting the blower motor and controls. Recirculated air shall be monitored to ensure concentration of vapors and dusts do not reach flammable or explosive threshold limits. Electric motors and controls shall be approved for installation in Class I and Class II hazardous locations as defined in Reference (r). Air mover blades should be nonmetallic.

C7.5.9. Mixing equipment shall be rigidly fixed and stabilized to preclude contact between fixed and movable parts during mixing. The mix bowl lift mechanisms (i.e., elevators) should be a strong-back design or similar design capable of lifting both sides of the bowl evenly to maintain adequate blade-to-bowl clearances during the complete lifting operation.

C7.5.10. Mixer design shall provide for the interruption of power to the mixer blades in the event of excessive loads or drive mechanism malfunction. An air clutch that disengages the motor from the transmission and shear pins in the gear train are examples of engineering controls that serve this purpose.

C7.5.11. Mix blades and mixer shaft shall be rigid and structurally strong to ensure minimum flex from viscosity of the mix and speed of the shaft.

C7.5.12. Electrical components of all mixers shall meet the appropriate electrical classification, be remotely located, or shrouded and purged with inert gas. Purge systems shall be inspected at regular intervals, maintained, and designed to provide automatic warning upon loss of inert gas pressure. When using purge systems, the inert gas storage tank should be checked prior to mixing operations to assure the supply is adequate for the complete process. The purge system design should prevent the creation of unsafe, oxygen deficient work areas.

C7.5.13. Mix bowl, blades, and drive unit shall be electrically bonded and grounded.

C7.5.14. Vacuum system components and piping used with mixers shall be disassembled (to the extent possible), inspected, and cleaned at regular intervals. Vacuum systems should be designed with flanged connections and external clamp fittings to facilitate disassembly. A high efficiency filter should be installed close to the mixer head to prevent explosive dusts from getting into vacuum piping.

C7.5.15. Mixer blade shafts shall be equipped with seals or packing glands that prevent migration of liquids or solvent vapors into bearings. Submerged bearings and packing glands should be avoided. However, if used they shall be periodically tested for contamination and cleaned.

C7.5.16. An inspection plan shall be established to detect significant changes in blade or shaft position relative to mixer head. (See section C3.17. for specific inspection requirement.)

C7.5.17. Propellant mixers should be equipped, inside and outside the mixing vessel, with a high-speed deluge system. Electric service to propellant mixers shall be interlocked with fire protection system controls so that the mixer cannot start when the fire protection system is inoperative. The interlock may be disabled for maintenance or similar situations when energetic materials are not present.

C7.5.18. All process equipment that applies energy to in-process propellant shall be inspected for wear and misalignment at frequencies based on historical experience and manufacturer's recommendations. A record of these inspections and any maintenance performed shall be maintained for the processing equipment.

C7.5.19. Mixers, grinders, and other propellant processing equipment should be equipped with sensors capable of detecting equipment malfunctions or other potentially hazardous abnormalities, particularly for remote-controlled operations. Machine tool power consumption monitors, tool force gages, sound or noise detectors, temperature indicators such as thermocouples or thermistors, and infrared sensors can alert the operator to non-standard conditions that require corrective action. Video monitoring systems should also be installed to provide real-time visual monitoring of remote-controlled operations and to record visual evidence at the time of an accidental initiation.

C7.5.20. Equipment performing sequential operations on propellants (e.g., extrusion and cutting) shall be controlled to prevent interference.

C7.5.21. Tool design for propellant operations should comply with specific guidelines.

C7.5.21.1. Coating metal surfaces such as molds and mandrels with Teflon or similar release materials will generally prevent the propellant from adhering. Coated surfaces should be inspected at regular intervals to detect wear, chipping, cracking, flaking of release material coating. Replace or recoat surfaces as necessary.

C7.5.21.2. Recommended materials for hand tools include aluminum, oil-resistant Neoprene, beryllium-copper alloy, ANSI 300 stainless steel, and tempered steel (for cutting tools such as exacto knives). Steel cutting tools shall not be allowed to cut through the propellant and contact metal surfaces. For example, during small sample cutting, the cutting board should be covered with a Teflon sheet. When ESD is a potential ignition source, hand tools shall be conductive.

C7.5.21.3. Tool design or selection shall incorporate safety considerations such as tool speed control, use of non-sparking metals in contact with or close proximity to the propellant, provision of limit switches to prevent over-ranging of tool and possible metal-to-metal contact, explosion proofing of machinery, use of effective coolant where necessary, effective dust and chip removal, ease of cleaning, and provision for adequate grounding.

C7.6. IN-PROCESS QUANTITIES AND STORAGE

C7.6.1. Propellant and propellant loaded subassemblies in operating buildings shall be limited to that quantity necessary to support safe and efficient operations. Short-term storage of larger quantities in an operating building is permissible when it is not being used for any other operations and the building meets all QD requirements.

C7.6.2. Operating buildings may be used for storage of completed assemblies (with or without installed ignition system) provided there are no other operations in progress and the building meets all QD requirements.

C7.6.3. Production igniters may be stored in designated areas within an assembly or disassembly facility.

C7.6.4. Indoor storage shall be provided for all AE. Temporary staging of AE materials outside operating buildings and at transportation transfer points is not considered storage. However, excessive quantities of these materials introduce additional risk which should be minimized. Accumulation of materials in these areas shall not exceed that which is consistent with efficient operation. AE, including propellant and propellant materials, should be protected from exposure to direct sunlight when in transit or on temporary hold.

C7.6.5. The probability of an unplanned ignition of potentially propulsive AE (i.e., propellant loaded devices, rocket motors, jet assisted take-off units, and missiles) shall be considered during all operations. When a hazard analysis indicates the risk of an unplanned ignition is unacceptable, the potentially propulsive AE shall be secured in a fixture using flight-restraining devices capable of withstanding at least 2.5 times the rated thrust of the unit. When doubt exists as to whether an AE item or its configuration (state of assembly) is propulsive or non-propulsive, treat the AE as propulsive until pertinent technical information can be obtained.

C7.7. INGREDIENTS PROCESSING

C7.7.1. Weighing, Measuring, and Handling Raw Materials

C7.7.1.1. Unless a hazard analysis indicates ESD is not a potential ignition source, the workstation, scales, and personnel shall be bonded and grounded per the requirements of Chapter 6 of this Manual during weighing, measuring, and handling raw materials. The hand tools used by operators shall be conductive. The hazard analysis shall also consider any potential presence of flammable vapors in the process and their sensitivity to ESD.

C7.7.1.2. During operations involving weighing and handling, oxidizers and fuels (metallic powders) shall be isolated from each other and from other materials by locating them in separate rooms, in different cubicles or in areas separated by physical barriers rather than by distance alone.

C7.7.1.3. To prevent inadvertent contact between fuels and oxidizers; containers, equipment, hand tools, scale pans, etc., used for weighing oxidizers shall not be used for weighing fuels and vice versa. Positive measures shall be implemented to ensure the complete separation of such equipment and tools so they will not be intermingled.

C7.7.1.4. The designated use of space and equipment shall not be changed without a thorough cleaning and inspection to assure the removal of all traces of the previous material when they could be incompatible.

C7.7.2. Oxidizer Processing. Oxidizers used in solid propellants are either organic (e.g., nitroesters, nitramines, and some nitrates) or inorganic (e.g., chlorates, perchlorates, peroxides, and nitrates of barium, sodium, potassium, strontium, ammonium, etc.). Screening, blending, grinding, and mechanized drying of organic oxidizers shall be conducted remotely. These same processing operations shall also be conducted remotely for inorganic oxidizers unless a hazard analysis indicates otherwise.

C7.7.2.1. Contaminating an oxidizer agent with any incompatible metal or chemical (fuel) shall be avoided to prevent the formation of a more sensitive composition. For example, copper alloys can form sensitive compounds when exposed to oxidizers such as ammonium perchlorate, and should not be used in oxidizer processing facilities. In addition, many organic lubricants are incompatible with strong oxidizing materials and may form sensitive or explosive compounds when allowed to mix. Oxidizer preparation operations shall be designed to avoid inadvertent contamination of the oxidizer with organic lubricants.

C7.7.2.2. Closed systems should be used to control dust, humidity, and tramp material.

C7.7.2.3. Flexible connections in pipes and duct systems through which oxidizers are conveyed shall be fabricated of fire retardant materials that are chemically compatible with the oxidizers.

C7.7.2.4. The pipes and duct systems shall be made electrically continuous. Threaded joints and fittings in contact with oxidizers should be avoided. Quick clamp neuter end pipe joints are preferred.

C7.8.2.5. ESD control measures shall be used to dissipate static charges to an acceptable level if transporting oxidizer by fluidization.

C7.7.3. Oxidizer Drying

C7.7.3.1. The maximum safe temperature for drying each type of oxidizer shall be established and shall not be exceeded at any point in the drying operation.

CHAPTER 7

C7.7.3.2. If the dryer is capable of exceeding the maximum safe temperature of the oxidizer being dried, dual, redundant thermostatic controls shall be used to prevent overheating.

C7.7.3.3. Electrical heating elements that may contact the oxidizer or oxidizer dust shall not be used.

C7.7.3.4. Dust should be held to a minimum in the drying process. A dust collection system shall be used if dusting can create a potential hazard.

C7.7.3.5. Incompatible materials shall not be dried simultaneously in the same heat conditioning device. Oxidizers shall not be dried in a heat conditioning device previously used for processing flammable or other incompatible materials until after cleaning and inspection shows it is free of any residual contamination.

C7.7.4. Screening Oxidizers

C7.7.4.1. Screening equipment shall be designed and constructed to protect oxidizer material from pinching, friction, or impact as a result of metal-to-metal contact. Rooms in which screening operations are conducted shall be cleaned as often as necessary to prevent hazardous accumulations of dust. The openings in screens shall always be smaller than the blade-to-blade and blade-to-bowl clearances of mixing equipment.

C7.7.4.2. Oxidizer screens shall be electrically grounded and bonded to the receiving vessel.

C7.7.4.3. Large scale mechanical screening of inorganic oxidizers like ammonium perchlorate shall be performed remotely unless a hazard analysis indicates otherwise. Small-scale manual screening of inorganic oxidizers is permissible when justified by a hazard analysis. The manual screening operation shall be isolated, the work area and the screening equipment shall be kept clean, and metal-to-metal contact shall not be allowed.

C7.7.5. Grinding Oxidizers and Nitramines

C7.7.5.1. When using impact-type mills, sufficient clearance shall be maintained between stationary and moving parts to prevent metal-to-metal contact. Clearances shall be checked as often as needed to ensure they are adequate. Mill bearings should be purged with air to prevent contamination. Impact-type grinders shall not be used to grind organic oxidizers and nitramines.

C7.7.5.2. Oxidizer feed materials shall be passed through a screen mesh with openings no greater than the clearance between hammer and plate. Screen mesh size for ammonium nitrate should be the smallest that allows free flow of the prills. Magnetic separators shall be used if screening is not possible.

C7.7.5.3. Only compatible lubricants shall be used in grinding equipment.

C7.7.5.4. Heat sensing devices should be installed on the bearing housing of grinding equipment.

C7.7.5.5. The cleaning method for grinding equipment and the appropriate cleaning frequency shall be determined and included in the SOP.

C7.7.5.6. Grinding operations should be equipped with wet dust collection systems, where appropriate.

C7.7.5.7. Pneumatic grinding operations shall be thoroughly grounded and bonded to provide for electrostatic charge dissipation.

C7.7.6. Preparations of Fuel Compositions

C7.7.6.1. Sensitivity characteristics of fuel compositions should be determined prior to production mixing operations.

C7.7.6.2. Compatibility of materials shall be established and controls incorporated into procedures to preclude the mixing of materials during processing at a time or in a manner that would result in sensitive compositions, e.g., dry AP and powdered metal mixtures.

C7.7.6.3. Due to the susceptibility of metal powders to ignition from ESD, all dumping, screening, weighing, and handling equipment should be bonded and grounded. When metallic powder or flammable liquids are transferred (poured) from one container to another, the containers should be bonded together prior to the transfer. Spatulas, scoops, and other tools used to dump, measure, or stir metal powders shall be conductive.

C7.7.6.4. Equipment design and handling methods shall minimize the formation and accumulation of dust during all preparation operations. Fume hoods, dust socks, closed systems, and dust and fume vacuum exhaust hoses shall be used, as appropriate, to prevent vapors and dust getting into the operating areas.

C7.7.6.5. Positive measures shall be taken to exclude moisture from metal powder operations. Waste metal powders should be immersed in a compatible non-reactive liquid until disposed.

C7.7.6.6. The introduction of an inert gas into process equipment in order to reduce oxygen content should be considered as a means to prevent dust explosions.

C7.7.7. Transfer Operations

C7.7.7.1. Finely divided powdered ingredients should be transferred by methods that control flow rate and minimize electrostatic charge generation.

C7.7.7.2. Before transferring flammable solvents, the transfer and receiving vessels should be bonded to eliminate electrostatic potential differences.

C7.8. MIXING

C7.8.1. Hardware and associated equipment shall be secured to prevent loose items falling into mixer bowls. (See paragraph C7.5.2. for more information.)

C7.8.2. All materials shall be screened prior to entering the mixer bowl. The size of the openings in the screen shall be less than the smallest clearance between the mixer blades and between the blades and the mix bowl. Where the physical characteristics of the material preclude screening, other methods such as magnetic separators or nondestructive testing should be used to remove foreign material before entering the mixer bowl. When necessary (e.g., during final weight adjustments), smaller amounts of material may be added directly, provided a positive means exists to ensure the material does not contain any foreign material.

C7.8.3. Oxidizers shall be introduced into mixers after the fuel-binder compositions to minimize the probability of the mixture undergoing a deflagration-to-detonation transition if an ignition occurs during mixing.

C7.8.4. Only non-sparking devices shall be used for hand scraping the sides and blades of mixers.

C7.8.5. Direct and unobstructed routes shall be provided for personnel egress from mixer buildings or bays. (See section C12.7. for additional egress information.)

C7.9. CASTING AND CURING. The three most common methods of casting are bayonet casting, in which the propellant is introduced into the top of the motor through hoses; bottom casting, in which the propellant is forced by pressure up through an opening in the bottom of the rocket case; and vacuum casting, in which the propellant is passed through a slit plate into a rocket motor case enclosed in a vacuum bell. High strength cases are also used as vacuum bells.

C7.9.1. Personnel may attend cast operations if justified by a thorough hazard analysis.

C7.9.2. Multiple or single production line type casting is permitted. However, when the survivability of the production facility is critical or the risk to the program is significant, the PCO may require the contractor to provide protection that prevents propagation of an incident from the casting operation to adjacent cast bells or pits.

C7.9.3. All cast piping and tooling in contact with propellant shall be smooth for ease of cleaning and be free of cracks, pits, crevices, and weld slag. Threaded joints should be avoided as much as possible. Joints requiring disassembly as a process operation or for cleaning should not be threaded type.

C7.9.4. Cast tooling and mandrel designs shall not permit metal-to-metal friction or impact points.

C7.9.5. Valves through which propellant flows shall be designed to prevent propellant from being pinched or compressed between metal surfaces, e.g., rubber diaphragm-type valves.

C7.9.6. Pressurized casting vessels shall be designed and capable of withstanding at least twice the maximum allowable working pressure.

C7.9.7. Lids shall be secured to pressurized casting vessels in such a manner that they will withstand the rated pressures of the vessels.

C7.9.8. Line pressure for pressurizing the casting vessel shall not exceed the working pressure of the vessel. Pressure lines shall have a relief valve downstream of the regulator.

C7.9.9. Each vessel shall be equipped with a blowout disk (burst diaphragm) designed to blow out at less than 120 percent of the vessel's maximum allowable working pressure. The design shall allow for the release of the potential rapid rise of pressure in the vessel if the propellant ignites.

C7.9.10. Pressure relief shall be provided when propellant is cured or cast under pressure.

C7.9.11. Pressurization and depressurization for propellant cure shall be done remotely.

C7.9.12. Casting vessels should be physically or electrically disconnected from lifting devices during cast operations.

C7.10. EXTRUSION PROCESSES

C7.10.1. Solvent-less extrusion presses and compression molding equipment should be designed to remove air from the propellant before compaction and extrusion begin. Procedures shall require checking operation of the vacuum system and for cleaning it to remove propellant residue and condensed vapors such as those generated from NG volatilization.

C7.10.2. Ramheads should be checked for alignment with the press bore to preclude metal-to-metal contact. Flashing removal should be included in the process procedures.

C7.10.3. Interlocks shall be provided to preclude press operation during loading or other attended operations.

C7.11. PROPELLANT LOADED AE

C7.11.1. When performing operations on cured propellant contained in pressure vessels or rocket motor cases that may be propulsive and where there is a risk of ignition due to energy inputs (e.g., electrical check of pyrotechnic devices), the unit should be secured in a fixture capable of withstanding a minimum of 2.5 times the rated thrust of the assembly.

C7.11.2. When the application of mechanical force is required to "breakaway" the mandrel or other tooling embedded in propellant, it should be applied by remote control. (See Table C7.T1 for exceptions.)

C7.11.3. Loaded motor cases or casting molds shall be secured during casting and handled in a manner that will prevent overturning or spillage of propellant. For large motors, casting cores shall be secured to prevent movement when loaded motors are transported in any manner.

C7.11.4. Propellant machining equipment shall be designed:

C7.11.4.1. To prevent contact of cutting tools or blades with motor cases and other metal objects.

C7.11.4.2. To minimize generation of heat.

C7.11.4.3. To facilitate removal of dust and chips and to provide personnel protection. The motor or grain should be X-rayed prior to machining or trimming if there is a possibility that metal or other foreign objects may be in the propellant.

C7.11.5. Propellant dust, chips, and shavings shall be removed frequently from the work area during machining and contouring. This process waste shall be physically removed from the work area and stored in appropriate containers prior to disposition.

C7.11.6. Rocket motors in the final assembly process should be positioned to permit ready access to all sides of the motor. Aisles and exit doors shall be kept clear and unobstructed. All exit doors shall have quick-release hardware.

C7.11.7. Grounding of propellant-loaded assemblies in storage is optional and shall be reviewed on a case-by-case basis.

C7.11.8. If the process requires removing an igniter-shorting clip, the igniter shall remain shorted until immediately before insertion. The igniter shall remain unshorted for only the minimum time required for the operation.

C7.11.9. When ESD is a potential ignition source during igniter insertion operations, the igniter and motor shall be bonded together and grounded to a single ground point. If analysis indicates the igniter or motor is sensitive to 0.1 joule of energy or less, personnel shall be grounded per paragraph C6.4.7.

C7.11.10. Operations that involve electrical continuity checking and/or testing of ignition systems installed in rocket motors shall be conducted according to thoroughly reviewed and approved procedures. These checks shall be conducted remotely with the motor secured in a fixture designed to withstand at least 2.5 times the thrust of the motor.

C7.12. DISASSEMBLY

C7.12.1. Equipment and tooling that require disassembly during the manufacturing process should be designed to prevent metal-to-metal contact and trapping of explosive material.

C7.12.2. Non-routine disassembly of equipment and tooling, such as that necessary for equipment repair, shall not be started until potential hazards from trapped material or process residuals have been evaluated and controls or safeguards have been implemented to mitigate the hazard.

C7.13. LOGISTICAL MOVES. Logistical moves involving large rocket motors and large quantities of propellants shall have hazard analyses and approved procedures. Operators involved shall be trained in the procedures.

Table C7.T1. Control and Personnel Protection Requirements for Certain Propellant Processing Operations

Operation	Remote Controls	Personnel Protected[1]
Blending, screening, grinding, and mechanized drying of perchlorates, including ammonium perchlorate	Mandatory[3]	Mandatory[3]
Blending and screening of nitramines	Mandatory[2]	Mandatory[2]
Screening, grinding, blending, and mechanized drying of nitramines	Mandatory	Mandatory
Grinding, blending, screening, and mechanized drying of ammonium nitrates	Advisory	Advisory
Rotating blade propellant mixing	Mandatory	Mandatory
Power-driven cutting, machining, sawing, planing, drilling, or other unconfined operations in which rocket motors or propellant of Hazard Division 1.1 and 1.3 are involved.	Mandatory[3]	Mandatory[3]
Mandrel break away removal from cured propellant	Mandatory[3]	Mandatory[3]
Pressing, extruding, palletizing, or blending propellant	Mandatory	Mandatory
Casting Propellants	Mandatory[3]	Mandatory[3]

NOTES:
1. Operating personnel shall be protected per the thermal and fragment requirements outlined in subparagraph C5.7.1.3.
2. Attended screening of wet material may take place if shown acceptable by hazard analysis.
3. Attended operation permitted if shown to be acceptable by hazard analysis.

CHAPTER 7

C8. CHAPTER 8

SAFETY REQUIREMENTS FOR MANUFACTURING
AND PROCESSING PYROTECHNICS

C8.1. <u>GENERAL</u>. The safety precautions for manufacturing and processing pyrotechnics are similar to those required for many types of explosives and other energetic materials. However, pyrotechnics exhibit many different characteristics because they are formulated for different purposes. Knowledge of the various pyrotechnic properties is critical to the establishment of proper hazard controls. Pyrotechnics can be divided into several general categories including: initiators (igniters), illuminants, smokes, gas generators, sound generators, heat producers, and timing compositions. Each of these categories has its own characteristics and attendant processing requirements. Knowledge of these characteristics is necessary to assure safety in processing. The range of characteristics associated with pyrotechnics includes compositions that are easily initiated, including compositions that burn in seconds at temperatures exceeding 5000 degrees Fahrenheit (°F) [2760 degrees Celsius (°C)] through compositions that require substantial energy for initiation and have relatively low output temperatures. As examples, the auto-ignition temperature for smoke compositions is typically about 356°F [180°C], while for illuminants it is about 932°F [500°C]. Illuminants burn approximately 2.7 times faster than smokes and the heat of reaction is 1.5 times as great. Infrared (IR) flare compositions are both hotter and faster burning than illuminants. Many of the compositions in the igniter or initiator class are as sensitive to ESD, friction, or impact as are initiating explosives such as lead azide and lead styphnate. Initiation thresholds to stimuli such as impact, friction, and ESD and energy output of initiator compositions shall be determined and understood to ensure adequate safety controls are implemented to provide personnel safety in specific processes. In addition to the safety precautions generally required for the handling of explosives and other energetic materials, section C8.2. provides specific guidance pertinent to pyrotechnic operations.

C8.2. <u>PROPERTIES OF PYROTECHNIC MATERIALS AND MIXTURES</u>. Knowledge of the various pyrotechnic properties is critical to the establishment of proper hazard controls. The summaries of various pyrotechnic terms provided in paragraphs C8.2.1. through C8.2.4. are not all inclusive and should only be used for general reference.

C8.2.1. <u>Oxidizers</u>. Oxidizers are oxygen-rich substances that decompose to liberate oxygen gas, or substances that act as oxidizers with active metal fuels. Typical inorganic oxidizers are nitrates, chlorates, perchlorates, oxides, chromates, and dichromates. Fluorine and chlorine, as in hexachloroethane and Teflon (brand of fluorine containing compound), are examples of organic compounds used as oxidizers. All oxidizers, if not well controlled, tend to increase the risk of undesired reactions, particularly in the presence of organic materials (including wood). Potassium chlorate compositions are particularly susceptible to accidental ignition. Impurities in process materials or those introduced by poor process control (e.g., oils, lubricants) can readily increase the sensitivity of mixtures or result in ignition. Some oxidizers with trace impurities (or by themselves, such as AP) can detonate when subjected to severe stimuli such as an adjacent explosion or thermal energy. Safety requires absolute control of oxidizers to prevent contamination, uncontrolled moisture absorption (many are hydroscopic), fires, or explosions from accidental mixing with fuels.

C8.2.2. Fuels. Fuels react with the oxidizers to produce heat and an oxidized product. It is the proper pairing of the fuel with an appropriate oxidizer that determines the reaction characteristics and the use for the mixtures. Metals such as magnesium or aluminum create high heat or light output. Fuels include an almost unlimited variety of organic (sugars and red gum) and a more limited variety of inorganic materials, e.g., sulfur, boron, phosphorus, and sulfides. Although generally more stable than oxidizers, fuels also have unique characteristics that contribute to risk. These include the liberation of hydrogen from magnesium and aluminum powders that become wetted. Storage and handling of fuels requires tight process controls that respect the characteristics of the specific materials and prevent contamination that may result in a reaction.

C8.2.3. Binders. Homogeneity of the mixtures governs the effectiveness of pyrotechnic compositions. Some pyrotechnics (e.g., black powder) are self-bound by the manufacturing process to maintain the charcoal, sulfur, and potassium nitrate in the correct, proportionate, intimate mixture needed. Other mixtures, because of differences in particle size or weight of ingredients, require the use of a binder to retain the homogeneous blend. Binders may include lacquers, epoxies, and a variety of polymers activated by heat or solvents. Some solvents are similar in composition to fuels, and the binder may also be a fuel or burn rate modifier. Some binders are flammable while others require the use of a highly flammable solvent, and thus the ignition characteristics of these materials are important risk factors.

C8.2.4. Types of Pyrotechnic Compositions. Pyrotechnic compositions are usually grouped by the function of the end item. There is no universal single grouping, but typical major groupings are heat and delay compositions, color and light compositions, and smoke. Delay compositions are used for or produce ignition, delay, heat, and propulsion. Smoke compositions are used for or produce obscurance, signal smokes, and noise. The range of sensitivity to initiation and the rate and/or amount of output energy varies greatly both within and between groups.

C8.2.4.1. Heat and Delay Compositions. Pyrotechnic fuses, electric matches, first fires, primers, igniters, and delay compositions are all members of this group. The end products must function with very little stimulus, and thus the mixtures as well as individual ingredients are sensitive to initiation. First fire, igniter, and primer mixtures are generally the most sensitive to initiation stimuli, i.e., heat, friction, impact, and static electricity. NOTE: Primer mixes containing initiating explosives such as lead azide or lead styphnate are properly classed as explosives. These mixtures often use black powder or potassium chlorate and metal combinations or potassium chlorate and phosphorous mixtures. This group also contains mixtures with high heat outputs for such purposes as document destroyers and welding. These high heat producers are generally metallic fuels and metallic oxidizers, as in the iron oxide and aluminum powder formulations for Thermite.

CHAPTER 8

C8.2.4.2. <u>Color or Light Producing Compositions</u>. There are a wide variety of mixes and compositions that produce light, color, or both. Illuminant candles, photoflash, and decoy flares all are part of this very broad category. Many of the compositions -- notably the photoflash and decoy flare compositions -- are characterized by very rapid reactions and extreme temperature outputs. Both have resulted in fatal accidents. Metallic fuels are characteristic of the high light (visible, IR) output mixtures. Output temperatures exceeding 2000°F [1093°C] characterize many of the items in this category. Accidental initiation of large mix batches of some compositions may have a significant pressurization effect in addition to the heat, with resultant structural damage.

C8.2.4.3. <u>Smoke and Noise Producing Compositions</u>. Obscurants, colored markers, weapons simulators, and weapons effects simulators comprise this category. Smoke compositions are characteristically slow burning in finished form, but must burn at a temperature high enough to vaporize the dye compound (usually organic). Chlorates are often the oxidizer in colored smoke mixes. "Flash-bang compositions" used in weapons simulators and weapons effects simulators are actually explosives in most instances and will detonate with adequate stimulus in unconfined bulk form. "Flash-bang" compositions, particularly in display or commercial fireworks but also in military items, are the cause of many injury-producing accidents. Similarly, "whistle" compositions are very sensitive to ignition and can detonate.

C8.3. <u>PROCESS REQUIREMENTS</u>

C8.3.1. <u>Housekeeping and Cleanliness Guidelines</u>. Pyrotechnic operations require stringent housekeeping and cleanliness due to the sensitive nature of the ingredients and compositions; the dangerous effects of contamination, including cross contamination of oxidizers and fuels; and the amount of open or exposed ingredients and mixtures. Materials control and cleanliness are mandatory not only to reduce the likelihood of accidental initiations, but also to minimize the effects of an accident.

C8.3.1.1. Do not allow ingredient or composition dusts to accumulate, whether on the exterior work surfaces or the interior of process equipment and ventilation systems. Accident investigations frequently identify dust buildups as the source of initiation when items are dropped on or scraped across them. Dust accumulations also can provide a propagation path from the initiation of a small quantity to a much larger quantity, thereby increasing the magnitude of an accident.

C8.3.1.2. Vapor recovery methods or ventilation shall prevent the accumulation of volatile vapors, and ignition sources shall be eliminated or controlled to prevent the initiation of a solvent vapor cloud. Where volatile flammable solvents are part of the process, solvent vapors in ventilation systems, hallways, conduits, or pipes may also provide a propagation path from the initiation of a small quantity to larger quantities.

C8.3.2. <u>Static Control Systems</u>. As many pyrotechnic ingredients, mixtures, or the solvents used in their production are highly susceptible to initiation by static electricity, static control systems are mandatory where hazard analysis indicates a need. Static control systems include conductive floors or mats, shoes, wrist straps, grounding of equipment, etc.

C8.3.3. <u>Hazard Analysis and Risk Assessment</u>. For all pyrotechnic operations, a documented hazard analysis and risk assessment is mandatory to validate the layout of operations, selection of materials and equipment, and process control parameters. (See Chapter 11 of this Manual.)

C8.3.4. <u>Machinery, Equipment, and Facilities</u>. Except as provided for in this chapter, the design, layout, and operation of facilities and equipment shall follow the mandatory provisions for the processing of explosives and other energetic materials contained elsewhere in this Manual. Where guidance is not provided, operations shall be governed by the results of hazard analyses performed and documented to address specific operations. Since most pyrotechnic compositions are sensitive to initiation by ESD, bonding and grounding, along with other means of static elimination and control, shall be considered.

C8.3.5. <u>Weighing Raw Materials</u>. Separate weight or measurement rooms, cubicles, or areas (dependent upon the quantity and sensitivity of the materials handled) shall be provided -- one for oxidizers and one for fuels (combustible materials and metallic powders). Containers, equipment, hand tools, scale pans, etc., used for weighing fuels or oxidizers shall not be interchanged or shared among incompatible operations, particularly where distance rather than physical barriers separates these areas. Positive measures shall be adopted to ensure the complete separation of such equipment and tools. A hazard analysis shall determine appropriate personnel protective equipment for personnel weighing or handling exposed oxidizers or fuels.

C8.3.6. <u>Drying Materials</u>. Drying pyrotechnic materials at elevated temperatures may increase their sensitivity and generate flammable vapors or dust that can create an explosive atmosphere. Contractors shall conduct hazard analyses to identify auto ignition temperatures and potential ignition sources and to implement controls to prevent unplanned ignition. The minimum temperature necessary to meet processing requirements shall be used to dry components and pyrotechnic materials. Heat conditioning devices used to dry pyrotechnics shall meet the requirements of section C13.4.

C8.3.7. <u>Mixing and Blending</u>. Mixing, blending, and cleanup of pyrotechnic compositions require close attention because most injury-producing accidents have occurred during the mixing, blending, or subsequent cleanup operations. Because of the variety within and among these compositions, no single type of mixer or blender can be the exclusively approved equipment for pyrotechnic mixing and blending operations.

C8.3.7.1. Each mixing device shall be considered separately with respect to the composition to be processed. When a history of safe operation has not been established, the type of mixer or blender and batch size shall be evaluated by appropriate hazard analysis or tests. Generally, devices that use a tumbling action are preferred to those using rotating blades, to minimize points where frictional heat may develop or where accidentally introduced foreign material can create hot spots through friction or crushing of composition. Mixers and blenders shall be equipped for pressure relief to preclude a transition from burning to detonation. Unless hazard analysis indicates otherwise, mixers and blenders shall be charged, operated, and emptied remotely. When mixers are charged or emptied manually, personnel exposures shall be minimized. Appropriate interlocks, clutch brakes, and similar devices shall be used to preclude the movement of mixer or blender parts during periods when operators are present.

C8.3.7.2. Mixing and blending operations shall be conducted in buildings or cubicles designed for such purposes. Multiple mixing or blending operations may be conducted in the same building, provided that each blender or mixer is located in a separate room, bay, or cell and separated from other operations in a manner that prevents propagation and protects personnel and production equipment. Two or more mixers or blenders may be located in the same cubicle, provided that the hazards are not increased by such installation. Normally, this would require that the materials in process be of significantly low energy content or slow energy release and the mixers be charged and emptied simultaneously. At least one wall or equivalent panel area in each bay shall be frangible so as to provide pressure relief in the event of an incident. Cell arrangement and pressure relief areas shall be located so that personnel cannot pass in front of these areas while mixers or blenders are operating.

C8.3.7.3. Exhaust ventilation equipment shall be installed on mixers or in bays where flammable solvents are used and shall be interlocked with the mixers. The interlock shall be designed to preclude mixer operation without ventilation. Vapor sensors should be used to provide automatic warning of flammable vapor concentrations approaching the lower explosive limit. Such sensors should be interlocked to personnel access control devices. Ventilation systems shall be designed to prevent propagation of an incident in one bay to others served by the same system.

C8.3.7.4. The operation of mixers or blenders may be observed by remote means such as closed-circuit television, mirrors, or transparent shields providing operator protection. Direct viewing of blender or mixer operation without intervening barriers shall be prohibited.

C8.3.7.5. Manual mixing, blending, or scraping of fuels and oxidizers shall be prohibited, unless hazard analysis indicates otherwise.

C8.3.7.6. Minimum criteria for rotating-blade mixing operations:

C8.3.7.6.1. The mix equipment shall be rigidly fixed and stable during mixing to preclude contact between the bowl and the mix blades.

C8.3.7.6.2. Positive controls (e.g., slip clutch, shear pins) shall be provided to disengage power from the drive shaft and blades in case of malfunction.

C8.3.7.6.3. Mixer blades and shaft shall be rigid and structurally strong to ensure minimum flex from viscosity of the mix and speed of the shaft.

CHAPTER 8

C8.3.7.6.4. All electrical components of the mixer shall meet the appropriate "Hazardous Location" classification defined in Reference (r).

C8.3.7.6.5. The mixer blade shaft shall include adequate and compatible seals or packing glands to prevent migration of mix or solvent vapor into bearings. Submerged bearings and packing glands should be avoided. If used, periodically test packing glands and bearings for contamination and clean them as often as necessary.

C8.3.7.6.6. A preventive maintenance and inspection program shall be established to monitor wear in the mixer blade shaft and bearings to avoid excess play. The program shall meet all the requirements in section C3.17. Perform operational checks of blade and/or plow and bowl clearances at least daily prior to the introduction of materials.

C8.3.7.6.7. Wet mixing shall not be started until adequate solvent is added to preclude dry mixing.

C8.3.7.6.8. Electrical service to mixers shall be interlocked with fire protection system controls to prevent mixer start-up when the fire protection system is inoperative. The interlock may be disabled as necessary when pyrotechnic materials are absent, e.g., maintenance operations.

C8.3.7.6.9. Mixers, mix bowls, and containers shall be bonded and grounded during charging and discharging of ingredients and pyrotechnic mixtures.

C8.3.7.6.10. Torque limits or amperage overload protection shall be defined and monitored.

C8.3.7.6.11. Solvent traps for vacuum mixing shall be maintained.

C8.3.8. Pressing, Extruding, and Pelleting

C8.3.8.1. Pressing operations shall be conducted with personnel protected by substantial dividing walls, barricades, or operational shields or shall take place at ILD from the operator and other operations. When it is necessary to repair, adjust, or otherwise clear a jam on a press or extruder, the pyrotechnic material shall be removed from the hopper and the bay or pressroom before such repairs or adjustments are made. Only those adjustments of ram speed or conveyor speed routinely controlled by the operator may proceed with material in the bay. Under no circumstances shall repair or adjustment requiring the use of tools be permitted with pyrotechnic material in the bay.

C8.3.8.2. The quantity of composition at the pressing location (behind the barricade) shall not exceed that required for the components undergoing the pressing operation. Separate all other quantities in the bay to prevent propagation from an event in the press.

C8.3.8.3. Each individual press, extruder, or loading device shall be located in a separate building, room, or cubicle and be designed to limit an incident to that area and protect operators. Multiple installations may be permitted within a bay or cubicle when tests or hazard analysis demonstrate that the facility and personnel are protected from the effects of the MCE. Adequate means of pressure relief shall be built into each bay or cubicle.

C8.3.9. Assembly Operations. Individual assembly operations shall be adequately separated from each other and shall be located in a separate cubicle or building from mixing, blending, and consolidation operations. Pyrotechnic composition shall be kept in closed or covered containers at all times except during processing. Surge, storage, and inprocess transit between operations shall also be accomplished with closed containers unless the operational configuration makes this impossible. Components in any assembly room, bay, or building shall be limited to the smallest quantity necessary for safe and efficient operations.

C8.3.10. Granulation, Grinding, and Screening

C8.3.10.1. Material to be reduced in particle size shall be screened or processed over a magnetic separator to remove foreign materials before grinding. Following grinding, the material should be re-screened or passed over a magnetic separator.

C8.3.10.2. In the operation of ball mills, hammer mills, granulators, or screeners, the operator shall be protected from the effects of a potential incident by an operational shield. The charging, discharging, and cleaning of grinding, granulating, and screening equipment shall be performed remotely, unless a hazard analysis indicates otherwise.

C8.3.10.3. Working surfaces, containers, and hand tools shall be appropriately bonded and grounded.

C8.3.11. Transportation. Pyrotechnic compositions shall be transported in closed containers only. Individual containers and the transport vehicle (e.g., handcart, hand truck) should be fabricated of the lightest materials compatible with the composition and having the requisite strength. This will minimize fragment generation if an incident occurs. Transport vehicles should be equipped with "dead man" brakes. On- and off-loading of transport vehicles should be conducted only in weather-protected areas designated for this purpose. Racks or other support suited to the size and shape of composition containers should be provided to prevent them from falling.

C8.3.12. Rebowling. Rebowling is the transfer of typically dry and sensitive materials in small quantities from one container to another, to recover remains of small quantities of materials or to subdivide large masses for processing. Operators rebowling dry pyrotechnics compositions with characteristics similar to initiating explosives shall be protected by operational shields.

C8.3.13. Machining of Pyrotechnic Material

C8.3.13.1. General Guidance for Machining

C8.3.13.1.1. Machining of pyrotechnic materials shall be conducted remotely unless a hazard analysis indicates otherwise.

C8.3.13.1.2. When coolant is required, it shall be compatible with the pyrotechnic composition. Positive automatic interlocking devices shall prevent the machine from starting until the coolant is flowing. These controls shall also be capable of stopping the machine if the flow of coolant is interrupted. When it is essential to cut off the coolant to adjust machine tools, the flow of coolant shall be restored and all automatic controls operating before machining resumes. Overheating of a cutting edge during machining is most dangerous when continuous contact with the pyrotechnic material is maintained after the machine has stopped; therefore, the coolant shall continue flowing until the cutter is removed from contact with the pyrotechnic material.

C8.3.13.1.3. Sensors are recommended to detect tooling malfunctions or other potentially hazardous conditions. Machine tool power-consumption monitors, tool force gages, sound or noise detectors, temperature-indicating devices, or IR detectors can be used in this regard.

C8.3.13.1.4. Cutting tools shall be chemically compatible with the pyrotechnic material to be machined and capable of maintaining a sharp cutting edge throughout the machine cycle.

C8.3.13.1.5. Control measures such as guides, bushings, and stops shall limit depth, diameter, and contour of the cut. The lineal and rotational speed of tools for the machining of pyrotechnic material shall be the minimum necessary for safe and efficient operation. Controls should be designed to prevent unintended operator adjustment.

C8.3.13.1.6. Drilling operations shall not impede the flow of chips and coolant in the bore. The drilling of small holes (one-quarter inch or less) and any size multiple drilling operation shall be performed by remote control, with operator protection, unless documented hazard analysis or tests demonstrate otherwise.

C8.3.13.1.7. Contoured cutting tools shall be completely retracted from contact with the pyrotechnic material before personnel are permitted to enter the machining area. Machine tools should be cleaned as often as necessary during operating hours to prevent residues from accumulating and shall be thoroughly cleaned at the end of each work shift. Pyrotechnic waste products shall be removed by vacuum accumulator systems, immersion in liquid coolant streams, or similar automatic means. When using compressed air as a coolant, only low pressure (10 pounds per square inch gauge (psig) [68.95 kPa]) may be used as a coolant, and then only when a vacuum collection system is used to reduce the scattering of pyrotechnic particles. The coolant delivery tube shall have a metallic tip or nozzle grounded to the machine to reduce static charges.

C8.3.13.2. Specific Guidance for Machining

C8.3.13.2.1. During drilling and facing operations, the feed rate should be adjusted to enhance the machinability of the composition and minimize friction and heat build-up. Hazard analysis should address factors including feed rate, type of composition, and tooling.

C8.3.13.2.2. Hand trimming and cutting of pyrotechnic candles may be permitted when supported by results of a hazard analysis specific to the particular composition and candle configuration.

C8.3.13.2.3. Sawing operations require particular care to prevent material from plunging into the saw blade and to ensure chip removal from saw teeth before subsequent cutting passes. Plunging can occur when thin sections are force fed into coarse pitch saw blades. To prevent this, either a minimum of two saw teeth must remain in contact with the material being cut while sawing, or the work feed rate shall be positively controlled. Chip accumulation in the saw teeth is a function of the material being sawed, rate of feed, blade speed, tooth design, and flushing arrangement. Additional chip removal equipment such as blade wiping brushes may be required.

C8.4. SPILL CONTROL

Spills of pyrotechnic composition and energetic ingredients pose potential hazards. In case of an accident, the responsible supervisor should be notified before taking any action to clean and contain the spills. SOP for pyrotechnic operations shall cover spill cleanup, either as part of the various operations detailed or as a separate procedure. The procedures shall specify which actions are to be taken by whom and in what order. The procedures shall also address recovery of the spilled material and decontamination of the area.

C8.5. COLLECTION OF PYROTECHNIC WASTE

C8.5.1. Waste material and scraps shall be removed at regular intervals from all operating areas. All waste material shall be segregated by type and compatibility and kept separate from common wastes. Containers for these materials shall be positively identified by color and labeled. Filled containers should be placed at designated collection points.

C8.5.2. Special care shall be taken to preclude the mixing of only small quantities of water with powdered or finely granulated metals that can react violently. Pyrotechnic waste may be maintained dry or submerged in water or oil, whichever is appropriate for disposal. Plastic liners should be used for waste containers to facilitate cleaning. Liners should be conductive when contents are subject to initiation by ESD.

C8.6. <u>CLEANING OF PYROTECHNIC PROCESSING EQUIPMENT</u>

C8.6.1. Since pyrotechnic materials are sensitive to friction, impact, or ESD, cleaning equipment contaminated with pyrotechnic materials poses hazards. Because of the required personnel proximity to the equipment being cleaned, hazards of cleaning may exceed those of processing. Therefore, cleaning shall receive the same planning and SOP coverage as production.

C8.6.2. Cleaning and solvent solution flushing by remote control is required for slurry-type mixing operations. For other applications, the process equipment shall be flushed with a compatible solvent and drained, with the process repeated as often as necessary to remove the pyrotechnic composition. High-pressure water wash may be used when compatible with the pyrotechnic composition. Precautionary measures shall be taken when a solvent represents a fire or toxicological threat. Runoff from cleaning operations shall be controlled to preclude the creation of a secondary hazard from the spread of contamination.

C8.6.3. When remote cleaning is not possible, selection of personal protective equipment (PPE) shall be based on a hazard analysis that demonstrates protection from the MCE at the cleaning operation. The use of PPE shall be required.

C8.7. <u>PERSONAL PROTECTIVE EQUIPMENT</u>

C8.7.1. PPE shall not be relied upon as the primary means of operator protection. The primary means should be the reduction of quantities being handled to the minimum necessary and the use of operational shields. Supplemental operator protection should be provided by high-speed deluge systems designed and installed for such purposes. The personal protective apparel prescribed in an SOP shall be based upon a hazards analysis of the operation.

C8.7.2. Unless a hazard analysis indicates otherwise, the minimum protective apparel for personnel exposed to open containers of pyrotechnic or energetic raw materials shall consist of:

C8.7.2.1. Cotton socks.

C8.7.2.2. Conductive-soled safety shoes.

C8.7.2.3. Flame-retardant coveralls.

C8.7.2.4. Hair coverings.

C8.7.3. Unless a hazard analysis indicates otherwise, all employees exposed to hazardous quantities of pyrotechnic compositions shall wear:

C8.7.3.1. Aluminized, thermally protective suit with hood and faceplate.

C8.7.3.2. Aluminized, thermally protective trousers.

C8.7.3.3. Aluminized, thermally protective gloves or equivalent. The definition of hazardous quantities will depend on the composition's energy output and sensitivity (as determined by hazard analyses or tests) and the nature of the operation.

C8.7.4. Required levels of protective apparel shall be specified in appropriate SOP steps.

C8.7.5. When the protective clothing described in paragraph C8.7.3. is required, the design and wearing shall ensure no exposure of any area of the body. Use appropriate seals or joints to preclude flame intrusion where apparel items overlap or join. Particular attention shall be given to possible gaps in coverage provided by the hood in order to prevent flame or hot gas impingement on the face, head, or neck. Protection of the employee's throat and lungs may require use of a self-contained breathing apparatus or supplied-air respirator to protect from the effects of a fireball.

C8.8. ADDITIONAL CONTROLS

C8.8.1. Many materials used to produce pyrotechnics are fire hazards, toxic hazards, or both. Operations shall provide protection from these hazards. Vapor and dust removal and collection systems shall be provided where toxic or flammable dusts or gases are generated. Design and installation of such equipment shall meet applicable safety requirements in sections C15.3., C15.4., and C15.5.

C8.8.2. Blankets should be provided in easily opened containers within 25 ft [8 m] of operations where they could be used to smother burning clothing. Alternate means of achieving the same effect should be provided when blankets are not available.

C8.8.3. When ESD is a potential ignition source, floors and workstations shall be conductive and personnel shall be grounded in accordance with applicable requirements in paragraph C6.4.7. Conductive shoes shall be tested for resistance to ground per subparagraph C6.4.7.5.4.

C8.9. REWORKING PYROTECHNIC COMPONENTS

C8.9.1. All repair, reassembly, or similar operations on loaded pyrotechnic compositions shall be performed in a separate bay used only for that purpose.

C8.9.2. Reworking and reusing pyrotechnic material may be desirable from both an economic and environmental basis; however, all potential rework and reuse of these materials require a careful hazard analysis to assure safety. Normally, consolidated or extruded pyrotechnic compositions are not pulverized for reblending operations and should be destroyed. Some relatively insensitive compositions, such as hexachloroethand (HC) smoke, may be reused. Other more sensitive materials, such as IR flare compositions, shall not be reused.

C8.10. FIRE PROTECTION

When compatible with process materials, deluge systems may be used for the protection of mixing, blending, screening, granulating, drying, pressing, or extrusion operations. The response time of the deluge system should be selected to minimize the damage to process equipment and facilities. Hazard analysis of the operation may dictate other applications.

CHAPTER 8

C9. CHAPTER 9

AE STORAGE

C9.1. GENERAL

A properly sited storage area is mandatory for AE. A properly segregated and separate storage area is preferred for explosives storage. ECMs offer the greatest protection for the stored AE and provide some mitigation of fragments and over pressures from internal explosions. Such magazines are preferred for the storage of HD 1.1 AE.

C9.2. MAGAZINE OPERATIONAL REGULATIONS

C9.2.1. Unpackaged AE and ammunition components, packing materials, conveyors, skids, empty boxes, or other such items shall not be stored in magazines containing AE. Limited dunnage lumber may be stored in the magazines, if it does not block exits or aisles.

C9.2.2. All AE containers shall be marked with a DoD hazard division, storage compatibility group, item nomenclature, and quantity.

C9.2.3. While crews are working inside magazines, doors shall remain open to permit rapid egress.

C9.2.4. Flammable liquids, except as the chemical filler of ammunition or as a prepackaged storable liquid propellant, shall not be stored in magazines containing AE.

C9.3. STACKING

C9.3.1. AE should be stored in original shipping containers or equivalent. AE in stacks should be grouped and identified according to lots.

C9.3.2. Adequate dunnage shall be used to provide ventilation to all parts of the stack.

C9.3.3. Aisles shall be maintained between each stack to allow inspection, inventory, and removal for shipment or surveillance tests. Block storage configuration is permitted, provided ventilation of stacks exists. Unobstructed aisles shall be maintained to permit rapid egress.

C9.3.4. Light (partially filled) boxes or pallets should be limited to one per lot, should be readily visible and immediately accessible, and shall be conspicuously marked to identify contents and quantities.

C9.4. UNPACKAGED AE ITEMS AND DAMAGED CONTAINERS

C9.4.1. Unpackaged AE items shall not be stored in magazines containing AE in their original shipping container, but may be stored in separate magazines.

C9.4.2. Damaged containers of AE should not be stored in a magazine with serviceable containers of AE. Such containers should be repaired or the contents transferred to new or serviceable containers. All containers of AE in magazines shall be closed with covers securely fastened. Containers that have been opened shall be properly closed before restoring them. Stored containers should be free from loose dust and grit.

C9.4.3. Do not permit loose powder, grains, powder dust, or particles of explosive substances from broken AE or explosive substance containers in magazines. In addition, clean up any spilled explosive substance as soon as possible following proper procedures established per section C8.4. and suspend all other work in the magazine until accomplished.

C9.5. MAINTENANCE AND REPAIRS TO MAGAZINES

C9.5.1. Repairs should not be made to the interiors of magazines containing bulk explosives. Repairs to roofs, ventilators, lightning rods, doors, and other parts of, or appendages to, the exteriors of magazines containing bulk explosives shall not normally require removing the explosives. Minor repairs may be made to the interiors of magazines containing finished ammunition or ammunition components.

C9.5.2. The general safety requirements set forth in this Manual -- particularly the elimination of fire hazards -- shall be followed when magazines are repaired. When necessary, baffles and screens should be used to confine sparks and flames to heating apparatus.

C9.6. OPEN STORAGE (OUTDOORS)

Contractors shall not store AE outdoors.

C9.7. STORAGE OF BULK INITIATING EXPLOSIVES

Bulk initiating explosives shall not be stored dry, nor shall they be stored with direct exposure to the sun. Containers of ample size to hold the double bag of explosives are used for normal storage. Covers designed and constructed to prevent friction and pinch points should be used. Covers of shipping containers used for long-term storage shall be equipped with a port for observing the level of the liquid contents. The viewing port shall have a transparent plastic cover proven compatible with the initiating explosives being stored. Bulk initiating explosives may, for expediency, be stored in shipping containers without viewing ports, provided they are stored in magazines that will prevent freezing; with containers on end, only one tier high; or in passageways for inspection and handling. Bags of initiating explosives in storage containers shall be under distilled water. Alcohol may be added to the distilled water to prevent freezing.

C9.8. HAZARDS OF LONG-TERM STORAGE

C9.8.1. AE may deteriorate in storage. The method of packaging, extremes of temperature and humidity during storage, the length of time the AE is stored, the nature of the deterioration, and the explosive substance compositions used are factors in the rate and criticality of the deterioration. Any deterioration that decreases the stability of the AE increases the risk of auto-ignition or a handling accident due to friction, impact, or ESD. The longer that AE remains in storage, the greater the likelihood that it will deteriorate. Older unstable AE material should be tracked, identified, and prioritized in the contractor inventory management programs.

C9.8.2. When facilities are available, store different types of unstable AE material in separate magazines. Dispose of unstable AE stock material in accordance with the procedures and requirements of Chapter 15 of this Manual. Disposition of unserviceable AE will be under local procedures based on the latest available technical data. Unstable AE includes substances with depleted stabilizer, misfired ordnance, explosive devices rendered safe by explosive ordnance disposal, and any similar items. Unstable AE material is incompatible with all other AE material in storage.

C9.8.3. Treat AE with unknown stability as unstable. Examples of AE to treat as unstable include non-stock material, dropped or damaged material, material in substandard packaging, unidentified material, and material not receipt inspected.

C9.9. ROCKETS AND ROCKET MOTORS

C9.9.1. In AGMs, rockets and rocket motor items (in a propulsive state) should be pointed in the direction with the least exposure to personnel and property in case of fire or explosion.

C9.9.2. Rockets should be stored in dry, cool magazines, out of the direct rays of the sun. Prolonged exposure of rocket ammunition to either high or low temperatures may increase the normal rate of deterioration or render the motors more susceptible to ignition if handled improperly later.

C10. CHAPTER 10

FIRE PROTECTION

C10.1. GENERAL

This chapter provides general requirements for developing and implementing fire protection and prevention programs, fire hazard identification systems, and firefighting procedures for fires involving AE.

C10.2. FIRE PLAN

C10.2.1. A written fire plan shall be prepared that itemizes the emergency functions of each department or outside agency and indicates responsible individuals and alternates.

C10.2.2. Voluntary and mutual fire fighting agreements with local municipalities or industrial centers shall include AE firefighting guidelines. (See section C10.7.) Contractor officials are responsible for informing the firefighters of AE hazards.

C10.3 SMOKING

Smoking may take place only in specifically designated and posted "smoking locations." Cigarettes, tobacco, and matches shall be discarded in ash receptacles only; they shall not be dropped into trashcans. Electric lighters with automatic pressure cutoffs shall be fixed, ensuring against removal. At least one fire extinguisher shall be provided at smoking locations. Personnel shall not wear clothing contaminated with explosives or other dangerous material in smoking locations.

C10.4. HOT WORK PERMITS

A written permit shall be required for the temporary use of heat-producing equipment or devices when explosives or highly flammable materials are involved or located in the near vicinity of the hot work.

C10.5 PORTABLE FIRE EXTINGUISHERS

Hand extinguishers within buildings can extinguish fires before major damage is done. Portable equipment may prove similarly valuable outside AGMs and other buildings with AE. Portable fire extinguishers shall be maintained in accordance with NFPA Standard No. 10 (Reference (v)).

C10.6. FIRE HAZARD IDENTIFICATION SYSTEM

C10.6.1. System and Posting Guidelines. At DoD installations, the contractor shall comply with the Military Service fire hazard identification system. The contractor shall establish a fire hazard identification system at contractor-owned facilities used on DoD contracts. The system described in C10.6.4. is acceptable for this purpose. This system shall assess the relative dangers up to the most hazardous material stored. The system shall require posting fire symbol placards that represent the most hazardous material present at the access road approach or on the exterior of AE buildings. When one fire symbol placard applies to all explosives within a storage area, it may be posted at the entry control point to the area. Posted placards shall be visible to responding emergency personnel from all access routes. Fire symbol placards shall be changed when the HD of the AE changes and shall be removed or covered when all AE is removed from the building. The supervisor is responsible for posting or changing placards. The contractor's fire services and security organization should be notified of fire symbol changes.

C10.6.2. DoD Fire Identification System. The DoD Fire Identification System consists of four fire divisions (1-4) and identifies HD 1.1 through HD 1.6. Fire Division 1 indicates the greatest hazard. The hazard decreases with ascending fire division numbers from 1 to 4.

C10.6.3. DoD Fire Division Symbols

C10.6.3.1. The four fire divisions are indicated by four distinctive symbols (see Table C10.T1. and Figure C10.F1.) in order to be visually recognized by the firefighting personnel from a distance. The number is shown on each symbol indicating the type of AE present. Reflecting or luminous symbols should be used. For application on doors or lockers inside buildings, half-sized symbols may be used.

C10.6.3.2. The symbols have an orange background and a black number identifying the fire division.

Table C10.T1. Fire Division Markings

Fire Division	Hazard Involved	Shape	HD
1	Mass detonation	Octagon	1.1 and 1.5
2	Explosion with fragment hazard	Cross	1.2.X and 1.6
3	Mass fire	Inverted triangle	1.3
4	Moderate fire	Diamond	1.4

C10.6.4. NFPA System. NFPA Standard No. 704 (Reference (w)) provides a simple, readily recognized and understood system of marking, which many fire departments prefer for response. This system identifies the hazard and severity of materials and may be used in lieu of the DoD fire hazard symbols on contractor facilities. The system identifies the hazards of a material in terms of three categories: health, flammability, and reactivity. This system indicates the degree of severity by a numerical rating that ranges from four (4), indicating severe hazard, to zero (0), indicating minimal hazard. The Reference (w) system is based on relative rather than absolute values.

Figure C10.F1. Fire Symbol Markings

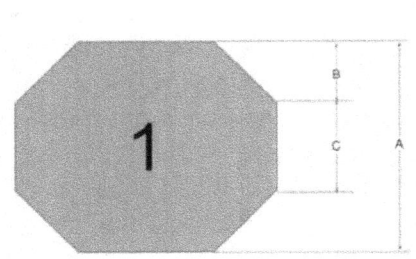

Fire Division 1 or 5
24 – inch: NSN 7690-01-082-0290
12 – inch: NSN 7690-01-081-9581

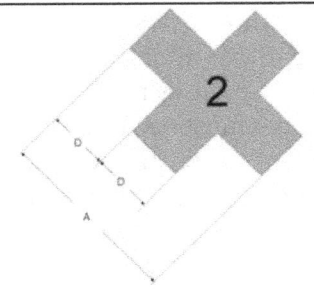

Fire Division 2 or 6
24 – inch: NSN 7690-01-082-0289
12 – inch: NSN 7690-01-087-7340

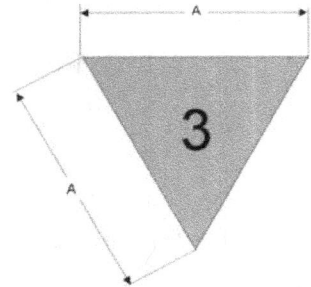

Fire Division 3
24 – inch: NSN 7690-01-081-9583
12 – inch: NSN 7690-01-081-9582

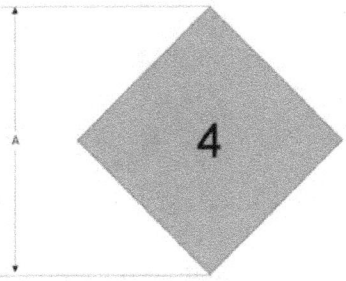

Fire Division 3
24 – inch: NSN 7690-01-082-6709
12 – inch: NSN 7690-01-081-9584

Dimensions	Large Symbol		Small Symbol	
	Inches	**Metric (mm)**	**Inches**	**Metric (mm)**
A	24	610	12	305
B	7	178	3.5	89
C	10	254	5	127
D	8	203	4	102
Letters (height)	10	254	5	127
Letters (thickness)	2	51	1	25

Colors (per Federal Standards 595A or GSA Catalog)
Background: Orange #12246
Letters: Black # 17038

C10.7. FIREFIGHTING PROCEDURES

C10.7.1. General

C10.7.1.1. Firefighters of AE fires shall have a thorough knowledge of the specific reactions of AE exposed to heat or to fire. The firefighting forces and other essential personnel shall be briefed before approaching the scene of the fire and shall be informed of the known hazards and conditions existing at the scene of the fire before proceeding to its location.

C10.7.1.2. Fire involving AE shall be fought according to the appropriate response for hazard or fire division and the stage of the fire.

C10.7.1.3. All fires starting in the vicinity of AE should be reported and should be fought immediately with all available means. However, if the fire involves explosive substances, is supplying heat to them, or if the fire is so large that it cannot be extinguished with the equipment at hand, the personnel involved shall evacuate to the applicable distances listed in Table C10.T2. and seek safety.

C10.7.1.4. Emergency withdrawal distances in Table C10.T2. for non-essential personnel are intended for application in emergency situations only and not for facility siting. The emergency withdrawal distances depend on fire involvement and on whether the HD, fire division, and NEW are known. Emergency authorities shall determine: (a) which personnel are essential and (b) the withdrawal distance for essential personnel at the fire.

C10.7.1.5. The initial withdrawal distance for non-essential personnel shall be at least IBD for the PES involved. If the fire involves AE, AE involvement is imminent, or the fire is or may become uncontrollable, then use the emergency withdrawal distances listed in Table C10.T2. If the fire does not involve explosive substances, emergency authorities shall determine the withdrawal distance based on the situation at hand.

C10.7.1.6. Structures or protected locations offering equivalent protection for the distances listed in Table C10.T2. may be used in lieu of relocating personnel from the structure or location to the specified emergency withdrawal distance.

C10.7.1.7. Contractors should develop evacuation plans that reference the appropriate withdrawal distances as part of the emergency response plan. Contractor personnel are responsible for alerting local authorities of any imminent explosive accident on the facility that may affect the local community and for providing local authorities with the appropriate emergency withdrawal distances.

C10.7.2. Specific

C10.7.2.1. Contractors shall train operational personnel on the characteristics of explosive substances, including their reactions to heat and fire, as well as what to do in case of fire. Personnel shall not attempt to fight fires involving HD 1.1 and HD 1.2.X AE. These AE detonate with a fragmentation hazard, and personnel shall evacuate immediately to the applicable distances listed in Table C10.T2., using protective cover where available and activating deluge systems and fire alarms while escaping. IBD provides protection from blast overpressure, but personnel in the open remain exposed to hazardous fragments and shall seek protective cover. Exit drills should be conducted annually. During exit drills, employees shall be advised of the safest escape routes and evacuation points.

Table C10.T2. Emergency Withdrawal Distances for Nonessential Personnel

HD	UNKNOWN QUANTITY (ft) [m]	KNOWN QUANTITY (ft) [m]
Unknown, located in facility, truck and/or tractor trailer	4,000 [1,219]	4,000 [1,219]
Unknown, located in railcar	5,000 [1,524]	5,000 [1,524]
1.1[2] and 1.5	Same as unknown facility, truck, trailer, or railcar as appropriate	**For Transportation:** NEWQD ≤ 500 lb D = 2,500 ft *NEWQD ≤226.8 kg D = 762 m* NEWQD > 500 lb D = 5,000 ft for railcars D = 4,000 ft for other modes *NEWQD > 226.8 kg D = 1,524 m for railcars D = 1,219 m for other modes* **For bombs and projectiles with caliber 5-in [127 mm] or greater:** D = 4,000 ft *D= 1,219 m* **For Facilities:** NEWQD ≤ 15,000 lb D = 2,500 ft *NEWQD ≤6,804 kg D = 762 m* 15,000 lbs < NEWQD ≤ 55,285 lbs D = 4,000 ft *6,804 kg < NEWQD ≤25,077 kg D = 1,219 m* NEWQD > 55,285 lbs $D = 105W^{1/3}$ *NEWQD > 25,077 kg D = 41.65Q^{1/3}*
1.2[2] and 1.6	2,500 [762]	2,500 [762]
1.3	600 [183]	Twice IBD with a 600 ft [183 m] minimum (C9.T13)
1.4	300 [91.5]	300 [91.5]

Notes:
1 Emergency withdrawal distances do not consider the potential flight range of propulsion units.
2 For HD 1.1 and HD 1.2 AE, if known, the maximum range fragments and debris shall be thrown (including the interaction effects of stacks of items, but excluding lugs, strongbacks, and/or nose and tail plates) may be used to replace the distances given.

C10.7.2.2. If the fire in a building that contains HD 1.1 or HD 1.2.X does not directly involve explosive substances and is small or in a segregated container, an attempt should be made to extinguish the fire. After summoning firefighters, responsible contractor personnel shall meet them as they approach the facility to brief them. When HD 1.1 or HD 1.2.X AE is directly involved, firefighting forces should maintain IBD from the fire. The safety of personnel fighting a HD 1.1 or HD 1.2.X fire depends on the accuracy of the information made available to all firefighting forces. No person shall re-enter a burning building containing HD 1.1 or HD 1.2.X AE.

C10.7.2.3. Personnel in the immediate vicinity of HD 1.3 AE should activate deluge systems and alarms and withdraw to the distance listed in Table C10.T2. Unless the fire is minor, involves no explosive, and appears controllable, firefighters shall confine their efforts to prevent it from spreading to other buildings. Fire in HD 1.3 AE creates a wide area of intense radiant heat, dangerous to personnel and equipment. The firefighters should exercise extreme caution.

C10.7.2.4. HD 1.4 AE presents a moderate fire hazard. Fires involving this material shall be fought until extinguished unless emergency authorities determine a need to evacuate. Non-essential personnel shall withdraw to the applicable distances listed in Table C10.T2.

C10.8. AUTOMATIC SPRINKLER SYSTEM

Properly installed and maintained automatic sprinklers reduce fire losses. They are particularly useful for load lines, AE manufacturing, receiving, shipping, inspection, workshops, and demilitarization.

C10.9. DELUGE SYSTEMS

C10.9.1. Contractors may use deluge systems to supplement sprinklers when the hazards are high, such as in powder hoppers and cutters. Rate of rise, light actuating, ultraviolet, or other quick-action devices for automatic control of deluge systems are recommended. Manual controls should serve as backup.

C10.9.2. To ensure immediate drenching of AE material, the distribution outlets (nozzles, sprays, heads, etc.) should be as near the explosive's exposed surface as permitted by the outlet discharge pattern. When explosives are under tight hoods or covers inside machines, distributing outlets should be located inside the enclosed space.

C10.9.3. Nonmetallic, internally spring held caps should protect distribution outlets exposed to explosive vapors, gases, or dust. Upon exertion of pressure within the outlet, the cap shall immediately pop. Caps should be attached to outlets to prevent their dropping into equipment during a deluge.

C10.9.4. Water flow and pressure should be determined for the hazard.

C10.9.5. Periodic inspections of deluge systems shall ensure that they are in proper operating condition.

C10.9.6. The deluge valve should allow for automatic and manual activation. Manual activation devices shall be placed at the operator station or at exits in explosives operating buildings as determine by a hazard analysis.

C10.9.7. NFPA Standard No. 13 (Reference (x)) and NFPA Standard No. 15 (Reference (y)) contain basic installation rules.

C10.10. FIREBREAKS

A firebreak is an area of bare ground or vegetation intended to limit the probability of fires causing a hazard to AE areas. A firebreak at least 50 ft [15 m] wide shall be maintained in all directions around magazines and AE operating buildings or locations. Barricades and other sloping ground, within the firebreak area, should retain enough vegetation to prevent significant erosion. Growth of vegetation within a firebreak shall be controlled to prevent rapid transmission of fire. Relatively tall vegetation of 6 to 8 inches [152 to 203 mm] in length, which is green or sparsely spread, is acceptable. Do not allow vegetation to become dry or dense. This could allow rapid transmission of fire.

C11. CHAPTER 11

RISK IDENTIFICATION AND MANAGEMENT

C11.1. GENERAL. AE operations involve many hazards and risks. These include the type of hazards associated with any industrial enterprise, e.g., AE reactivity, lifting, slipping, tool use, toxic chemicals, potential exposures to environmental extremes.

C11.1.1. The evaluation of hazards and risk of accidents addressed in this section relate to processes, not end products. The safety of operations is a contractor responsibility.

C11.1.2. A basic risk identification and management system is a necessary element of a comprehensive AE safety program. The purpose of this chapter is to address risk identification and management for all AE processes.

C11.2. RISK MANAGEMENT SYSTEM. Contractors shall have a risk identification and management system and perform a hazard analysis resulting in the evaluation of processes, materials, equipment, and personnel hazards. This analysis will aid in the development of a written SOP for AE contract operations. The analysis may include such factors as: initiation sensitivity; quantity of AE; heat output, burn rate, potential ignition and initiation sources; protection capabilities of shields; personnel protective equipment and clothing; fire protection; and personnel exposure with special considerations (such as toxic or corrosive chemicals). The contractor shall document the analysis and keep it as long as the SOP is active. The risk analysis should identify normal and abnormal (planned and unplanned) energy input into the AE, documenting the comparison between energy input and the sensitivity of the AE.

C11.2.1. The contractor shall perform risk analyses using personnel knowledgeable in the process, materials, equipment, and relevant safety requirements.

C11.2.2. A hazard is any condition, which, by itself or by interacting with other variables, may result in death or injury to personnel or damage to property. Controls only reduce the likelihood or severity of hazards. Controls do not eliminate hazards.

C11.2.2.1. After identifying a hazard, qualified contractor personnel shall determine the associated risk. The risk analysis of a potential accident shall address both the severity and the probability of occurrence of an accident.

C11.2.2.2. Evaluation of the hazard provides information useful for ranking the degree of risk associated with a hazard. The degree of risk indicates which hazardous conditions should receive priority for corrective action when compared to other hazardous conditions. One technique for ranking hazardous conditions is the assignment of a risk assessment code. The evaluation of the hazard results in the assignment of a narrative or numerical risk assessment that enables management to evaluate the seriousness of the risk before and after action is taken to control it. Table C11.T1. is an example format of a risk matrix used by the Department of Defense. Definitions of the code numbers and letters are contained in Table C11.T2.

Table C11.T1. Risk Matrix Format Example

Accident Severity	Accident Probability			
	A	B	C	D
I	1	1	2	4
II	1	2	3	4
III	2	3	4	5
IV	4	4	5	5

Table C11.T2. Risk Assessment Definitions Example

Accident Severity	Accident Probability	Risk Assessment Codes
I. An accident that could result in the death or permanent disability or the inability to deliver the contract item.	A. Likely to occur immediately	1. Critical
II. An accident that could result in permanent partial disability or temporary total disability, in excess of 3 months, or result in late delivery, 30 days or more, of the contract item.	B. Probably will occur in time	2. Serious
III. An accident that could result in lost workdays or compensation for employees or result in the late delivery (less than 30 days) of the contract item.	C. Possible to occur in time	3. Moderate
IV. An accident that could result in first aid or minor supportive medical treatment to personnel or damage to process equipment or product, but would not affect the delivery of the contract item.	D. Unlikely to occur	4. Minor 5. Negligible

C11.3. ANALYTICAL METHODS. There are a number of analytical methods or approaches to the performance of hazard and risk analyses. The complexity of the process involved, the number of variables, and the severity of the consequences of failure should determine the level and methodology of the analysis used. The contractor shall select the level and best method for performing the analysis.

C11.3.1. As a minimum, contractors shall break the total process into successive steps and assess the hazards and risks for each process step. For specific guidance, contractors may refer to the latest version of MIL-STD 882D (Reference (z)) or part 1910 of Reference (f).

C11.3.2. A significant percentage of accidents occur during intermittent operations such as setup, startup, maintenance, repair, response to out-of-tolerance operation, and shut down or clean-up. Therefore analyses shall consider intermittent operations as well as normal operations.

C11.4. <u>INFORMATION FOR ANALYSIS</u>

C11.4.1. Contractors shall develop and use a methodology to determine if AE process changes present a new hazard or increase the risk of a present hazard before incorporating the change into a process. If the change increases baseline hazards or risks, contractors shall document any controls necessary to mitigate those risks.

C11.4.2. Contractors shall use the information acquired from the hazard analysis and generated by process changes to revise SOPs and train employees.

C12. CHAPTER 12

AE BUILDING DESIGN AND LAYOUT

C12.1. GENERAL

The design and layout of AE buildings are critical considerations in explosives safety and directly impact QD requirements and hazardous exposures to operating personnel and valuable equipment. Proper preplanning, layout, and design can significantly reduce risk of injury and property loss. Fire, fragment generation, venting, and evacuation shall be considered when designing facilities and laying out operations.

C12.2. BUILDING EXTERIORS

Exterior wall and roof coverings of AE operating buildings should be noncombustible. Whenever possible, construction should be frangible (breakaway) to allow venting an internal explosion without collapsing and to limit fragmentation to only a few large fragments. Firewalls and dividing walls are exceptions. AE buildings should be one story, except to meet process requirements. Basements should be avoided, since they may expose personnel to AE hazards and make evacuation difficult.

C12.3. INTERIOR WALLS, ROOFS, AND CEILINGS

Interior walls, roofs, and ceilings of AE buildings should be made of non-combustible material or, if combustible, should be treated or covered with fire retardant material. The recommended practice for roofs is to install insulation and covering directly on the underside of the roof deck. Interior wall surfaces and ceilings of AE operating buildings that might house loose, finely divided explosive substances shall be smooth, free from cracks and crevices, fire resistive and, if painted, covered with high gloss paint to minimize dust accumulation and facilitate cleaning. To further prevent dust accumulation, ledges should be avoided and, if present, shall be beveled or kept clean. Wall joints and openings for wiring and plumbing shall be sealed against dust. Suspended ceilings and hollow walls shall be prohibited in AE facilities classified as Class II hazardous locations as defined by Reference (r).

C12.4. FLOORS AND WORK SURFACES

Floors and work surfaces shall be constructed to facilitate cleaning, with no cracks or crevices in which explosives could lodge. Non-sparking floors and work surfaces shall be provided in all locations where exposed explosives or hazardous concentrations of flammable vapor or gas, capable of initiation by mechanical sparks, are present. When required by Chapter 6 of this Manual, conductive floors (mats or similar static-dissipating floor surfaces), tabletops, and other work surfaces shall be provided. Cove bases at the junctions of walls and floors are preferred. No exposed nails, screws, or bolts in work surfaces shall be permitted.

C12.5. SUBSTANTIAL DIVIDING WALLS

C12.5.1. Substantial dividing walls, constructed in accordance with the requirements of Reference (n), prevent simultaneous detonation of limited quantities of high explosives on opposite sides of the wall so they do not need to be added when determining QD requirements.

C12.5.2. Openings in dividing walls for conveyors, pass-through boxes, or other uses should be avoided. However, in locations where operationally necessary, the opening(s) shall not be larger than the minimum needed for the material's safe passage and their closures shall be designed with equivalent wall-strength characteristics. Closures shall be equipped with fusible links to help prevent the spread of fire.

C12.6. EXITS AND DOORS

Explosive hazards should not occupy space between operators and an exit. Exit doors in buildings containing explosives, except storage magazines, should be casement-type and glazed with non-shatter plastic material. All doors should be equipped with panic hardware for rapid egress, should open in the direction of the flow of material through the building, and should open onto unobstructed passageways. Additional information can be found in NFPA Standard No. 101 (Reference (aa)) for exits and doors and in NFPA Standard No. 80 (Reference (ab))for fire doors and fire windows.

C12.7. EMERGENCY EGRESS

When standard exits and fire escapes do not provide for rapid egress from work levels above the ground floor, other means of emergency egress (e.g., safety chutes) shall be provided. Operators should not be exposed to AE hazards while working below ground level. When personnel exposure to AE hazards below ground level is unavoidable, a hazard analysis shall be performed to identify and control all potential ignition sources and to investigate the feasibility of operator shielding, PPE, and alternative emergency egress systems.

C12.8. PASSAGEWAYS

Weather-protected passageways and ramps for travel between buildings or magazines should include design features such as non-combustible construction, fire stops, fire doors, and fire suppression systems to help prevent fire from spreading from one building to another. Designing weak sections, openings, or abrupt change in direction of passageways will help to prevent funneling the explosion forces from one building to another.

C12.9. ROADS AND WALKWAYS

Only roads serving a single magazine or explosives processing building (including its service facilities) may dead end and, in that case, only at the magazine or building. All buildings or magazines on dead end roads shall be provided with sufficient apron space either in front or around all four sides, to permit the safe turn-around of the largest vehicle that could service the structure.

C12.10. WINDOWS AND SKYLIGHTS

C12.10.1. The use of conventional glass in areas with a potential blast overpressure hazard creates a serious secondary fragmentation hazard. Safety glass or non-shatter plastic materials such as Lexan or Plexiglas should be used when practical to reduce this hazard. When glazing with conventional glass is used, properly fixed plastic or wire mesh screening on the inside surface of the glass may also reduce the hazard.

C12.10.2. Since IBD do not protect against glass breakage and the hazards of flying glass, exposures at IBD should not have windows or other glass surfaces exposed to PESs. If windows are present, personnel exposure to hazards from flying glass can be minimized by building orientation or by limiting the number and size of glass panels.

C12.10.3. Prior to new construction or major modification of existing ESs, a glass hazard risk assessment shall be conducted and windows shall be blast resistant and of sufficient strength based on engineering analysis to control flying glass. The framing and sash of such windows must be of sufficient strength to retain the glass panel in the structure.

C12.11. DRAINS, SUMPS, AND SEWERS

C12.11.1. All drain lines handling explosive wastes shall have sumps or basins of sufficient capacity for the removal of explosives by settling. The drains shall be of adequate capacity; free of pockets; and with slopes of at least one-quarter inch per foot to prevent explosives settling-out in the drain line before reaching the collection point in the sump or settling basin. Sumps shall be so designed that suspended and settleable solid explosive material cannot be carried beyond the sumps in the wash waters, and so that overflow shall not disturb any floating solids. The settling rate of the material and the usual rate of flow shall be taken into account in determining the sump's capacity. The design shall also permit easy removal of collected explosives, and shall allow for retention of those that float on water until they can be skimmed off. Bolted sump tanks or other types of construction that permit the explosives to settle in obscure or hidden spaces are prohibited.

C12.11.2. Care shall be taken to prevent deposits of explosives from sump effluent onto the surfaces of the collection system due to drying, temperature changes, or interaction with other industrial contaminants. Sweeping and other dry collecting measures should be used to keep appreciably water-soluble explosives out of the drainage system.

C12.11.3. Drains between the source of explosive and the sump shall have troughs with rounded bottoms and with removable ventilated covers to facilitate inspection for accumulation of explosives. Waste liquids shall not run into closed drains and sewers. Inspect and clean out drains periodically to prevent the buildup of explosives. Drains and sewers containing explosive waste materials shall not connect into the normal sewage systems

C12.12. HARDWARE

C12.12.1. Hardware in buildings containing exposed explosive materials, explosive dusts, or vapors should be of non-sparking material. Installation of hardware (piping and ducts) should not be affixed to blowout panels or walls.

C12.12.2. Fasteners such as nuts and bolts that could accidentally drop into explosives or explosive constituents shall be prevented from doing so by being drilled and thonged or otherwise secured.

C12.13. VENTILATION SYSTEMS

Contractors shall equip exhaust fans in "Hazardous (Classified) Locations" (as defined by Reference (r)) -- through which combustible dust or flammable vapor pass -- with nonferrous blades or line the casing with nonferrous material. Fan motors shall meet the requirements for the applicable Hazardous (Classified) Locations as defined by Reference (q). Contractors shall bond and ground the entire exhaust system and shall clean and service the system on a regular schedule. For more guidance for exhaust systems, refer to Reference (r).

C12.14. STEAM FOR HEATING AND PROCESSING

C12.14.1. Steam used for heating operating buildings containing explosives shall have a maximum pressure of 5 psi (228°F) [34.45 kPa (109°C)], except for facilities where freeze protection is required. Steam pressures in lines or vessels that may inadvertently come in contact with propellants or explosives shall not exceed 15 psi (250°F) [103.35kPa (121°C)].

C12.14.2. Process steam is that which is in direct contact with explosives and used directly in their manufacture, or which, in case of equipment failure, would exhaust directly into contact with explosives or explosive fumes. Process steam should be limited to 5 psi (228°F) [34.45 kPa (109°C)]. Where necessary, process steam may exceed 5 psi [34.45 kPa], but shall not exceed 15 psi (250°F) [103.35kPa (121°C)] for routine operations. Requirements for steam pressure exceeding 15 psi [103.35 kPa] shall require a hazard analysis and approval by the contracting officer on a case-by-case basis.

C12.14.3. The exterior of steam or hot water pipes in contact with wood, paper, or other combustible materials shall not exceed 160°F [71°C]. An insulating pipe covering capable of reducing the surface temperature of the covering to 160 °F (71 °C) or less is acceptable. Piping containing hot water or steam in excess of 140°F [60°C] should be insulated in areas where personnel may contact them.

C12.14.4. Where steam temperatures must exceed 228 degrees Fahrenheit (5 psi) [109°C (34.45kPa)] in hazardous locations, steam lines shall be covered and painted with an impervious material or otherwise protected against contact with explosives. Where a reducing valve is used, a relief valve should be installed on the low-pressure piping. Pressure reducing valves shall not be bypassed in a manner permitting circumvention of pressure reduction requirements. The production of super-heated steam that results from the throttling action of reducing valves shall be prevented by positive means. The use of a "water leg" or water column for control of steam pressure of 5 psi [34.45 kPa] or less is recommended. Where close control of steam temperature is necessary, indicating and recording pressure or temperature gages should be installed. Such devices shall be periodically tested and the test results recorded. When electrical resistance to ground is high, steam lines shall be properly grounded where they enter buildings.

C12.15. TUNNELS

Tunnels between buildings that contain AE shall incorporate features that resist the shock wave of an explosion. This is important in order to minimize the possibility of an explosion in one building from affecting the operations in the other building. (For further information on tunnels, see Chapter 5 of Reference (c).)

CHAPTER 12

C13. CHAPTER 13

SAFETY REQUIREMENTS FOR SPECIFIC AE AND AE OPERATIONS

C13.1. GENERAL

This chapter provides the minimum safety requirements necessary for the prevention of mishaps involving specific AE and AE operations. The contractor is responsible for analyzing each operation and developing procedures to control or eliminate hazards.

C13.2. PROPERTIES OF EXPLOSIVES. Knowledge of properties of specific types of explosives is critical to the establishment of proper hazard controls.

C13.2.1. Primary (Initiating) Explosives. Initiating explosives include lead azide, lead styphnate, and tetracene. They are extremely sensitive to friction, heat, ESD, and impact. When involved in a fire, they may detonate.

C13.2.1.1. In storage, initiating explosives shall be kept wet with distilled water or water and alcohol mixtures to reduce sensitivity. Take every precaution to prevent the liquid from freezing, since this increases sensitivity. Handling of frozen initiating explosives is prohibited. Assure the water used for storage is free of bacteria-forming impurities that could react to form gases and rupture containers.

C13.2.1.2. Operators shall keep work areas and equipment clean and maintain good housekeeping to prevent contamination of these explosives with foreign (particularly gritty) material that markedly increases their sensitivity.

C13.2.1.3. Do not allow lead azide to contact copper, zinc, or alloys containing any concentration of such metals because of the likely formation of other azides that are more sensitive than the original lead azide. Similar hazards exist for other explosives.

C13.2.2. Secondary (Boostering and Bursting) Explosives. Boostering and bursting explosives include tetryl, RDX, PETN, octogen, nitroamine high explosive (HMX), and compositions manufactured with these explosives. These explosives have sensitivities between initiating explosives and those of explosives used as main charges such as TNT. They may be ignited by heat, friction, or impact and may detonate when burned in large quantities or at too great a depth. Some of these materials are toxic when taken internally or by skin contact, and special precautions are necessary to protect personnel. Local exhaust ventilation, enclosed process systems, automatic handling systems, etc., should be used to minimize dust in the employee's breathing zone.

C13.2.3. <u>Main Charge Explosives</u>. Main charge explosives include TNT, tritonal, RDX, HMX, ammonium picrate (Explosive D), and compositions manufactured with these explosives. Process hazard analysis shall be used to evaluate the safety of the processing methodology, e.g., melt-cast, extrusion, press and machine, and mix-cast-cure versus sensitivity characteristics. Alkaline cleaning agents or other alkaline products should not be permitted in buildings where large quantities of these explosives are handled. Amatol forms sensitive compounds with copper and brass. Where Explosive D is processed, lead fusible links and solder-type sprinkler heads should not be used. Depth bomb explosive (DBX) is an aluminized explosive that is somewhat hygroscopic and reacts with metals in the same manner as amatol. High blast explosive (HBX) is also an aluminized explosive that outgases when exposed to water and may create internal pressure when loaded into ammunition. HMX compositions usually result in a very powerful explosive with a high degree of thermal stability. Pentolite tends to separate into its ingredients (PETN and TNT) and should, therefore, be handled as carefully as PETN. Picratol is a mixture of TNT and Explosive D; the precautions necessary when handling either shall be observed. Picric acid is highly acidic, corrosive, and toxic; it shall be isolated from lead and lead compounds. Tetrytol is a mixture of tetryl and TNT which is stable in storage but exudes at 149°F. Dry tetrytol slightly corrodes magnesium and aluminum alloys, and wet tetrytol slightly corrodes copper, brass, aluminum, magnesium, mild steel, and cadmium-plated mild steel. TNT is stable and does not form sensitive compounds with metals. It will, however, form sensitive compounds in the presence of alkalies. TNT also exhibits well-recognized toxic properties. Torpex is an aluminized explosive used mainly in underwater ordnance. Non-hygroscopic and non-corrosive, torpex is stable in storage but may outgas (hydrogen) and produce internal pressure when loaded into ammunition. Tritonal is a mixture of TNT and aluminum powder and is more sensitive to impact than TNT. Tritonal shall not be exposed to water. Plastic bonded explosives are conventional high explosives with plastic binders such as polystyrene, viton, estane, etc. Their sensitivity varies with the composition. The plastic bonded explosives series most frequently encountered are identified by the prefixes "PBX" or "LX" and a number.

C13.2.4. <u>Other Explosives</u>. Other common military explosives encountered include black powder and NG. Black powder is a mixture of potassium or sodium nitrate, charcoal, and sulfur and is highly sensitive to friction, heat, and impact. It deteriorates rapidly after absorption of moisture, but retains its explosive properties indefinitely if kept dry. NG's extreme sensitivity to impact and friction is such that it is manufactured only as needed. Frozen NG, while less sensitive than liquid, may undergo internal changes upon thawing and, if enough heat is generated, may detonate.

C13.2.5. <u>Research of Additional Properties</u>. Contractors must investigate and understand pertinent properties before handling explosive substances. Sensitivity data for the same characteristic, generated on different types of equipment, are not necessarily comparable. Contractors must thoroughly understand the sensitivity test method employed, the unit of measure in which data are presented, and the relative sensitivity ranking of the explosive as compared to other similar explosives. The size and mass of some explosives can change some characteristics. For example, 100 lb [45-kg] billets of LX-14 may detonate when subjected to the same drop test that causes only minor reaction in lighter billets of the same material.

CHAPTER 13

C13.3. LABORATORY OPERATIONS

C13.3.1. Research and development laboratories and testing facilities constitute a separate category involving guidance, restrictions, and relief from certain requirements prescribed elsewhere in this Manual.

C13.3.2. Each operation at facilities designed for blast and fragment confinement shall be reviewed to ensure that the explosives limits are within the laboratory or test area capability. Explosives limits shall be decreased and safe separation distances shall be increased as the capability to confine fragment and blast decreases.

C13.3.3. A total confinement facility shall be inspected after a detonation to ensure structural integrity. Reduction of the explosives limits may be necessary to prevent future blasts from exceeding the retention capability.

C13.3.4. Each proposed program for the laboratory or test facility shall be reviewed to determine all potential hazards. Considerations shall include:

C13.3.4.1. Structural limitations of the facility.

C13.3.4.2. Remote control viewing and operating equipment, if required.

C13.3.4.3. Special safety precautions for personnel elsewhere in the building.

C13.3.4.4. Safe separation distances.

C13.3.4.5. Required deviations from other sections of this Manual.

C13.3.5. SOP shall, at a minimum, include:

C13.3.5.1. Protective clothing.

C13.3.5.2. Warning signals.

C13.3.5.3. Fire and other emergency procedures.

C13.3.5.4. Pre-operation and special testing of required equipment, e.g., stray voltage and calibration checks.

C13.3.5.5. Removal of all explosives not needed for the operation.

C13.3.5.6. Arrangements for overnight storage of necessary explosives.

C13.3.5.7. Inspection and cleanup procedures after a test or detonation.

C13.3.6. Laboratories shall use no more explosives than absolutely required for a given operation. Particularly hazardous laboratory operations involving new or relatively unknown explosives shall be performed by remote control. Operational shields shall be used in these operations and in new or untested applications of explosives.

C13.4. HEAT CONDITIONING OF AE

C13.4.1. All ovens, conditioning chambers, dry houses, and other devices and facilities that are capable (in ordinary service) of heating AE to temperatures in excess of 90°F [32°C] are heat-conditioning devices. Heat-conditioning devices shall be provided with dual independent fail-safe heat controls. For devices or facilities heated by steam only, the requirement for dual heat controls is satisfied if the steam pressure is controlled by a reducing valve (maximum pressure of 5 psi [34.45 kPa] unless otherwise authorized) on the main building steam supply and a thermostat.

C13.4.2. Heat-conditioning devices shall be able to discharge overpressure from an internal explosion. Barriers or catching devices shall restrain blowout panels, doors, and other venting apparatus and prevent excessive displacement during an accidental explosion.

C13.4.3. Heat-conditioning devices shall be vented to allow any gases produced during conditioning to escape.

C13.4.4. Steam heat conditioning devices are preferred; however, when the use of electrical heating elements is unavoidable, they shall be located where there is no possibility of contact with explosives or flammable materials.

C13.4.5. The blades of fans in a heat-conditioning device shall be of non-sparking material and the device's electric motor shall be installed externally. The air shall not re-circulate if the heating surfaces exceed 228°F [109°C] or if the air contains materials that could collect on the heating coils.

C13.4.6. Electrical equipment and fixtures in or on a heat-conditioning device used for explosives or flammable material shall be approved for use in the hazardous atmosphere in question.

C13.4.7. The interior of a heat-conditioning device shall be free of crevices, openings, and protuberances not easily cleaned, where dust or flammable material could lodge.

C13.4.8. All non-current-carrying metal parts of a heat-conditioning device shall be interconnected and electrically grounded.

C13.4.9. Heat-conditioning devices should be installed in isolated locations and set up to give personnel maximum protection from the effects of an explosion. When indicated by hazard analysis, operational shields and other personnel protection measures shall be used.

C13.4.10. Heat-conditioning devices should be separated by QD or protective construction to prevent an explosives accident in one heat-conditioning device from propagating to others. Hazardous materials shall not be placed in a room or cubicle containing a heat-conditioning device, unless proof has been shown that a mishap in the heat-conditioning device would not involve the other materials.

C13.4.11. Operating procedures for heat-conditioning devices shall:

C13.4.11.1. Limit the explosive materials in the device to the type and quantity authorized for the specific device.

C13.4.11.2. Address the critical temperatures of explosive compositions before processing in a heat-conditioning device and ensure the device does not exceed these temperature limits.

C13.4.11.3. Require checking heat-conditioning device temperatures at specified intervals during operation.

C13.4.11.4. Require cleaning the conditioning devices, ducts, vacuum lines, and other parts of the equipment subject to contamination by hazardous materials before introducing a different item or composition for conditioning.

C13.5. SPRAY PAINTING LOADED AE

C13.5.1. Loaded AE shall not be electrostatically spray-painted.

C13.5.2. Water wash or dry filter-type spray booths shall be used for loaded AE.

C13.5.3. Controls for ventilating fan motors for spray painting booths shall be interlocked with the controls for the paint sprayer. With this arrangement, failure of the ventilating system will shut off power to the paint sprayer.

C13.5.4. High-voltage, electrically powered paint-spraying equipment shall be installed in accordance with the requirements of NFPA Standard No. 33 (Reference (ac)) as applicable.

C13.5.5. Conventional equipment used for spray painting in standard spray booths shall meet the requirements of Reference (ac). The nozzles of all spray guns shall be electrically grounded to control the ESD hazard.

C13.6. DRYING FRESHLY PAINTED LOADED AE. Ovens used to dry loaded AE shall comply with Reference (r). Other requirements include:

C13.6.1. Automatic thermostatic controls shall regulate temperatures once they reach a maximum determined by the AE involved. It is recommended that temperatures not exceed 170°F.

C13.6.2. Each oven shall be equipped with automatic internal sprinkler systems that conform to Reference (x). Approved electrical heat actuated devices, installed as required for Reference (r), Class I, Division 1, Group D hazardous locations, may be used for automatic operation of the system.

C13.6.3. Hot air or other means may supply heat, provided AE does not contact coils, radiators, and heating elements.

C13.6.4. In case of power failure, the heat supply for any conveyor system shall automatically stop.

C13.6.5. Electric drying units not approved for use in Class I hazardous locations should be designed so that solvent vapor concentration in the oven is kept below 25 percent of its lower explosive limit.

C13.7. REWORK, DISASSEMBLY, RENOVATION, AND MAINTENANCE

C13.7.1. AE rework and disassembly operations shall not be conducted with other AE or inert operations. When concurrent scheduling cannot be avoided, operations shall be sufficiently separated from one another to protect adjacent personnel and equipment and prevent propagation to adjacent AE. Separation may be accomplished with a minimum of ILD protection, operational shielding, or the remote control of operations.

C13.7.2. The operator and all other personnel shall be fully protected during rework and disassembly operations known or expected to use force exceeding assembly specifications.

C13.7.3. If AE items have been assembled normally, the same equipment, tools, methods, and applied forces may be used to disassemble them. In such cases, personnel protection required during the assembly operations is also required during the rework or disassembly operations. Care shall be taken, however, to verify that the assembly was normal and that the surfaces to be separated are not corroded and not sealed with metallic applicants.

C13.7.4. The contractor shall request specific safety guidance through contract channels when renovation or maintenance is not adequately addressed in the contract.

C13.8. AE LOADING AND ASSOCIATED OPERATIONS

C13.8.1. Screening and Blending HE. Bulk HEs intended for processing shall be screened or visually inspected and passed over a magnetic separator to detect extraneous material for removal. Screening equipment shall not subject explosives to pinching, friction, or impact. Explosives screening units without exhaust ventilation shall be thoroughly cleaned as often as necessary and after every shift, to prevent hazardous accumulations of explosives dusts.

C13.8.2. <u>Screening and Blending Initiating Explosives</u>. Suitable operational shields shall be provided for screening and blending operations involving initiating explosives, or operators shall be located at a minimum of ILD from screening and blending facilities.

C13.8.3. <u>Explosives Melting</u>

C13.8.3.1. Temperatures used for melting explosives and keeping explosives molten should not exceed 228°F [109°C]. However, steam pressures up to 15 psi [103.35 kPa] (250°F [121°C]) may be used to melt Composition B and similar binary explosives and to maintain a molten state.

C13.8.3.2. Melt unit valves and melt mix draw-off or other lines carrying molten explosives shall be constructed and maintained to prevent friction or impact capable of igniting the explosives. Diaphragm-type valves should be disassembled and inspected regularly. Damaged or old diaphragms shall be replaced so no cracks allowing metal-to-metal contact can develop. Draw-off lines should be constructed to prevent exposure of threads, fastening screws, and bolts both outside and between the flanges. A sealing compound should be used to prevent explosives seepage or vapor condensation on the contacting surfaces of the bolts, flanges, screws, and nuts. Melt mix kettle draw-off pipes should be electrically connected to items being filled during draw-off operations. Items shall be individually grounded unless tests show that grounding through contact surface is adequate.

C13.8.3.3. Wet-type collectors remove dust and vapors from exhausted air and are effective for melt mix exhausting systems. Water in the wet collector shall not be re-circulated unless the system removes hazardous suspensions. Water retaining explosives shall be discharged to a containment unit designed to keep them wet. The exhaust and collecting equipment shall be regularly inspected and flushed of explosives accumulations. When protective construction prevents propagation of a detonation between melt kettles, each kettle shall be equipped with a complete and separate dust and vapor collection system to prevent propagation through the collection system.

C13.8.4. <u>Agitation</u>. Agitation nitrators, washers, and other machines that -- because of the hazard of the process and the possibility of the process material decomposing -- are equipped with mechanical agitators shall have at least two means of agitation. Each shall operate from an independent power source to maintain agitation if one fails.

C13.8.5. <u>Explosives Machining</u>. Awareness of the friction sensitivity of explosives to be machined is required. Friction sensitivity values of explosives listed in subparagraphs C13.8.5.2. and C13.8.5.3. are available for comparison. Compare sensitivity values only for identical test methods and equipment.

C13.8.5.1. High explosives (cased or uncased) that may be machined without special personnel protection and without coolant, if no metal-to-metal contact is involved, include amatol, octol, TNT, Composition B, Explosive D, and RDX/TNT compositions containing 60 percent or less RDX.

C13.8.5.2. High explosives (cased or uncased) that may be machined without special personnel protection -- provided a coolant is directed on the tool and explosives at their point of contact and no metal-to-metal contact is involved -- include octol, pentolite (50-50 and 10-90), tetrytol, and cyclotols (Composition B less than 60-40; that is, 70-30).

C13.8.5.3. When essential, other HEs may be machined by remote control, with the operator protected by a suitable operational shield. Initiating explosives should not be machined.

C13.8.5.4. When an unprotected operator is involved in drilling, only a single drill with a diameter greater than 1/4 inch [0.64 cm] shall be used.

C13.8.5.5. Machining of cased explosives is permitted in an operation requiring removal of metal before or after tool contact with the explosives filler, provided that operators are protected by operational shields and perform the work by remote control.

C13.8.5.6. Where wet machining is performed, automatic interlocking devices shall be used to prevent machining from starting until coolant is flowing. These controls shall be capable of stopping the machining if the coolant flow is interrupted. When coolant flow must stop for adjustment of machining tools, positive means shall be provided to ensure that flow of coolant is restored and all automatic control devices are operating before machining can resume.

C13.8.5.7. The lineal and rotational speeds of tools used for the machining of explosives shall be maintained at the minimum required to perform the operation safely and efficiently. The rate of feed should be determined by hazard analysis.

C13.8.5.8. Pneumatically or hydraulically driven machine tools are preferred for all machining operations on HEs. Control mechanisms for hydraulic and pneumatic equipment shall prevent unauthorized personnel from tampering with speeds.

C13.8.5.9. For all machining operations on cased or uncased HEs, procedures during tool adjustments shall prevent contact between moving parts of the machining equipment and metallic parts of the case or holding fixtures.

C13.8.5.10. Machining tools shall be compatible with the explosives being processed. Dull or damaged tools shall not be used for machining HEs.

C13.8.5.11. The explosives products resulting from machining operations shall be removed by an exhaust system meeting Reference (r) requirements or by immersion in a stream of liquid flowing away from the operation.

C13.8.5.12. Machining of HE of questionable quality during an ammunition and explosives demilitarization process shall be accomplished by remote control, with operators protected by operational shields.

CHAPTER 13

C13.8.6. <u>Assembly and Crimping of Complete Rounds</u>. Each assembly and crimping operation shall be separated from other operations by structures or shielding sufficient to contain any fragments produced by an accidental detonation.

C13.8.7. <u>Pressing Explosives</u>

C13.8.7.1. Each pelleting operation involving black powder, tetryl, TNT, or other explosives of similar sensitivity and each operation involving the pressing or reconsolidation of explosives shall be conducted in a separate room or cubicle having walls of sufficient strength to withstand an explosion of all explosives present.

C13.8.7.2. Pressing or reconsolidating of explosives in small caliber rounds, tracer bodies, tetryl lead-ins, detonators, and similar items shall be performed on machines having consolidating stations designed to preclude propagation between stations and provide adequate operator protection. Operators shall stay behind tested protective barriers during such operations.

C13.8.7.3. Punches and dies used in explosives pressing operations shall be in matched sets that have been inspected and calibrated prior to use to verify dimensional fit and finish characteristics. Punches and dies shall undergo a rigid test, such as a magnaflux or X-ray, before use and at locally determined intervals to detect hairline cracks and verify structural integrity.

C13.8.8. <u>Protection of Primers</u>. Equipment, transportation, and operations shall be designed to protect loose primers or primers in components from accidental impact or pressure. When feasible, a protecting cap shall cover the primer.

C13.8.9. <u>Explosives Washout and Flashing Facilities</u>. Washout operations in operating buildings or other locations shall be separated from other operations by operational shields or a minimum of ILD. AE subjected to washout operations shall be inspected to ensure against residual explosives contamination. When contamination is detected, the AE shall be decontaminated prior to disposal.

C13.8.10. <u>Heat-Sealing Equipment</u>. Electric heat-sealing machines should be separated from other operations. Temperature limits for heat-sealing equipment shall be established with a safety factor below the ignition temperature of the explosives, propellants, or pyrotechnics involved.

C.13.8.11. <u>Rebowling Operations</u>. Rebowling operations involving primary explosives or primer mixes shall be performed by remote control, with the operator protected by an operational shield.

C13.8.12. <u>Thread Cleaning</u>

C13.8.12.1. Nonferrous picks shall be used for thread cleaning. Stainless steel brushes may be used to clean threads of explosives-loaded projectiles if a fuse seat liner separates the thread cleaning operation from the explosive charge. Operators do not need operational shields; however, thread cleaning operations should be separated from unrelated operations by ILD.

C13.8.12.2. Power-actuated, thread-chasing tools may be used to clean loaded projectiles when threads are imperfect because of previously applied sealants; however, the operation must be performed within a separate cubicle and by remote control. Hand-operated thread-chasing tools may be used when no explosives are present in the threads.

C13.8.12.3. Thread cutting shall not be performed on projectiles containing explosives. Straightening crossed threads is considered thread cutting.

C13.8.13. Profile and Alignment Gaging Operations

C13.8.13.1. Operational shields shall enclose each profile and alignment gaging operation, excluding small arms ammunition, to protect adjacent operations from fragments. The layout of equipment and operational procedures shall be developed to minimize personnel injury and property damage in case of an accident.

C13.8.13.2. When chamber gaging large caliber fixed ammunition, the gage should be pointed toward a dividing wall or other barrier and the round inserted and removed by the same operator. The round shall never be left in the gauge. Rounds of mortar ammunition shall be gaged before attaching propellant increments and, unless prohibited by the design characteristics, before assembly of the ignition system.

C13.8.14. AE Handling and Movement

C13.8.14.1. Only trained personnel who understand the hazards and risks involved will handle AE. (See paragraph C3.3.3.) Supervisors in AE operations will be trained to recognize and abate hazards in those operations.

C13.8.14.2. Personnel handling packed or unpacked AE will not tumble, drag, drop, throw, roll, or walk that AE. Containers designed with skids may be pushed or pulled into position, unless marked otherwise.

C13.8.14.3. Hoists, slings, and other lifting devices used to lift or move AE shall:

C13.8.14.3.1. Be designed and evaluated for use with that AE.

C13.8.14.3.2. Positively secure or hold the AE to prevent shifting or falling.

C13.8.14.3.3. Only be used for the intended purpose and in the intended manner.

C13.8.14.3.4. Be clearly marked with rated load capacities and special hazard warnings or instructions.

C13.8.14.3.5. Be inspected and load tested at regularly scheduled intervals and a record maintained of the inspection dates and results.

C14. CHAPTER 14

TESTING REQUIREMENTS

C14.1. GENERAL

The contractor is responsible for the safety of testing programs and shall designate an individual to be responsible for each program. Technical information about the ammunition items, explosives, and weapon systems shall be considered so that the required safety measures may be engineered into the test plans.

C14.2. OPERATING PRECAUTIONS. An SOP shall be prepared for all testing operations and the SOP shall consider these special safety precautions:

C14.2.1. Protection for AE percussion elements (primers, caps, etc.) shall be provided in the design of equipment, transportation, and operations to protect these elements from accidental initiation.

C14.2.2. Cartridges and projectiles larger than 2.36 inches [60 mm], when hand carried, shall be handled one at a time.

C14.2.3. Fused projectiles shall not be handled by the fuses alone.

C14.2.4. Powder charges shall be transported in closed containers to prevent accidental ignition.

C14.2.5. Only trained personnel shall perform operations on explosives-loaded ammunition components.

C14.2.6. No work, adjustment, or observation should be permitted on a weapon system that is loaded and ready for firing, except to check and adjust azimuth and elevation. In no case shall a lanyard be attached until the piece is ready to be fired. No one shall step over the lanyard once it is attached. On weapons equipped with safety locks, the lock may be released after the lanyard has been attached. In the case of small arms, the bolt shall be kept open at all times except when actually firing.

C14.2.7. AE material, except inert components, shall not be delivered to machine shops or other locations not specifically designated for work or modification without approval by a responsible contractor authority.

C14.2.8. The premature or improper mixing of fuels and oxidizers, as associated with liquid propellants, shall be prevented. This applies particularly at test stands and test facilities when transferring liquid propellants.

C14.2.9. Remote control of mechanical devices shall replace manual activation whenever possible.

C14.2.10. Guns operated by remote control shall be equipped with cease-fire devices for halting operations when a hazardous condition occurs. These devices shall be independent of the regular controls so operations can be stopped if the regular controls fail.

C14.2.11. The design and control of electrical circuits used to arm and initiate squibs, igniters, blasting caps, detonators, and similar EEDs on a test range or in a test facility shall meet the manufacturer's instructions or these criteria and guidelines:

C14.2.11.1. Every electrical "ARM" and "FIRE" circuit shall include an interlock device consisting of a safety plug or a key-operated switch to prevent inadvertent application of energy.

C14.2.11.2. The safety plug design and configuration shall be unique for its application and use to prevent unauthorized or accidental activation of a firing circuit. Key-operated switches for "ARM" and "FIRE" circuits shall be designed to lock in the safe (off) position when the control key is removed. Duplicate keys or safety plugs shall not be permitted in any test area.

C14.2.11.3. All fire control circuits in test operation areas shall be properly documented for operational control purposes. Documentation shall include complete wiring diagrams or running sheets, electrical schematics, and cable functions lists. All changes or modifications to fire control circuits shall be approved by contractor safety personnel before being incorporated into the fire control circuits.

C14.2.11.4. Whenever feasible, each fire control circuit shall be grounded and isolated from all other circuits. A shielded, twisted pair of wires with an outer insulating jacket is preferred for each circuit. The fire conductors shall be physically isolated and shall not be run in the same cable with any other circuits.

C14.2.11.5. The fire control shall include both an "ARM" switch and a "FIRE" switch. The safe mode of the arming circuit shall not only interrupt the firing circuit, but should also short-circuit and earth-ground the terminals.

C14.2.11.6. The firing circuit shall be tested for stray voltage per subparagraph C15.8.2.2.7.2. The test SOP shall assure that personnel are adequately protected (in case of initiation) before testing circuit continuity with EEDs installed.

C14.2.11.7. Firing circuits shall be clearly marked or otherwise identified in a distinctive manner and installed so as to prevent them from becoming inadvertently energized from other circuits.

C14.2.11.8. When conducting multiple repetitive test firings using electric initiators and power sources equipped with capacitors, the safe plug or key-operated safety switch shall interrupt, short-circuit, and ground the firing circuit. If this is not possible, the firing wires shall be disconnected from the power source, shorted, and grounded after each test firing to prevent energizing the firing circuit during subsequent test set ups.

C14.2.11.9. Contractor safety personnel may specify alternate shorting and grounding techniques of either or both requirements. However, initiating circuits shall include some type of grounding to prevent static potentials from building up.

C14.2.11.10. The test SOP shall include steps to ensure necessary control over test operations and to ensure security of "ARM" and "FIRE" circuit protective devices.

C14.3. TEST HAZARDS

C14.3.1. Inert-loaded or minimum-charged ammunition should be used in lieu of explosives-loaded items when the test objectives are not affected.

C14.3.2. When temperature-conditioning rooms or boxes are utilized, subparagraphs C14.3.2.1. through C14.3.2.3. shall apply:

C14.3.2.1. Firings from temperature-controlled facilities shall be on an azimuth approved by the contractor's responsible representative. No weapon shall be fired in an enclosed area unless the muzzle is located outside the port opening. Destruction tests, excess pressure tests, and tests of classes of guns known to be unsafe (where the possibility of breech failures exists) shall be conducted with portable shields or equivalents placed on each side of the breech and with a protective plate to the rear of the mount, forming a barrier.

C14.3.2.2. All equipment used in the temperature conditioning of explosives shall comply with QD requirements in Chapter 5 of this Manual. If the equipment is located inside a sited building, the QD for the building applies.

C14.3.2.3. Heat-conditioning equipment shall meet the requirements of section C13.4.

C14.3.3. No firing shall be permitted unless people in the area are under adequate cover.

C14.4. TEST CLEARANCE

C14.4.1. Clearance, to be obtained before performing each test, shall be granted only by responsible contractor personnel with jurisdiction in the danger area where the test is to be performed. When required, air space clearances shall be obtained in accordance with local and Federal Aviation Administration Handbook (Reference (ad)) requirements.

C14.4.2. The contractor personnel responsible for the test areas where the weapon system is located shall obtain the necessary coordination and clearance from their counterparts when a test may encroach upon other danger areas.

C14.4.3. To ensure that danger areas are clear of personnel and ships, vessels, and other craft, clearance for impact and airburst danger areas shall be obtained before firing on or over water.

C14.5. WARNING AND COMMUNICATION SYSTEMS

A warning system shall be established for each testing program, comprising some combination of flags, lights, and sound signals. If visitors or personnel authorized to enter a test area are not familiar with the system, knowledgeable personnel shall escort them. Test areas should be equipped with primary and back-up communication equipment that is readily available, such as telephone or radio.

C14.6. SPECIFIC ITEMS FOR TEST. The safety requirements for testing specific items of ammunition vary according to the type of ammunition, design features, explosives characteristics, test facilities, climate and terrain environment, and other related factors. These factors shall be considered and specific test criteria included in the test plan.

C14.6.1. Recoilless Weapons

C14.6.1.1. All personnel shall be protected against breech blast and malfunction of the round. The danger area in open range firing shall extend to the rear of the weapon: 300 ft [91.44 m] for calibers up to and including 2.95 inches [75 mm] and 450 ft [137.16 m] for all others. The danger zone may be reduced only when effective barricades direct the blast effects away from personnel.

C14.6.1.2. The safety switch on a rifle shall not be advanced to the firing position until the breechblock is closed and all preparations for firing are completed.

C14.6.1.3. Because the blast from salvo firing can obscure a misfire, ripple firing is preferred. When salvo firing cannot be avoided, a wait of at least 2 minutes shall precede the opening of any breechblock after a one-volley salvo.

C14.6.1.4. Unburned propellant from any test firing shall not accumulate in the surrounding area. Safe methods shall be developed for cleanup, decontamination, and disposal.

C14.6.2. Pyrotechnics. Shielded enclosures should be used when testing pyrotechnic items inside a building. Enclosures should be vented to the outside, preferably through the roof, to prevent exposure of personnel to flame, toxic gases, and heat and to prevent rupture of the enclosures.

C14.6.3. Static Tests of Propellant Motors and Engines. Static test stands shall be used for solid propellant motors and liquid propellant engines in any combination. Fire, blast, and fragments shall be considered in establishing safe distances. Static test stands shall be designed to restrain motors and engines undergoing tests.

C14.7. <u>MALFUNCTIONS</u>. For the purposes of this Manual, malfunction applies to the ammunition and the weapon systems or pieces involved.

C14.7.1. <u>Cook-off</u>. Automatic function, or cook-off, of a round left in a hot gun for an extended period is possible in tests involving a high rate of fire, particularly with machine guns and anti-aircraft guns. This possibility largely depends upon the gun's rate of heat dissipation. High air temperature, low wind velocity, low elevation of the gun, and confinement of the gun are also factors. To prevent cook-off, the barrel of the empty gun shall be frequently cooled. If a round is retained or remains in a hot gun with the breech closed, people in the vicinity shall remain under cover until the gun has cooled. If a round jams and the breech fails to close, personnel in the danger zone shall take cover and remain there until the gun has cooled.

C14.7.1.1. Adequate cooling periods are:

Type of Cooling	Time (minutes)
Water	5
Air (machine guns)	15
Air (other guns)	30

C14.7.1.2. When the possibility of a cook-off exists, the danger zone for personnel in the vicinity of the gun firing explosive ammunition shall be:

Type of Gun	Radius[1] (feet)
Machine guns	600
Less than or equal to 75 mm	1,200
Over 75 mm through 105 mm	1,800
Over 105 mm	2,400

[1] When ball ammunition or rounds with inert projectiles are used, radii may be reduced by half. When hazard or engineering analysis demonstrates barricades direct the blast effects away from personnel, the danger zone may also be reduced.

C14.7.1.3. The danger zone down range shall be maintained as for actual firing until the danger of cook-off has passed.

C14.7.2. <u>Premature Burst</u>. If a premature burst occurs, contractor personnel responsible for the test program shall investigate and evaluate the situation. The test shall either be suspended or the lateral limits of the danger zone shall be increased in accordance with prescribed safety distances before the test resumes. The increased lateral limits shall be maintained until the particular test is completed.

C14.7.3. <u>Misfire</u>. After a misfire, all persons shall stand clear of the breech in case the round functions and the gun recoils. All electrical connections that could cause firing of the gun shall be disconnected. The appropriate danger zone for the actual firing shall be maintained during the waiting period, until the danger of cook-off has passed. The removed round shall immediately be placed where subsequent detonation could not cause injury or damage. In the case of misfires involving small-caliber rockets and small-arms ammunition, the rounds should be immersed in water (unless the results of prior analyses or investigations preclude such practice). Misfire procedures shall be established to include attempts to refire weapons, waiting periods, cooling, operational precautions, and disposition of ammunition. Once these procedures have been carried out, the firing pin and mechanism shall be checked, and the barrel of the gun examined to ensure that it is clear; then firing may resume. Additional misfire procedures may be found in technical and field manuals for specific weapons and ammunition items.

C14.7.4. <u>Hangfire</u>. A hangfire is a delayed firing occurring as a short time lag between the striking of the firing pin on the primer and the ignition of the primer, igniter, or propellant. All hangfires shall be reported immediately to responsible personnel, including the ACO and PCO for hangfires involving government-furnished AE. Testing shall be suspended and the cause of the hangfire investigated. In cases of hangfire, the firing of a particular lot of ammunition shall be suspended unless responsible authorities advise differently.

C14.8. <u>AMMUNITION AND DUD RECOVERY</u>. Open-air test area recovery requirements shall be followed:

C14.8.1. <u>Marking</u>. When projectiles or bombs with live fuses, live boosters, or HEs are fired for impact on, or burst over, a recovery field, observers stationed in a protected place shall record the location of duds and exploded rounds. Before leaving a recovery field or impact area, personnel in charge of cleaning the fields shall mark duds and unexploded rounds with the appropriate color-coded flag or device. Where locations cannot be marked, fields shall be posted with warning signs and entry shall be restricted.

C14.8.2. <u>Policing</u>. Except for those specifically trained in disposal procedures, personnel shall not touch or in any way disturb dud ammunition.

C14.8.3. <u>Destruction</u>. All types of AE shall be disposed of in accordance with this Manual, contract requirements, or instructions provided by the contracting officer.

C14.9. <u>PERSONNEL SHELTERS</u>

C14.9.1. <u>General</u>. During tests involving explosives, all energetic material shall be located in a substantial barricade or in an isolated area with adequate cover for all operating personnel and equipment within the danger zone. On tests where there is a possibility of fragmentation, the test supervisor shall require all personnel within the danger zone to move to an approved personnel bombproof (shelter). Only the minimum number of personnel required to conduct the test will be involved in the firing operations. The person assigned to attach the lanyard shall be the last to leave the emplacement or stockade, and no firing shall be attempted until he or she has informed the test officer that all personnel are clear of the weapon and in an approved personnel bombproof (shelter).

C14.9.2. <u>Portable Bombproofs for Fire Observation</u>. All portable bombproofs (shelters) used for fire observation shall be emplaced behind the firing line in the sectors between compass headings 100 and 135 degrees and between 225 and 260 degrees (compass centered on firing point with 0 and 360 degrees at the impact point) as shown in Figure C14.F1. The distances from the bombproof to the firing points shall be those indicated in Table C14.T1. Portable bombproofs (shelters) shall be adequately secured and supported to prevent overturning. Observations from bombproofs shall be indirect, using mirrors, periscopes, or other suitable devices. When emplacement of bombproofs on the impact side of the firing line is required, contractors shall request specific safety guidance through contract channels. (See Table C14.T2 for a listing of portable bombproofs (shelters) and their uses.)

Figure C14.F1. <u>Emplacement of Bombproofs at Firing Points</u>

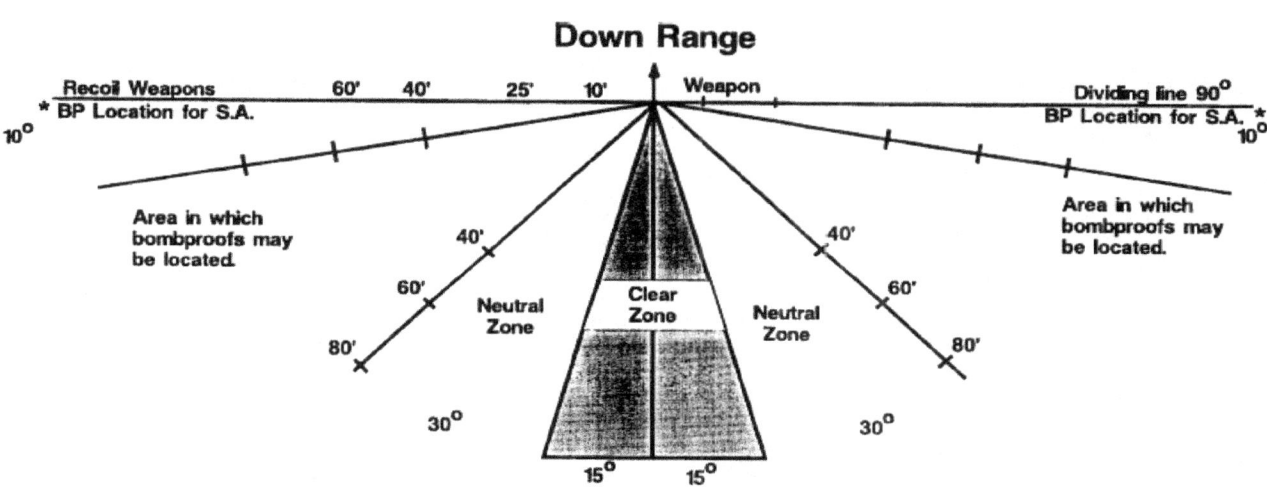

Note: Emplacing of bombproofs in the neutral zone requires prior approval from the responsible agency.
No bombproofs permitted in the clear zone.
The dividing line is center line of trunnions.

* Locating BP in 10° small arms area requires approval of the Range Safety Office.

Table C14.T1. <u>Separation of Firing Points and Bombproofs</u>

Category of Firing	Firing Point to Bombproof Distances (in feet)			
	Class A	Class B	Class C	Class X
Small Arms up to 30MM Inclusive, Shoulder Fired Rockets up to 3.5" Inclusive	5'	5'	5'	*
Artillery Items, Incl Rockets, up to & Including 175MM Gun. All Howitzer Incl 8" Howitzer (Propellant Charges up to 54 lbs.)	40'	40'	Not Permitted	*
Artillery Items, 8" Gun and Over (Propellant Charges 55 to 160 lbs.)	80'	80'	Not Permitted	*
Recoilless Rifles up to 120MM	At 10' or beyond 40'	At 10' or beyond 40'	Not Permitted	*
Recoilless Rifles Above 120MM	At 25' or beyond 60'	At 10' or beyond 60'	Not Permitted	*
Propellant Charges Above 160 lbs.	**	**	Not Permitted	*

* Class X to be used only for cameras, X-Ray equipment, ammo (no personnel).
** Distance of bombproofs to be established by the official responsible for range safety.

Table C14.T2. <u>Portable Bombproofs and Uses</u>

CLASS	TYPE OF ARMOR	TYPE OF VISION	TYPE OF PORTS	NUMBER OF PERSONNEL	TO BE USED ON LOCATIONS	CALIBER OF WEAPON
A	3" Homogenous	Indirect	Safety Glasses with Periscope	*	Firing Front & Impact Area	All
B	+2" Green	Indirect	Safety Glasses with Periscope	*	Firing Fronts	All
C	+3/4" Boiler Plate or Mild Steel	Direct	+1" Safety Glass	*	Firing Fronts Trajectory Line	Up to and Incl 30MM
X	1/4" to 3" Homogenous	Direct or None	Open or None	No	Cameras, X-Ray, Ammo Shields	All

* Each bombproof will be marked as to the number of personnel permitted.

C14.10. TESTING OF AMMUNITION OR DEVICES FOR SMALL ARMS

C14.10.1. Ammunition shall not be placed in any gun until the gun is in firing position and ready to shoot.

C14.10.2. Safety devices on gun mounts and ranges shall be kept in operating condition and tested before use. If a malfunction occurs, test operations shall cease and a report be made to the responsible supervisors.

C14.10.3. Every weapon removed from a firing position, storage case, rack, or picked up by any operator shall be inspected for the presence of ammunition in the chamber, magazine, or feed mechanism, and for obstruction in the bore.

C14.10.4. The chamber, magazine, and feed mechanism of all guns should be open during handling and transportation. When practicable, a safety block should be used in the chambers of weapons.

C14.10.5. Primers of misfired rounds may be hypersensitive; precautions should be taken during their removal from the gun, handling, and disposal.

C14.10.6. Firing on ballistic ranges, except in function and casualty tests, shall be from fixed rests.

C14.10.7. When sand butts are used to stop bullets, a reinforced concrete wall should be constructed at sufficient distance behind the retaining wall to permit inspection. This is necessary because bullets tend to tunnel through the sand and penetrate the retaining wall after continued firing. To discover any such penetration, the inner face of the second wall should be inspected frequently. If terrain effectively protects the rear of the range, no concrete wall is necessary.

C14.10.8. Because bullets tend to ricochet from a sand bank, the roofs of enclosed ranges should be protected to prevent penetration.

C14.10.9. When water traps are used to receive a fired bullet, interlocks shall be provided to prevent firing of the test weapon if water pressure failure occurs.

C14.10.10. Unburned propellant from any test firing shall not accumulate in the surrounding area. Safe methods shall be developed for cleanup, decontamination, and disposal.

C14.11. VELOCITY AND PRESSURE TESTS

Special high-pressure tests or tests of ammunition with unknown pressure characteristics shall be performed only when personnel are protected against injury from gun failures. Operational shields or remote control firing of guns serve this purpose.

C15. CHAPTER 15

COLLECTION AND DESTRUCTION REQUIREMENTS FOR AE

C15.1. GENERAL

C15.1.1. This chapter provides safety requirements for the collection and destruction of AE. It contains more detailed information than other portions of this Manual due to the higher risks of these operations. The Environmental Protection Agency has developed regulations that apply to contractors and may impose requirements beyond those in this Manual. Explosives safety should not be compromised while meeting environmental considerations.

C15.1.2. For specific policies and procedures necessary to provide protection to personnel as a result of DoD ammunition, explosives, or chemical agent contamination of real property currently and formerly owned or used by the Department of Defense, refer to Chapter 12 of Reference (c). This includes manufacturing areas such as pads, pits, basins, ponds, streams, burial sites, and other locations incident to such operations. This requires identification and control measures that are in addition to, not substitutes for, those generally applicable to DoD real-property management. As used hereinafter, "contamination" refers to contamination with ammunition, explosives, or chemical agents. Contractors shall comply with the requirements of Chapter 12 of Reference (c), as implemented by the DoD Components, for all contracts involving explosives remediation of real property. Contractors shall also comply with the minimum qualification standards of DDESB TP 18 (Reference (ae)) for personnel performing unexploded ordnance-related operations in support of the Department of Defense.

C15.2. PROTECTION DURING DISPOSAL OPERATIONS

C15.2.1. Operational shields and special clothing shall protect personnel during disposal operations. Fragmentation hazards require, at a minimum, overhead and frontal protection for personnel. Shelters should be located at the IBD appropriate for the quantity and type of materials being detonated. Personnel shall use protective structures when destroying AE by detonation and when burning AE that may detonate. Personnel shall not approach the burning site but shall observe an appropriate waiting period after the fire is out.

C15.2.2. Personnel shall never work alone during disposal and destruction operations. Warning signs or lights, roadblocks, or other effective means shall restrict the area. One person, available in an emergency, should observe from a safe distance while another performs the operations.

C15.3. COLLECTION OF AE

C15.3.1. Water-Soluble Materials. Enough water should be used to neutralize Explosive D, black powder, and other soluble materials to ensure their complete dissolution. As little material as practicable should be dissolved at one time. Sweeping floors before washing them down reduces the amount of dissolved material in the wash water. Experts shall be consulted when uncertainty exists concerning the purity and composition of wash water.

C15.3.2. Solid Wastes. Explosives-contaminated solid waste material shall be collected, place in closed containers, and promptly delivered to buildings for treatment or holding or to the burning ground for destruction.

C15.3.3. Explosives Dusts

C15.3.3.1. HE dusts such as TNT, tetryl, Explosive D, Composition B, and pentolite should be removed by a vacuum system. A "wet collector" that moistens the dust near the point of intake and keeps it wet until the dust is removed for disposal is preferred for all but Explosive D, which should be collected in a dry system.

C15.3.3.2. The contractor may collect more sensitive explosives such as black powder, lead azide, lead styphnate, tracer, igniter, incendiary compositions, and pyrotechnic materials by vacuum, provided they are kept wet close to the point of intake. Collect each type representing a different hazard separately so that black powder, for example, cannot mix with lead azide. The vacuum system should be designed to vent any gases that may be formed. The use of vacuum systems for collection of sensitive explosive substances should be confined to operations involving small quantities of explosives, that is: operations with fuses, detonators, small-arms ammunition, and black powder igniters. Scrap pyrotechnic, tracer, flare, and similar mixtures shall be collected in No. 10 mineral oil or equivalent to minimize the fire and explosion hazard. Materials collected in the dry state shall be placed in an oil-filled receptacle available at each operation throughout the shift. The oil level should be about 1 inch [2.54 cm] above the level of any pyrotechnic mixture in the container. Remove containers of scrap explosive for disposal from the operating buildings at least once per shift. The appropriate rated Class B firefighting equipment shall be available when oil is used as a desensitizer.

C15.4. DESIGN AND OPERATION OF COLLECTION SYSTEMS

C15.4.1. Collection systems and chambers shall be designed to prevent pinching thin layers of explosives or explosives dust between metal parts.

C15.4.1.1. Pipes or ducts used to convey dusts shall require flanged, welded, or rubber connections. The contractor shall not use threaded connections. The system shall prevent explosive dusts from accumulating in parts outside the collection chamber.

C15.4.1.2. Pipes or ducts conveying HEs shall have long radius bends. Systems for propellant powder may use short radius bends, provided they are stainless steel, with polished interiors.

C15.4.1.3. Vacuum application points should be kept to a minimum. The design of the vacuum collection system should provide a separate exhaust line to the primary collection chamber from each room or bay. If this is not possible, no more than two bays shall be serviced by a common header.

C15.4.1.4. Wet primary collectors are preferred (except with Explosive D). The length of vacuum line from the vacuum application points to the wet collectors should be short. A single secondary collector shall service as few primary collectors as possible.

C15.4.1.4.1. The contractor shall not connect more than two dry primary collectors to a single secondary collector (wet or dry type).

C15.4.1.4.2. Since permanently attaching the collection system to the explosive dust-producing machine increases the likelihood of propagation through the collection system from a detonation at the machine, manual operation of the suction hose to remove explosives dust is preferred.

C15.4.1.4.3. For the same reason, manually operated suction hoses connected to explosives dust-producing machines should not interconnect. However, when potential dust concentrations pose a severe health hazard, the collection system shall be permanently attached to the explosive dust-producing machine and should be interlocked with the machine.

C15.4.2. Two collection chambers shall be serially installed in series ahead of the pump or exhauster to prevent explosives dust from entering the vacuum pump in a dry vacuum collection system.

C15.4.3. Slide valves for vacuum collection systems are permitted; however, there shall be no metal-to-metal contact. An aluminum slide operating between two ebonite spacer bars or similar compatible materials will eliminate unacceptable metal-to-metal contact.

C15.4.4. The design of wet collectors shall provide for:

C15.4.4.1. Proper immersion of explosives.

C15.4.4.2. Breaking up of air bubbles to release airborne particles.

C15.4.4.3. Removal of moisture from the air leaving the collector to prevent moistened particles of explosives from entering the small piping between the collector and the exhauster or pump.

C15.4.5. At least once every shift, explosives dust shall be removed from the collection chamber to eliminate unnecessary and hazardous concentrations of explosives. The entire system should be cleaned weekly to remove residual contamination, with parts dismantled as necessary.

C15.4.6. The entire explosives dust collection system shall be electrically grounded. Test the electrical bonding and grounding system in accordance with paragraph C6.4.5.

C15.4.7. Small vacuum systems positioned close to workstations shall be shielded.

C15.5. LOCATION OF COLLECTION CHAMBERS

C15.5.1. Dry-type stationary vacuum collection chambers should be located in the open, outside operating buildings, or in buildings set-aside for that purpose. To protect operating personnel from blast and fragments from the collection chamber, a barricade or operational shield appropriate for the NEW involved shall be provided between the operating building and the outside location or separate building. At least 3 ft [1 m] shall separate the collection chamber from the barricade or operational shield.

C15.5.2. When it is not practicable to locate dry-type stationary vacuum collection chambers outside the operating building, a separate room or bay within the building may be set aside for the purpose. This room shall not contain other operations and shall not be used as a passageway between other operating locations within the building when explosives are being collected. Walls separating the room or bay from other portions of the operating building shall meet the requirements for operational shields for the NEW in the collection chamber. If more than one collection chamber is to be placed in the room, walls meeting the requirements for operational shields or barricades shall subdivide the room into cubicles. Only one chamber shall be placed in a single cubicle.

C15.5.3. Walls separating the room, bay, cubicle, or the outside location holding the dry-type portable vacuum collectors shall be separated from other portions of the operating building as described in paragraphs C15.5.1. and C15.5.2. and shall meet the requirements of an operational shield for the quantity of explosives in the collection chamber.

C15.5.4. Stationary and portable wet-type collectors may be placed in operating bays or cubicles if they are limited to 5 lbs [2.3 kg] or less NEW TNT equivalency. When placed in separate cubicles, the limits for each collector may increase to 8 lbs [3.65 kg] NEW. If the collectors contain more than 8 lb. [3.65 kg] NEW, the location requirements for dry collectors (paragraphs C15.5.1., C15.5.2., and C15.5.3.) will apply.

C15.6. AE AWAITING DESTRUCTION

When stored in the open, AE awaiting destruction shall be separated by IBD from the AE disposal site. When adequately protected from frontal and overhead hazards, AE awaiting destruction shall be separated by at least ILD from the AE disposal site. All AE awaiting destruction shall be protected from accidental ignition or explosion caused by ambient storage conditions or by fragments, grass fires, burning embers, or blast overpressure originating at the disposal site.

CHAPTER 15

C15.7. <u>CONTAINERS FOR WASTE EXPLOSIVES</u>

Containers for AE awaiting destruction shall be the original closed packages or equivalent. Closures shall prevent spillage or leakage of contents when handled or overturned and shall not pinch or rub explosives during closing and opening. Containers shall be marked clearly to identify contents. Containers constructed with spark-producing or easily ignited material shall not be used.

C15.8. <u>DESTRUCTION SITES</u>

C15.8.1. <u>Site Criteria</u>

C15.8.1.1. AE destruction sites shall be located as far as possible from magazines, inhabited buildings, public highways, runways, taxiways, and operating buildings. (See paragraph C5.19.5. to determine the minimum separation distance for AE destruction sites from other ESs.) To prevent secondary fragments, do not burn or detonate AE on concrete or in areas having large stones or crevices.

C15.8.1.2. Firefighting equipment should be available to extinguish grass fires and to wet down the area between burnings and at the close of operations.

C15.8.1.3. Ordinary combustible rubbish should not be disposed of near AE and AE-contaminated material destruction sites.

C15.8.2. <u>Materials and Equipment for Detonating Explosives</u>

C15.8.2.1. Detonations of AE should be initiated with electric blasting caps and blasting machines or permanently installed electric circuits energized by storage batteries or conventional power lines. When using earth to cover AE for disposal, the blasting cap shall not be buried. The donor charge shall be primed with a sufficient length of detonating cord to allow connecting the blasting cap above ground level.

C15.8.2.2. Special requirements for using electric blasting caps and electric blasting circuits are:

C15.8.2.2.1. A blasting cap shall never be held at the explosive (output) end. The wire lead end of the cap should be held between the thumb and the index finger with the explosive end pointed down, away from the body, and to the rear.

C15.8.2.2.2. Except during electrical continuity testing of the blasting cap and lead wires, the shunt shall not be removed from the lead wires of the blasting cap until the moment of connection to the blasting circuit,. If the shunt is removed to test the blasting cap, short circuit the lead wires again following the test by twisting the bare ends of the wires together. The wires shall remain short-circuited in this manner until the moment of connection to the blasting circuit.

C15.8.2.2.3. The lead wires shall be carefully held so that there is no tension where they connect to the cap and shall be straightened as necessary by hand. The lead wires shall not be thrown, waved through the air, or uncoiled by snapping as a whip.

C15.8.2.2.4. Blasting circuit wires shall be twisted pairs. Operators shall keep blasting circuit wires twisted together and connected to ground at the power source and twisted at the opposite end at all times except when actually firing the charge or testing circuit for continuity and current or voltage. Never connect the blasting cap to the blasting circuit wires unless the blasting circuit wires are shorted and grounded at the ends near the power source.

C15.8.2.2.5. Electric blasting or demolition operations and unshielded electric blasting caps shall be separated from radio frequency (RF) energy transmitters by safe distances.

C15.8.2.2.6. When transported by vehicles with two-way radios, and when in areas presumed to have extraneous electromagnetic pulse, blasting caps shall be in closed metal boxes.

C15.8.2.2.7. Operators should follow these procedures when connecting electric blasting cap lead wires to the blasting circuit wires.

C15.8.2.2.7.1. The blasting circuit wires shall be tested for electrical continuity.

C15.8.2.2.7.2. The blasting circuit shall be tested for extraneous current and voltage. To test, arrange a dummy test circuit similar to the actual blasting circuit, except substitute a radio pilot lamp of suitable voltage for the blasting cap. If the pilot lamp glows, indicating potentially dangerous amounts of RF energy, blasting operations using electric blasting caps shall stop. Blasting operations may proceed using non-electric blasting caps and a safety fuse. The contractor may substitute other test instruments such as the DuPont "Detect-A-Meter" or "Voltohmeter" for the radio pilot lamp. If the potential source of extraneous electromagnetic pulse is from a radar, a television, or a microwave transmitter, the actual blasting circuit -- including the blasting cap (without other explosives) -- shall be tested for extraneous effects. Personnel performing such tests shall be protected from the effects of an exploding blasting cap.

C15.8.2.2.7.3. The blasting cap and its lead wires shall be tested for electrical continuity. Personnel performing such tests shall be protected from the effects of an exploding blasting cap. The individual who removes the shunt should ground himself or herself by grasping the blasting circuit wire prior to performing the operation in order to prevent accumulated static electricity from firing the blasting cap.

C15.8.2.2.7.4. Personnel shall first assure the blasting circuit wires are shorted and grounded at the power source and then connect the blasting cap lead wires to the blasting circuit wires.

CHAPTER 15

C15.8.2.2.7.5. All but two persons shall evacuate from the area. One person shall partially retreat and act as safety observer. The other person shall maintain physical possession of a safety device that locks out the blasting circuit (e.g., plug, key, pigtail) and shall place the blasting cap onto the charge. Both persons will then retreat to the personnel shelter.

C15.8.2.2.7.6. The operator shall disconnect the blasting circuit wires from ground at the power source, untwist the wires, and use a galvanometer to test the firing circuit for electric continuity before connection to the blasting machine or firing panel.

C15.8.2.2.7.7. The individual assigned to make the connections shall confirm that everyone in the vicinity is in a safe place before connecting the blasting circuit wires to the power source and signaling for detonation. This individual shall not leave the blasting machine or its actuating device for any reason and, when using a panel, shall lock the switch in the open position until ready to fire, retaining the only key. After accounting for all personnel, the blasting circuit wires shall be connected to the power source and the charge fired.

C15.8.2.2.7.8. After firing, the blasting circuit wires shall be disconnected from power source, the wires twisted together, and connected to ground.

C15.8.2.2.7.9. Blasting and destruction operations shall be suspended when electrical storms are in the vicinity. At the first sign of an electrical storm, short-circuit the blasting cap lead wires, short-circuit and ground the blasting circuit wires, and evacuate all personnel from the demolition area to a safe location.

C15.8.2.2.8. When conditions prevent the use of electrical initiators for detonation, non-electric blasting caps and safety fuses shall be used. At the beginning of each day's operation and whenever using a new coil, the safety fuse's burning rate shall be tested. The fuse shall be long enough for personnel to evacuate to a safe distance. Under no circumstances shall the fuse length be less than that required for a 2-minute burn time. Appropriately designed crimpers shall be used to affix fuses to blasting caps. Only fuses small enough in diameter to enter the blasting cap without forcing shall be used. All personnel, except the operator lighting the fuse, shall retreat to the personnel shelter or leave the disposal area before ignition.

C15.8.3. Servicing of Destruction Site

C15.8.3.1. Vehicles transporting AE to burning or disposal sites shall meet the requirements of section C3.16. and paragraph C8.3.12. No more than two persons shall ride in the cab. No one shall ride in the truck bed.

C15.8.3.2. Vehicles should be unloaded immediately and withdrawn from the burning or disposal area until destruction operations are completed. Containers of explosives shall not be opened before the vehicle has departed.

CHAPTER 15

C15.8.3.3. Containers of explosives or ammunition items to be destroyed at the destruction site shall be spotted and opened at least 10 ft [3.05 m] from each other and from explosive material set out earlier, to prevent rapid transmission of fire if premature ignition should occur.

C15.8.3.4. Empty containers shall be closed and removed to prevent charring or damage during burning of explosives. Delivery vehicles shall pick up and remove empty containers on the next trip.

C15.9. DESTRUCTION BY BURNING

C15.9.1. No mixing of an explosive with extraneous material, other explosives, metal powders, detonators, or similar items shall occur without authorization.

C15.9.2. Because of the danger of detonation, AE shall not be burned in containers or in large quantities.

C15.9.3. A bed of easily combustible material at least 2 inches [.61 mm] thick should be positioned under the explosive bed to ensure complete consumption of wet explosives. The combustible material should extend at least 2 inches [.61 mm] beyond the edges of the explosive bed. If necessary, the thickness and extent of the combustible material may be adjusted, based on actual experience at the site.

C15.9.3.1. The explosive bed shall be no more than 3 inches [76 mm] deep.

C15.9.3.2. An ignition train of combustible material leading to the explosives shall be arranged so that both it and the explosives can be burned in such a fashion to avoid any ignited material from propagating to itself in an uncontrolled manner or from propagating to any other explosives treatment areas.

C15.9.3.3. No burning shall take place when wind velocity exceeds 15 mph [24 km/h].

C15.9.3.4. For direct ignition of a combustible train, either a safety fuse long enough to permit personnel to reach protective shelter or a black powder squib initiated by an electric current controlled from a distance or protective structure shall be used. Tying two or more squibs together may be necessary to ensure ignition of the combustible train. Contractors should consider designing ignition systems to facilitate removal from the combustible train in the event of a misfire. When using electrically initiated firing devices, comply with testing requirements in subparagraph C15.8.2.2.7.

C15.9.3.5. Combustible materials are not required for burning solid propellants ignited by squibs.

CHAPTER 15

C15.9.3.6. The sites of misfires shall be evacuated for at least 30 minutes. Operators shall implement misfire procedures and shall notify safety and emergency response personnel to ensure all appropriate safety precautions are taken before approaching the explosives burn bed. Only two trained and qualified operators shall approach the position of the explosives. One shall examine the misfire and the other shall act as backup. The backup shall watch the examination from a safe distance, behind natural or artificial barriers or other obstructions for protection. The backup shall follow contractor procedures should an accident occur.

C15.9.4. If burning is expected to be complete and to leave the ground uncontaminated, loose, dry explosives may be burned without combustible material. For the safety of personnel and operations, the ground shall be checked for residual unburned explosives. Volatile flammable liquids shall not be poured over explosives or the underlying combustible material at any stage of the disposal process to accelerate burning.

C15.9.5. Wet explosives shall always be burned on beds of non-explosive materials.

C15.9.6. Explosive powders such as RDX, HMX, etc., should be burned in desensitized form to promote safe handling and prevent detonation.

C15.9.7. Pyrotechnic materials in oil containers shall be emptied into shallow metal pans before burning. The empty containers may be burned with the explosives.

C15.9.8. Parallel beds of explosives prepared for burning shall be separated by not less than 150 ft [46 m]. Care shall be taken to prevent material igniting from smoldering residue or from heat retained in the ground from previous burning operations. Unless a burned-over plot has been saturated with water and passed a safety inspection, 24 hours shall elapse before the next burning.

C15.10. DESTRUCTION BY DETONATION

C15.10.1. Detonation of AE should occur in a pit at least 4 ft [1.3 m] deep and with the AE covered by at least of 2 ft [0.6 m] of earth. The components should be placed on their sides or in that position exposing the largest area to the influence of initiating explosives. Demolition blocks shall be placed in intimate contact on top of the item to be detonated, secured by earth packed over them. Under certain circumstances, the contractor may substitute bangalore torpedoes or bulk HE for the demolition blocks. NOTE: Detonations at remote demolition areas do not require a pit.

C15.10.2. Local regulations, atmospheric conditions, earth strata, etc., shall determine the maximum quantities destroyed at one time, both in pits and open sites. Considering these variables, determine the acceptable NEW based on criteria in Chapter 5 of this Manual. This procedure should be used for destruction of fragmentation grenades, HE projectiles, mines, mortar shells, bombs, photoflash munitions, and HE rocket heads separated from their motors.

C15.10.3. After each detonation, the surrounding area shall be searched for unexploded AE.

C15.10.4. The sites of misfires shall be evacuated for at least 30 minutes. Operators shall implement misfire procedures and shall notify safety and emergency response personnel to ensure all appropriate safety precautions are taken before approaching the explosives. Contractors should consider designing initiation systems to facilitate removal from the explosives in the event of a misfire.

C15.11. DESTRUCTION BY NEUTRALIZATION

Methods of neutralization include dissolving in water-soluble material or chemical decomposition. The contractor is responsible for investigating which of these is most appropriate. The contractor shall comply with all applicable local, State, and Federal requirements.

C15.12. DESTRUCTION CHAMBERS AND INCINERATORS

C15.12.1. General. The contractor should destroy small, loaded AE components (e.g., primers, fuses, boosters, detonators, activators, relays, delays, and all types of small-arms ammunition) in destruction chambers or deactivation furnaces. The contractor should use explosives scrap incinerators for burning tracer and igniter compositions, small quantities of solid propellant, magnesium powder, sump cleanings, absorbent cleaning materials, and similar materials. Destruction chambers and incinerators should be equipped with suitable pollution control devices (e.g., multiple chamber incinerators with thermal incinerator afterburners) and concrete barricades. The final incineration should take place at a minimum temperature of 1400°F [760°C].

C15.12.2. Operation of Incinerators

C15.12.2.1. Personnel shall not operate the feeding conveyor until the incinerator temperature is high enough to ensure complete destruction. Temperature recording devices should be installed.

C15.12.2.2. To remove accumulated residue, incinerators shall be shut down and thoroughly cooled. Repairs shall be made only during shutdown. Personnel entering the incinerator to clean it shall wear respiratory protection to prevent inhalation of toxic dusts or fumes, e.g., mercury from tracers or lead from small-arms ammunition.

C15.12.3. Operation of Destruction Chambers and Deactivation Furnaces

C15.12.3.1. Operation of destruction chambers and deactivation furnaces shall be by remote control.

C15.12.3.2. Operators shall not approach the unprotected side of the concrete barricade for any reason until enough time has elapsed for explosives in the chamber to react. Regular inspections shall be performed to ensure the feed-pipe chute or conveyor is free of obstructions.

C15.12.3.3. Components shall be fed into the chamber a few at a time. The exact number permitted at one time for each type of component shall be posted in a place easily seen from the operator's working position.

C15.12.3.4. Guards shall be installed on conveyor-feeding mechanisms to facilitate feeding and to prevent items from jamming or falling.

C15.13. SUPPORT IN DISPOSAL OF EXPLOSIVES WASTE

The contractor shall request instructions from the responsible ACO if, at end of contract, there is excess or residual government-owned AE and the contract does not address disposition.

AP1. APPENDIX 1

GLOSSARY

AP1.1. Aboveground Magazine. Any open area or any structure not meeting the requirements of an earth-covered magazine that is used for explosives storage.

AP1.2. Administration Area. The area encompassing administrative buildings that serve the entire installation. This excludes offices located near and directly serving explosives storage and operating areas.

AP1.3. Ammunition and Explosives. For the purpose of the document, any liquid and solid propellants and explosives, pyrotechnics, incendiaries and smokes in the following forms: bulk; ammunition; rockets; missiles; warheads, devices; and components of all of the above, except inert items. This definition does not include inert components containing no explosives, propellants, or pyrotechnics; flammable liquids; acids; oxidizers; powdered metals; or other materials having fire or explosive characteristics, unless these materials are being used for or incorporated into initiation, propulsion, or detonation as a integral or component part of an explosive, an ammunition or explosive end item of a weapon system. This may include, but not necessarily limited to, all items of U.S.-titled (i.e., owned by the U.S. Government through the DOD Components) ammunition; propellants, liquid and solid; pyrotechnics; high explosives; guided missiles; warheads; devices; and chemical agent substances and components presenting real or potential hazards to life, property, and the environment. Excluded are wholly inert items and nuclear warheads and devices, except for considerations of storage and stowage compatibility, blast, fire, and nonnuclear fragment hazards associated with the explosives (DoD 6055.9-STD, Appendix 1, para AP1.1.12). See the definition of 'military munitions' at 10 U.S.C. § 101(e)(4).

AP1.4. Ammunition and Explosives Area. An area specifically designated and set aside from other portions of a facility for the development, manufacture, testing, maintenance, storage, or handling of ammunition and explosives.

AP1.5. Auxiliary Building. Any building accessory to or maintained and operated to serve an operating building or ammunition and explosives area. Explosive materials are not present in an auxiliary building such as power plants, change houses, paint and solvent lockers, and similar facilities.

AP1.6. Barricade. An intervening barrier, natural or artificial, of such type, size, and construction as to limit in a prescribed manner the effect of an explosion on nearby buildings or exposures.

AP1.7. Blast Impulse. The product of the overpressure from the blast wave of an explosion and the time during which it acts at a given point, i.e., the area under the positive phase of the overpressure-time curve.

AP1.8. <u>Blast Overpressure</u>. The pressure, exceeding the ambient pressure, manifested in the shock wave of an explosion.

AP1.9 <u>Bombproof (Shelter)</u>. A structure designed to resist fragments and explosive effects for the protection of personnel conducting and observing ammunition and explosives testing and destruction.

AP1.10. <u>Change House</u>. A building provided with facilities for employees to change to and from work clothes. Such buildings may be provided with sanitary facilities, drinking fountains, lockers, and eating facilities.

AP1.11. <u>Classification Yard</u>. A railroad yard used for receiving, dispatching, classifying, and switching of cars.

AP1.12. <u>Compatibility</u>. Ammunition or explosives that may be stored or transported together without significantly increasing either the probability of an accident or, for a given quantity, the magnitude of the effects of such an accident.

AP1.13. <u>Deflagration Reaction.</u> Ignition and rapid burning of the confined energetic materials builds up high local pressures leading to non-violent pressure release as a result of a low strength case or venting through case closures (e.g., loading ports or fuze wells). The case may rupture but does not fragment; closure covers might be expelled, and unburned and burning energetic materials might be thrown about and spread the fire. Propulsion may launch an unsecured test item, causing an additional hazard. No blast or significant fragmentation damage to the surroundings is expected, only heat and smoke damage from the burning explosive substances. A rapid chemical reaction in which the output of heat is enough to enable the reaction to proceed and be accelerated without input of heat from another source. Deflagration is a surface phenomenon with the reaction products flowing away from the unreacted material along the surface at subsonic velocity. The effect of a true deflagration under confinement is an explosion. Confinement of the reaction increases pressure, rate of reaction, and temperature and may cause transition into a detonation.

AP1.14. <u>Demilitarize</u>. Any disarming, neutralizing, and any other action rendering ammunition and explosives innocuous or ineffectual for military use.

AP1.15. <u>Detonation Reaction</u>. (1) A supersonic decomposition reaction propagates through the energetic materials and produces an intense shock in the surrounding medium and very rapid plastic deformation of metallic cases, followed by extensive fragmentation. All energetic materials will be consumed. Effects will include: large ground craters for items on or close to the ground; holing, plastic flow damage, and fragmentation of adjacent metal structures; and blast overpressure damage to nearby structures. (2) A violent chemical reaction with a chemical compound or mechanical mixture evolving heat and high pressure. A detonation proceeds through the reacted material toward the unreacted material at a supersonic velocity. The result of the chemical reaction is exertion of extremely high pressure on the surrounding medium, forming a propagating shock wave which is initially of supersonic velocity.

AP1.16. <u>Dividing Wall</u>. A wall designed to prevent, control, or delay propagation of an explosion between quantities of explosives on opposite sides of the wall.

AP1.17. <u>Earth-Covered Magazine (ECM)</u>. Any earth-covered structure that meets soil cover depth and soil requirements of Reference (c). An ECM has three possible structural strength designations: "7-Bar," "3-Bar," or "Undefined." The strength of an ECM headwall and door(s) determines its designation.

AP1.18. <u>Energetic Liquid</u>. A liquid, slurry, or gel consisting of or containing an explosive, oxidizer, fuel, or combination that may undergo, contribute to, or cause rapid exothermic decomposition, deflagration, or detonation.

AP1.19. <u>Engineering Controls</u>. Regulation of facility operations through the use of prudent engineering principles such as facility design, operation sequencing, equipment selection, and process limitations.

AP1.20. <u>Explosion</u>. (1) A reaction of any chemical compound or mechanical mixture which, when initiated, undergoes a very rapid combustion or decomposition, releasing large volumes of highly heated gases that exert pressure on the surrounding medium. (2) A mechanical reaction in which failure of the container causes the sudden release of pressure from within a pressure vessel; for example, pressure rupture of a steam boiler. Depending on the rate of energy release, an explosion can be categorized as a deflagration, a detonation, or pressure rupture.

AP1.21. <u>Explosive</u>. For the purpose of this Manual, any chemical compound or mechanical mixture that, when subjected to heat, impact, friction, detonation, or other suitable initiation, undergoes a very rapid chemical change with the evolution of large volumes of highly heated gases that exert pressures in the surrounding medium. The term applies to materials that either detonate or deflagrate.

AP1.22. <u>Explosives Facility</u>. Any structure or location containing ammunition and explosives (AE) excluding combat aircraft parking areas or AE aircraft cargo areas.

AP1.23. <u>Exposed Site (ES)</u>. A location exposed to the potential hazardous effects (blast, fragments, debris, and heat flux) from an explosion at a potential explosive site (PES). The distance to a PES and the level of protection required for an ES determine the quantity of ammunition or explosives permitted in a PES.

AP1.24. <u>Fire Protection Distance</u>. The distance between refueling vehicles and refueling operations and structures or sites containing ammunition and explosives. This distance is at least 100 feet [30.48 m] (50 feet [15.24 m] from non-combustible structures).

AP1.25. <u>Firebrand</u>. A projected burning or hot fragment whose thermal energy is transferred to a receptor.

AP1.26. <u>Fire-Resistive</u>. Combustible materials or structures that have been treated or have surface coverings designed to retard ignition or fire spread.

AP1.27. <u>Flame-Resistant</u>. Combustible materials, such as clothing, that have been treated or coated to decrease their burning characteristics.

AP1.28. <u>Flammable</u>. A material that ignites easily and burns readily.

AP1.29. <u>Fragmentation</u>. The breaking up of the confining material of a chemical compound or mechanical mixture when an explosion takes place. Fragments may be complete items, subassemblies, pieces thereof, or pieces of equipment or buildings containing items.

AP1.30. <u>General Public</u>. Persons not associated with the contractor's ammunition and explosives facilities or operations such as visitors, to include guests of personnel assigned to the facilities, or persons not employed or contracted by the Department of Defense or DoD contractors or subcontractors.

AP1.31. <u>Hangfire</u>. Temporary failure or delay in the action of a primer, igniter, or propelling charge.

AP1.32. <u>Hazard Analysis</u>. The logical, systematic examination of an item, process, condition, facility, or system to identify and analyze the probability, causes, and consequences of potential or real hazards.

AP1.33 <u>Hazardous Fragment</u>. A fragment having an impact energy of 58 feet/pound [79 joules] or greater.

AP1.34. <u>Hazardous Fragment Density</u>. A density of hazardous fragments exceeding one per 600 square feet [55.7 square meter].

AP1.35. <u>High Explosive Equivalent or Explosive Equivalent</u>. The amount of a standard explosive that, when detonated, will produce a blast effect comparable to that which results at the same distances from the detonation or explosion of a given amount of the material for which performance is being evaluated. For the purpose of these standards, TNT is used as the standard for comparison.

AP1.36. <u>Holding Yard</u>. A location for groups of railcars, trucks, or trailers used to hold ammunition, explosives, and dangerous materials for interim periods before storage or shipment.

AP1.37. <u>Hybrid Propellants</u>. A propellant charge using a combination of physically separated solid and liquid (or jelled) substances as fuel and oxidizer.

AP1.38. <u>Hygroscopic</u>. A tendency of material to absorb moisture from its surroundings.

AP1.39. <u>Hypergolic</u>. A property of various combinations of chemicals to self-ignite upon contact with each other without a spark or other external initiation.

AP1.40. <u>Inhabited Building</u>. A building or structure other than an operating building occupied in whole or in part by human beings, both within and outside DoD contractor plants. They include but are not limited to schools, churches, residences, stores, shops, factories, hospitals, theaters, and post offices.

AP1.41. <u>Inhabited Building Distance</u>. The separation distance between potential explosive sites and non-associated exposed sites requiring a high degree of protection from an accidental explosion. Such exposed sites include facility boundaries, wholly inert administrative facilities, the public, etc.

AP1.42. <u>Inspection Station</u>. A designated location at which trucks and railcars containing ammunition and explosives are inspected.

AP1.43. <u>Interchange Yard</u>. An area set aside for the exchange of railroad cars or vehicles between the common carrier and DoD contractors.

AP1.44. <u>Intraline Distance</u>. The distance to be maintained between any two operating buildings and sites within an operating line, at least one of which contains or is designed to contain explosives.

AP1.45. <u>K-Factor</u>. The factor in the formula $D = kW^{1/3}$ used in quantity distance determinations where D represents distance in feet and W is the net explosive weight in pounds. The K-factor is a constant and represents the degree of damage that is acceptable. Typical constants range from 1.25 to 50; the lower the factor, the greater the level of acceptable damage.

AP1.46. <u>Launch Pad</u>. The load-bearing base, apron, or platform upon which a rocket, missile, or space vehicle and its launcher rest during launching.

AP1.47. <u>Liquid Propellants</u>. Substances in fluid form (including cryogenics) used for propulsion for operating power for missiles, rockets, ammunition, and other related devices. (See Reference (c).) For purposes of this Manual, liquid fuels and oxidizers are considered propellants even when stored and handled separately.

AP1.48. <u>Loading Density</u>. Quantity of explosive per internal volume of structure usually expressed as either pounds per cubic foot (lbs/ft^3) or kilograms per cubic meter (kg/m^3).

AP1.49. <u>Loading Docks</u>. Facilities, structures, or paved areas designed and installed for transferring ammunition and explosives between any two modes of transportation.

AP1.50. <u>Lunchroom</u>. A facility where food is prepared or brought for distribution by food service personnel. It may serve more than one potential explosion site (PES). A break room in an operating building may be used by personnel assigned to the PES to eat meals.

AP1.51. <u>Magazine</u>. Any building or structure, except an operating building, used for the storage of ammunition and explosives. (See Reference (m) for more detailed descriptions.)

APPENDIX 1

AP1.52. <u>Mass-Detonating Explosives</u>. High explosives, black powder, certain propellants, certain pyrotechnics, and other similar explosives (alone or in combination, or loaded into various types of ammunition or containers) most of which can be expected to explode virtually instantaneously when a small portion is subjected to fire, to severe concussion or impact, to the impulse of an initiating agent, or to the effect of a considerable discharge of energy from without. Such an explosion normally will cause severe structural damage to adjacent objects. Explosion propagation may occur immediately to other items of ammunition and explosives stored sufficiently close to and not adequately protected from the initially exploding pile with a time interval short enough so that two or more quantities must be considered as one for quantity distance purposes.

AP1.53. <u>Maximum Credible Event (MCE)</u>. In hazards evaluation, the MCE from a hypothesized accidental explosion, fire, or agent release is the worst single event that is likely to occur from a quantity and disposition of ammunition and explosives (AE). The event must be realistic with a reasonable probability of occurrence considering the explosion propagation, burning rate characteristics, and physical protection given to the AE involved. The MCE evaluated on this basis may then be used as a basis for effects calculations and casualty predictions.

AP1.54. <u>Misfire.</u> Failure of a component to fire or explode as intended.

AP1.55. <u>Navigable Streams</u>. For purposes of this Manual, those parts of streams, channels, or canals capable of being used in their ordinary or maintained condition as highways of commerce over which trade and travel are, or may be, conducted in the customary modes, not including streams that are not capable of navigation by barges, tugboats, and other large vessels unless they are used extensively and regularly for the operation of pleasure boats.

AP1.56. <u>Net Explosive Quantity</u>. Expressed in kilograms, the total weight of all explosive substances (i.e., high explosive weight, propellant weight, and pyrotechnic weight) in the ammunition and explosives.

AP1.57. <u>Net Explosive Weight (NEW)</u>. Expressed in pounds, the total weight of all explosive substances (i.e., high explosive weight, propellant weight, and pyrotechnic weight) in the ammunition and explosives.

AP1.58. <u>Net Explosive Weight for Quantity Distance (NEWQD)</u>. The total weight, expressed in pounds [kilograms], of all explosive substances (high explosive weight, propellant weight, and pyrotechnic weight) in the ammunition and explosives (AE), unless testing has been conducted to support an approved different value due to the contribution of high explosives, propellants, or pyrotechnics. For all hazard division 1.3 or 1.4 (other than S) AE, NEWQD is equal to net explosive weight. NEWQD is used when applying quantity distance and other criteria in this document.

AP1.59. <u>Nitrogen Padding (or Blanket)</u>. The practice of filling the void or ullage of a closed container with nitrogen gas to prevent oxidation of the chemical contained therein and to avoid formation of a flammable fuel and air mixture, or to maintain a nitrogen atmosphere in or around an operation or piece of equipment.

AP1.60. <u>Non-combustible</u>. Not burnable.

AP1.61. <u>Non-Robust Munitions</u>. Those hazard division 1.1 and 1.2 ammunition and explosives that are not members of: robust munitions or fragmenting munitions, e.g., air-to-air missile warheads; cluster bomb unit-type munitions; or sympathetic detonation sensitive. Examples of non-robust munitions include torpedoes and underwater mines.

AP1.62. <u>Operating Building</u>. Any structure, except a magazine, in which operations pertaining to manufacturing, processing, handling, loading, assembling, testing, and packaging of ammunition and explosives are performed.

AP1.63. <u>Operating Line</u>. A group of buildings, facilities, or related work stations so arranged as to permit performance of the consecutive steps in the manufacture of an explosive or in the loading, assembly, modification, and maintenance of ammunition.

AP1.64. <u>Operational Shield</u>. A barrier constructed at a particular location or around a particular machine or operating station to protect personnel, material, or equipment from the effects of a possible localized fire or explosion.

AP1.65. <u>Parallel Operating Lines</u>. Adjacent operating lines processing ammunition and explosives (AE) that present similar sensitivities to initiation. Such AE at related work stations in the same building or facility are not parallel operating lines, but may require physical separation or other control measures to limit the maximum credible event and protect personnel and equipment.

AP1.66. <u>Passenger Railroad</u>. Any steam, diesel, electric, or other railroad that carries passengers for hire.

AP1.67. <u>Potential Explosive Site (PES)</u>. The location of a quantity of explosives that will create a blast, fragment, thermal, or debris hazard in the event of an accidental explosion of its contents. Quantity limits for ammunition and explosives at a PES are determined by the distance to an exposed site.

AP1.68. <u>Propellant</u>. Explosives compositions used for propelling projectiles and rockets and to generate gases for powering auxiliary devices.

AP1.69. <u>Public Highway</u>. Any street, road, or highway used by the general public for any type of vehicular travel.

AP1.70. Public Traffic Route. Any public street, road (including any on a DoD contractor facility or military reservation), highway, navigable stream, or passenger railroad that is routinely used for through traffic by the general public.

AP1.71. Pyrotechnic Material. The explosive or chemical ingredients, including powdered metals, used in the manufacture of military pyrotechnics.

AP1.72. Quantity Distance (QD). The quantity of explosive material and distance separation relationships that provide defined types of protection. These relationships are based on levels of risk considered acceptable for the stipulated exposures and are tabulated in the appropriate QD tables. Separation distances are not absolute safe distances but are relative protective or safe distances.

AP1.73. Renovation. The work performed on ammunition, missiles, or rockets to restore them to a completely serviceable condition; this usually involves the replacement of unserviceable or outmoded parts.

AP1.74. Service Magazine. A building of an operating line used for the intermediate storage of explosives materials.

AP1.75. Spall. Pieces of a material (and the process by which they are formed) that are broken loose from the surface of a parent body by tensile forces created when a compression shock wave travels through the body and reflects from the surface.

AP1.76. Static Test Stand. Locations on which liquid propellant engines or solid propellant motors are tested in place.

AP1.77. Substantial Dividing Wall. An interior wall designed to prevent simultaneous detonation of explosives on opposite sides of the wall; however, such walls may not prevent propagation (depending on quantities and types of explosives involved).

AP1.77.1. Substantial dividing walls are one way of separating explosives into smaller groups to minimize the results of an explosion and allow a reduction in quantity distance (QD). These walls do not protect personnel near the wall from high explosives, because the spalling of wall surface opposite the explosion source may form dangerous secondary fragments.

AP1.77.2. Reinforced concrete-type walls may vary in thickness, but will be at least 12 inches [305 mm] thick. At a minimum, both will be reinforced with rods at least .5 inches [12.7 mm] in diameter. The rods will be spaced not more than 12 inches [305 mm] on centers horizontally and vertically, interlocked with footing rods and secured to prevent overturning. Rods on one face will be staggered with regard to rods on the opposite face and should be approximately 2 inches [50.8 mm] from each face. Concrete should have a design compressive strength on 2,500 pounds per square inch (17.24 Mega Pascal MPa) or more. The capability to prevent simultaneous detonation is based on a limit of 425 net lbs [193 kg] of mass-detonating explosives. All storage plans and QD calculations shall be based on the total quantity of mass-detonating explosives on both sides of a dividing wall when the quantity of either side exceeds

425 lbs [193 kg]. Explosives should be 3 feet [0.91 m] or more from the wall. (See Reference (n) for specific construction details.)

AP1.77.3. Retaining walls filled with earth or sand must be at least 5 feet [1.5 m] wide, with earth or sand packed between concrete, masonry, or wooden retaining walls.

AP1.78. <u>Suspect Truck and Rail Car Site</u>. A designated location for placing trucks and railcars containing ammunition and explosives that are suspected of being in a hazardous condition. These sites are also used for trucks and railcars that may be in a condition that is hazardous to their contents.

AP1.79. <u>Waiver</u>. A written authority that provides a temporary exception, permitting deviation from mandatory requirements of this Manual. It is generally granted for a single contract and may apply for a short period during that contract performance until correction of the waived conditions.

AP2. APPENDIX 2

QD TABLES EXTRACTED FROM DOD 6055.9-STD

AP2.1. QD TABLES

The tables in this appendix are extracted copies of the tables found in Reference (c). The tables are provided to make this publication a more complete source of information for contractors. NOTE: Criteria provided by these Standards are provided in English units (ft, lb, psi, etc.) with metric equivalents shown in brackets ([m, kg, kPa], etc.) or highlighted.

AP2.2. NUMBERING OF TABLES

Tables are sequentially numbered for this publication, with the Reference (c) table number shown in parentheses immediately after the table's title. Within the tables and table notes, the numbers and equations from Reference (c) are used.

AP2.3. LIST OF TABLE NUMBERS

For convenience, the table numbers from this Manual and Reference (c) are listed below:

DoD 4145.26-M	DoD 6055.9-STD
AP2.T1	C9.T1
AP2.T2	C9.T2
AP2.T3	C9.T3
AP2.T4	C9.T4
AP2.T5	C9.T5
AP2.T6	C9.T6
AP2.T7	C9.T7A
AP2.T8	C9.T7B
AP2.T9	C9.T8
AP2.T10	C9.T9
AP2.T11	C9.T10
AP2.T12	C9.T11
AP2.T13	C9.T12
AP2.T14	C9.T13
AP2.T15	C9.T14
AP2.T16	C9.T15
AP2.T17	C9.T16
AP2.T18	C9.T17
AP2.T19	C9.T18
AP2.T20	C9.T19
AP2.T21	C9.T20
AP2.T22	C9.T21
AP2.T23	C9.T22

AP2.T24   C9.T35
AP2.T25   C9.T36

Table AP2.T1. <u>HD 1.1 IBD and PTRD</u>
(Table C9.T1.)

NEWQD	IBD From:				PTRD From:			
	ECM			Other PES[4]	ECM			Other PES[5]
	Front[1,2]	Side[1]	Rear[3]		Front[5,6]	Side[5]	Rear[5]	
(lbs)	(ft)	(ft)	(ft)	(ft)	(ft)	(ft)	(ft)	(ft)
[kg]	[m]	[m]	[m]	[m]	[m]	[m]	[m]	[m]
1	500	250	250	NOTE 4	300	150	150	NOTE 5
0.45	152.4	76.2	76.2		91.4	45.7	45.7	
1.5	500	250	250		300	150	150	
0.68	152.4	76.2	76.2		91.4	45.7	45.7	
2	500	250	250		300	150	150	
0.91	152.4	76.2	76.2		91.4	45.7	45.7	
3	500	250	250		300	150	150	
1.4	152.4	76.2	76.2		91.4	45.7	45.7	
5	500	250	250		300	150	150	
2.3	152.4	76.2	76.2		91.4	45.7	45.7	
7	500	250	250		300	150	150	
3.2	152.4	76.2	76.2		91.4	45.7	45.7	
10	500	250	250		300	150	150	
4.5	152.4	76.2	76.2		91.4	45.7	45.7	
15	500	250	250		300	150	150	
6.8	152.4	76.2	76.2		91.4	45.7	45.7	
20	500	250	250		300	150	150	
9.1	152.4	76.2	76.2		91.4	45.7	45.7	
30	500	250	250		300	150	150	
13.6	152.4	76.2	76.2		91.4	45.7	45.7	
50	500	250	250		300	150	150	
22.7	152.4	76.2	76.2		91.4	45.7	45.7	
70	500	250	250		300	150	150	
31.8	152.4	76.2	76.2		91.4	45.7	45.7	
100	500	250	250		300	150	150	
45.4	152.4	76.2	76.2		91.4	45.7	45.7	
150	500	250	250		300	150	150	
68.0	152.4	76.2	76.2		91.4	45.7	45.7	
200	700	250	250		420	150	150	
90.7	213.6	76.2	76.2		91.4	45.7	45.7	
300	700	250	250		420	150	150	
136.1	213.6	76.2	76.2		128.0	45.7	45.7	
450	700	250	250	↓	420	150	150	↓
204.1	213.6	76.2	76.2		128.0	45.7	45.7	
500	1,250	1,250	1,250	1,250	750	750	750	750
226.8	381.0	381.0	381.0	381.0	228.6	228.6	228.6	228.6
700	1,250	1,250	1,250	1,250	750	750	750	750
317.5	381.0	381.0	381.0	381.0	228.6	228.6	228.6	228.6
1,000	1,250	1,250	1,250	1,250	750	750	750	750
453.6	381.0	381.0	381.0	381.0	228.6	228.6	228.6	228.6

Table AP2.T1. <u>HD 1.1 IBD and PTRD</u> (Table C9.T1.) (continued)

NEWQD	IBD From:				PTRD From:			
	ECM			Other PES[4]	ECM			Other PES[5]
	Front[1,2]	Side[1]	Rear[3]		Front[5,6]	Side[5]	Rear[5]	
(lbs)	(ft)	(ft)	(ft)	(ft)	(ft)	(ft)	(ft)	(ft)
[kg]	*[m]*	*[m]*	*[m]*	*[m]*	*[m]*	*[m]*	*[m]*	*[m]*
1,500	1,250	1,250	1,250	1,250	750	750	750	750
680.4	*381.0*	*381.0*	*381.0*	*381.0*	*228.6*	*228.6*	*228.6*	*228.6*
2,000	1,250	1,250	1,250	1,250	750	750	750	750
907.2	*381.0*	*381.0*	*381.0*	*381.0*	*228.6*	*228.6*	*228.6*	*228.6*
3,000	1,250	1,250	1,250	1,250	750	750	750	750
1,360.8	*381.0*	*381.0*	*381.0*	*381.0*	*228.6*	*228.6*	*228.6*	*228.6*
5,000	1,250	1,250	1,250	1,250	750	750	750	750
2,268.0	*381.0*	*381.0*	*381.0*	*381.0*	*228.6*	*228.6*	*228.6*	*228.6*
7,000	1,250	1,250	1,250	1,250	750	750	750	750
3,175.1	*381.0*	*381.0*	*381.0*	*381.0*	*228.6*	*228.6*	*228.6*	*228.6*
10,000	1,250	1,250	1,250	1,250	750	750	750	750
4,535.9	*381.0*	*381.0*	*381.0*	*381.0*	*228.6*	*228.6*	*228.6*	*228.6*
15,000	1,250	1,250	1,250	1,250	750	750	750	750
6,803.9	*381.0*	*381.0*	*381.0*	*381.0*	*228.6*	*228.6*	*228.6*	*228.6*
20,000	1,250	1,250	1,250	1,250	750	750	750	750
9,071.8	*381.0*	*381.0*	*381.0*	*381.0*	*228.6*	*228.6*	*228.6*	*228.6*
30,000	1,250	1,250	1,250	1,250	750	750	750	750
13,607.7	*381.0*	*381.0*	*381.0*	*381.0*	*228.6*	*228.6*	*228.6*	*228.6*
45,000	1,250	1,250	1,250	1,423	750	750	750	854
20,411.6	*381.0*	*381.0*	*381.0*	*433.7*	*228.6*	*228.6*	*228.6*	*260.3*
50,000	1,289	1,289	1,250	1,474	774	774	750	884
22,679.5	*392.9*	*392.9*	*381.0*	*448.9*	*235.7*	*235.7*	*228.6*	*269.4*
70,000	1,442	1,442	1,250	1,649	865	865	750	989
31,751.3	*439.5*	*439.5*	*381.0*	*502.2*	*263.7*	*263.7*	*228.6*	*301.3*
100,000	1,625	1,625	1,250	1,857	975	975	750	1,114
45,359.0	*495.0*	*495.0*	*381.0*	*565.6*	*297.0*	*297.0*	*228.6*	*339.4*
150,000	2,177	2,177	1,804	2,346	1,306	1,306	1,083	1,408
68,038.5	*663.5*	*663.5*	*550.0*	*715.2*	*398.1*	*398.1*	*330.0*	*429.1*
200,000	2,680	2,680	2,469	2,770	1,608	1,608	1,481	1,662
90,718.0	*816.8*	*816.8*	*752.5*	*844.4*	*490.1*	*490.1*	*451.5*	*506.6*
250,000	3,149	3,149	3,149	3,151	1,889	1,889	1,889	1,891
113,397.5	*959.8*	*959.8*	*959.8*	*960.4*	*575.9*	*575.9*	*575.9*	*576.2*
300,000	3,347	3,347	3,347	3,347	2,008	2,008	2,008	2,008
136,077.0	*1,020.5*	*1,020.5*	*1,020.5*	*1,020.5*	*612.3*	*612.3*	*612.3*	*612.3*
500,000	3,969	3,969	3,969	3,969	2,381	2,381	2,381	2,381
226,795.0	*1,209.9*	*1,209.9*	*1,209.9*	*1,209.9*	*725.9*	*725.9*	*725.9*	*725.9*

Notes for Table AP2.T1. (Table C9.T1. and subparagraph C5.8.1.7.):

1. For NEWQD < 45,000 lbs [20,412 kg], the distance is controlled by fragments. When fragments are absent or if the HFD ($1/600$ ft^2 [$1/55.7$ m^2]) is less than the blast hazard range, then the blast criteria in this note may be used.

    (NEWQD in lbs, d in ft)

NEWQD ≤ 45,000 lbs:	$d = 35NEWQD^{1/3}$	**[EQN C9.T1-1]**
45,000 lbs < NEWQD ≤ 100,000 lbs:	$d = 35NEWQD^{1/3}$	**[EQN C9.T1-2]**
100,000 lbs < NEWQD ≤ 250,000 lbs:	$d = 0.3955NEWQD^{0.7227}$	**[EQN C9.T1-3]**
250,000 lbs < NEWQD:	$d = 50NEWQD^{1/3}$	**[EQN C9.T1-4]**

(NEWQD in kg, d in m)		
$NEWQD \leq 20,412$ *kg:*	$d = 13.88NEWQD^{1/3}$	**[EQN C9.T1-5]**
20,412 kg < NEWQD $\leq$ 45,359 kg:	$d = 13.88NEWQD^{1/3}$	**[EQN C9.T1-6]**
45,359 kg < NEWQD $\leq$ 113,398 kg:	$d = 0.2134NEWQD^{0.7227}$	**[EQN C9.T1-7]**
113,398 kg < NEWQD:	$d = 19.84NEWQD^{1/3}$	**[EQN C9.T1-8]**
(d in ft, NEWQD in lbs)		
$d \leq 1,245$ ft:	$NEWQD = d^3/42,875$	**[EQN C9.T1-9]**
1,245 ft < d $\leq$ 1,625 ft:	$NEWQD = d^3/42,875$	**[EQN C9.T1-10]**
1,625 ft < d $\leq$ 3,150 ft:	$NEWQD = 3.60935d^{1.3837}$	**[EQN C9.T1-11]**
3,150 ft < d:	$NEWQD = d^3/125,000$	**[EQN C9.T1-12]**
(d in m, NEWQD in kg)		
d $\leq$ 379.3 m:	$NEWQD = d^3/2,674.04$	**[EQN C9.T1-13]**
379.3 m < d $\leq$ 495.0 :	$NEWQD = d^3/2,674.04$	**[EQN C9.T1-14]**
495.0 m < d $\leq$ 960.3 m:	$NEWQD = 8.4761d^{1.3837}$	**[EQN C9.T1-15]**
960.3 m < d:	$NEWQD = d^3/7,809.53$	**[EQN C9.T1-16]**

2. IBD for frontal exposures applies to all directions from HPM. The MCE in the HPM is used as the NEWQD. The limit on the design MCE in an HPM is 60,000 lbs [27,215 kg].

3. For NEWQD < 100,000 lbs [45,359 kg], the distance is controlled by fragments and debris. When fragments and debris are absent or the range to a hazardous debris density of $1/600$ ft^2 [$1/55.7$ m^2] is less than the blast hazard range, then the blast criteria may be used.

(NEWQD in lbs, d in ft)		
$NEWQD \leq 100,000$ lbs:	$d = 25NEWQD^{1/3}$	**[EQN C9.T1-17]**
100,000 lbs < NEWQD $\leq$ 250,000 lbs:	$d = 0.004125NEWQD^{1.0893}$	**[EQN C9.T1-18]**
250,000 lbs < NEWQD:	$d = 50NEWQD^{1/3}$	**[EQN C9.T1-19]**
(NEWQD in kg, d in m)		
NEWQD $\leq$ 45,359 kg:	$d = 9.92NEWQD^{1/3}$	**[EQN C9.T1-20]**
45,359 kg < NEWQD $\leq$ 113,398 kg:	$d = 0.002976NEWQD^{1.0893}$	**[EQN C9.T1-21]**
113,398 kg < NEWQD:	$d = 19.84*NEWQD^{1/3}$	**[EQN C9.T1-22]**
(d in ft, NEWQD in lbs)		
$d \leq 1,160$ ft:	$NEWQD = d^3/15,625$	**[EQN C9.T1-23]**
1,160 ft < d $\leq$ 3,150 ft:	$NEWQD = 154.2006d^{0.9750}$	**[EQN C9.T1-24]**
3,150 ft < d:	$NEWQD = d^3/125,000$	**[EQN C9.T1-25]**
(d in m, NEWQD in kg)		
d $\leq$ 353.8 m:	$NEWQD = d^3/976.19$	**[EQN C9.T1-26]**
353.8 m < d $\leq$ 960.3 m:	$NEWQD = 208.0623d^{0.9750}$	**[EQN C9.T1-27]**
960.3 m < d:	$NEWQD = d^3/7,809.53$	**[EQN C9.T1-28]**

4. For NEWQD < 30,000 lbs [< 13,608 kg], the distance is controlled by fragments and debris. Lesser distances may be permitted for certain situations (see subparagraph C5.8.1.7.).

(NEWQD in lbs, d in ft)		
30,000 lbs < NEWQD $\leq$ 100,000 lbs:	$d = 40NEWQD^{1/3}$	**[EQN C9.T1-29]**
100,000 lbs < NEWQD $\leq$ 250,000 lbs:	$d = 2.42NEWQD^{0.577}$	**[EQN C9.T1-30]**
250,000 lbs < NEWQD:	$d = 50NEWQD^{1/3}$	**[EQN C9.T1-31]**
(NEWQD in kg, d in m)		
13,608 kg < NEWQD $\leq$ 45,359 kg:	$d = 15.87NEWQD^{1/3}$	**[EQN C9.T1-32]**
45,359 kg < NEWQD $\leq$ 113,398 kg:	$d = 1.1640NEWQD^{0.577}$	**[EQN C9.T1-33]**
113,398 kg < NEWQD:	$d = 19.84NEWQD^{1/3}$	**[EQN C9.T1-34]**
(d in ft, NEWQD in lbs)		
1,243 ft < d $\leq$ 1,857 ft:	$NEWQD = d^3/64,000$	**[EQN C9.T1-35]**
1,857 ft < d $\leq$ 3,150 ft:	$NEWQD = 0.2162d^{1.7331}$	**[EQN C9.T1-36]**
3,150 ft < d:	$NEWQD = d^3/125,000$	**[EQN C9.T1-37]**
(d in m, NEWQD in kg)		
378.6 m < d $\leq$ 565.6 m:	$NEWQD = d^3/3,989.42$	**[EQN C9.T1-38]**
565.6 m < d $\leq$ 960.3 m:	$NEWQD = 0.7686d^{1.7331}$	**[EQN C9.T1-39]**
960.3 m < d:	$NEWQD = d^3/7,809.53$	**[EQN C9.T1-40]**

5. Computed as 60 percent of applicable IBD.

6. PTRD applies to all directions from HPM. The MCE in the HPM is used as the NEWQD.

Table AP2.T2. <u>HD 1.1 HFD</u> (Table C9.T2.)

NEWQD (lbs) [kg]	OPEN (ft) [m]	STRUCTURE (ft) [m]
≤ 0.5	236	200
≤ 0.23	*71.9*	*61.0*
0.7	263	200
0.3	*80.2*	*61.0*
1	291	200
0.45	*88.8*	*61.0*
2	346	200
0.91	*105.5*	*61.0*
3	378	200
1.4	*115.3*	*61.0*
5	419	200
2.3	*127.7*	*61.0*
7	445	200
3.2	*135.6*	*61.0*
10	474	200
4.5	*144.4*	*61.0*
15	506	200
6.8	*154.2*	*61.0*
20	529	200
9.1	*161.1*	*61.0*
30	561	200
13.6	*170.9*	*61.0*
31	*563.0*	200
14.1	*171.7*	*61.0*
50	601	388
22.7	*183.2*	*118.2*
70	628	519
31.8	*191.3*	*158.1*
100	658	658
45.4	*200.4*	*200.4*
150	815	815
68.0	*248.5*	*248.5*
200	927	927
90.7	*282.6*	*282.6*
300	1085	1085
136.1	*330.6*	*330.6*
450	1243	1243
204.1	*378.7*	*378.7*
> 450	1250	1250
>204.1	*381.0*	*381.0*

Notes for Table AP2.T2. (Table C9.T2. and subparagraph C5.8.1.7.):

(1) OPEN

NEWQD < 100 lbs: $\quad$ HFD = 291.3 + [79.2 x ln(NEWQD)]; $\quad$ **[EQN C9.T2-1]**

NEWQD ≥ 100 lbs: $\quad$ HFD = -1133.9 + [389 x ln(NEWQD)]; $\quad$ **[EQN C9.T2-2]**

NEWQD in lbs, HFD in ft, with a minimum distance of 236 ft; ln is natural logarithm.

NEWQD < 45.4 kg: $\quad$ HFD = 107.87 + [24.14 x ln(NEWQD)]; $\quad$ **[EQN C9.T2-3]**

NEWQD ≥ 45.4 kg: $\quad$ HFD = -251.87 + [118.56 x ln(NEWQD)]; $\quad$ **[EQN C9.T2-4]**

NEWQD in kg, HFD in m, with a minimum distance of 71.9 m; ln is natural logarithm.

(2) OPEN

HFD < 658 ft: $\quad$ NEWQD = exp [(HFD/79.2) - 3.678]; $\quad$ **[EQN C9.T2-5]**

658 ft ≤ HFD < 1250 ft: $\quad$ NEWQD = exp [(HFD/389) + 2.914]; $\quad$ **[EQN C9.T2-6]**

NEWQD in lbs, HFD in ft; exp [x] is e^x.

HFD < 200.5 m: $\quad$ NEWQD = exp [(HFD/24.14) – 4.4685]; $\quad$ **[EQN C9.T2-7]**

200.5 m ≤ HFD < 381 m: $\quad$ NEWQD = exp [(HFD/118.56) + 2.1244]; $\quad$ **[EQN C9.T2-8]**

NEWQD in kg, HFD in m; exp [x] is e^x.

(3) STRUCTURES

NEWQD ≤ 31 lbs $\quad$ HFD = 200 ft

31 lbs < NEWQD ≤ 450 lbs $\quad$ HFD = -1133.9 + [389 x ln(NEWQD)]; $\quad$ **[EQN C9.T2-9]**

NEWQD in lbs, HFD in ft; ln is natural logarithm.

NEWQD ≤ 14.1 kg $\quad$ HFD = 61.0 m

14.1 kg < NEWQD ≤ 204.1 kg $\quad$ HFD = -251.87 + [118.56 x ln(NEWQD)]; $\quad$ **[EQN C9.T2-10]**

NEWQD in kg, HFD in m; ln is natural logarithm.

(4) STRUCTURES

HFD ≤ 200 ft $\quad$ NEWQD ≤ 31 lbs

200 ft < HFD ≤ 1250 ft $\quad$ NEWQD = exp[(HFD/389) + 2.914] $\quad$ **[EQN C9.T2-11]**

NEWQD in lbs, HFD in ft, exp [x] is e^x

HFD ≤ 61.0 m $\quad$ NEWQD ≤ 14.1 kg

61.0 m < HFD ≤ 381.0 m $\quad$ NEWQD = exp[(HFD/118.56) + 2.2144] $\quad$ **[EQN C9.T2-12]**

NEWQD in kg, HFD in m, exp [x] is e^x

(5) Use of equations given in Notes (1) through (4), to determine other HFD-NEWQD combinations, is allowed.

(6) PTRD is 60 percent of HFD.

Table AP2.T3. <u>HFD for Open Stacks of Selected HD 1.1 AE</u>
(Table C9.T3.)

Nomenclature[a]	Number of Units									
	1	2	3	4	5	6	7	8	9	10
Sparrow, AIM-7[b]	280	565	770	955	1120	1245				
	85.3	*172.2*	*234.7*	*291.1*	*341.4*	*379.5*				
Sidewinder, AIM-9	400	400	400	400	400	400	400	400	400	400[1]
	121.9	*121.9*	*121.9*	*121.9*	*121.9*	*121.9*	*121.9*	*121.9*	*121.9*	*121.9[1]*
Chaparral, MIM-72H	400	400	400	400	400	400	400	400	400	400[1]
	121.9	*121.9*	*121.9*	*121.9*	*121.9*	*121.9*	*121.9*	*121.9*	*121.9*	*121.9[1]*
Maverick, AGM 65 A/B/D	400	500	500							
	121.9	*121.9*	*152.4*							
Maverick, AGM 65 E/F/G	670	900[2]	1200[2]							
	204.2	*274.3[2]*	*365.8[2]*							
ASROC	500	500	500							
	152.4	*152.4*	*152.4*							
CBU-87*	800	800	910	945	965	982	1000	1020	1035	1055[3]
	243.8	*243.8*	*277.4*	*288.0*	*291.4*	*299.3*	*304.8*	*310.9*	*315.5*	*321.6[3]*
Improved Hawk	900	900	900	900	900	900	900	900	900	900[1]
	274.3	*274.3*	*274.3*	*274.3*	*274.3*	*274.3*	*274.3*	*274.3*	*274.3*	*274.3[1]*
Penguin*	500	500	500							
	152.4	*152.4*	*152.4*							
Projectile, 105 mm[c]	340	355	525	660	725	775	810	845	870	890[3]
	103.6	*108.2*	*160.0*	*201.2*	*221.0*	*236.2*	*246.9*	*257.6*	*265.2*	*271.3[3]*
Projectile, 155 mm	415	590	770	955	1035	1095	1145	1195	1235	
	126.5	*179.8*	*234.7*	*291.1*	*315.5*	*333.8*	*349.0*	*364.2*	*376.4*	
Projectile, 5"/54	300	375	475	570	680	790	860	925	1005	1085
	91.4	*114.3*	*144.8*	*173.7*	*207.3*	*240.8*	*262.1*	*281.9*	*306.3*	*330.7*
Harpoon*	500	600[4]	600[4]	600[4]						
	152.4	*182.9[4]*	*182.9[4]*	*182.9[4]*						
Tomahawk*	500	600[4]	600[4]	600[4]						
	152.4	*182.9[4]*	*182.9[4]*	*182.9[4]*						
Bomb, 500-pound, MK 82	670									
	204.2									
Bomb, 1000-pound, MK 83	815									
	248.4									
Bomb, 2000-pound, MK 84	925									
	281.9									
Bomb, BLU-109	880									
	268.2									
Bomb, 750-pound, M117	690									
	210.3									
Torpedo, MK 46	500	500	500	500	500	500	500	500		
	152.4	*152.4*	*152.4*	*152.4*	*152.4*	*152.4*	*152.4*	*152.4*		
Torpedo, MK 48[d,e] (motor vehicles, unshielded)	630	775	875	925						
	192.0	*236.2*	*266.7*	*281.9*						
Torpedo, MK 48[d,f]	500	500	550	600	635	670	700	725	755	780[3]
	152.4	*152.4*	*167.6*	*182.9*	*193.5*	*204.2*	*213.4*	*221.0*	*230.1*	*237.7[3]*

Notes for Table AP2.T3. (Table C9.T3.):

1. Ten units or more until the point is reached at which this distance is exceeded by the distance requirements of Table C9.T1.
2. Use the distance shown only where there are less than 25 unrelated people exposed in any arc encompassing 45 degrees from 900 ft [274 m] to 1250 ft [381 m] from the PES.
3. More than 10 units may be involved before 1250 ft [381 m] is exceeded. For distances involving more than 10 units, consult the applicable Service guidance.
4. When handling more than one missile, the missiles must be transported or handled in a nose-to-tail configuration and in their launch capsule or shipping container; furthermore, they must be aligned and handled so that each group of two missiles is located outside of the warhead fragment beam spray region of the other two missiles.

General Comments for Table AP2.T3. (Table C9.T3.):

(a) Items identified by an asterisk "*" include fragments from shipping or storage container(s). However, all of the HFD in this table may be applied to both packaged and unpackaged configurations.
(b) Those items with WAU-17 warhead.
(c) 105-mm projectiles and 105-mm complete rounds not in standard storage or shipping containers are HD 1.1.
(d) All Modification (includes Torpedo MK48 ADCAP).
(e) These distances must be used when handling torpedo(es) from motor vehicles where sandbag (or other equivalent) shielding (as described in Note (f)) is not present between the leading edge of the torpedo(es) warhead and the motor vehicle engine compartment/crew cab to prevent the engine compartment/crew cab from contributing to the debris.
(f) These distances may be used when handling torpedo(es) from:
  (i) Motor vehicles with sandbag (or other equivalent) shielding between the leading edge of the torpedo(es) warhead and the motor vehicle engine compartment/crew cab to prevent the engine compartment/crew cab from contributing to the debris, or
  [Note: Sandbag shield requirement is equivalent to a minimum thickness of 2 ft [0.61 m] of sand between the engine compartment/crew cab and the torpedo(es). The sandbags must shield all parts of the engine compartment/crew cab from the torpedo warhead.]
  (ii) Other means of transport such as boats, torpedo transporters, forklifts, or portable cranes.

APPENDIX 2

Table AP2.T4. <u>HD 1.1 ILD from ECM</u> (Table C9.T4.)

NEWQD	Barricaded			Unbarricaded		
	Front[1]	Side[2]	Rear[3]	Front[4]	Side[5]	Rear[6]
(lbs)	(ft)	(ft)	(ft)	(ft)	(ft)	(ft)
[kg]	[m]	[m]	[m]	[m]	[m]	[m]
50	37	26	22	66	59	44
22.7	11.2	7.9	6.7	20.2	18.0	13.5
70	41	29	25	74	66	49
31.8	12.6	8.8	7.5	22.6	20.1	15.1
100	46	32	28	84	74	56
45.4	14.2	9.9	8.5	25.5	22.6	17.0
150	53	37	32	96	85	64
68.0	16.2	11.3	9.7	29.1	25.9	19.4
200	58	41	35	105	94	70
90.7	17.8	12.5	10.7	32.1	28.5	21.4
300	67	47	40	120	107	80
136.1	20.4	14.3	12.2	36.7	32.7	24.5
500	79	56	48	143	127	95
226.8	24.2	17.0	14.5	43.5	38.7	29.0
700	89	62	53	160	142	107
317.5	27.1	19.0	16.2	48.7	43.3	32.5
1,000	100	70	60	180	160	120
453.6	30.5	21.4	18.3	54.9	48.8	36.6
1,500	114	80	69	206	183	137
680.4	34.9	24.5	20.9	62.8	55.9	41.9
2,000	126	88	76	227	202	151
907.2	38.4	26.9	23.0	69.1	61.5	46.1
3,000	144	101	87	260	231	173
1,360.8	44.0	30.8	26.4	79.1	70.4	52.7
5,000	171	120	103	308	274	205
2,268.0	52.2	36.5	31.3	93.8	83.4	62.5
7,000	191	134	115	344	306	230
3,175.1	58.4	40.9	35.0	104.9	93.3	70.0
10,000	215	151	129	388	345	259
4,535.9	65.7	46.0	39.4	118.2	105.1	78.8
15,000	247	173	148	444	395	296
6,803.9	75.2	52.7	45.1	135.3	120.3	90.2
20,000	271	190	163	489	434	326
9,071.8	82.8	58.0	49.6	148.9	132.4	99.3
30,000	311	218	186	559	497	373
13,607.7	94.8	66.4	56.8	170.5	151.6	113.6
50,000	368	258	221	663	589	442
22,679.5	112.4	78.7	67.4	202.1	179.7	134.7

APPENDIX 2

Table AP2.T4. <u>HD 1.1 ILD from ECM</u> (Table C9.T4.) (continued)

NEWQD	Barricaded			Unbarricaded		
	Front[1]	Side[2]	Rear[3]	Front[4]	Side[5]	Rear[6]
(lbs)	(ft)	(ft)	(ft)	(ft)	(ft)	(ft)
[kg]	[m]	[m]	[m]	[m]	[m]	[m]
70,000	412	288	247	742	659	495
31,751.3	125.7	88.0	75.4	226.1	201.1	150.7
100,000	464	325	278	835	743	557
45,359.0	141.6	99.1	84.9	254.6	226.5	169.8
150,000	531	372	319	956	850	653
68,038.5	162.1	113.5	97.2	291.5	259.2	199.1
200,000	585	409	351	1,053	936	746
90,718.0	178.4	124.9	106.9	320.8	285.3	227.4
300,000	669	469	402	1,205	1,071	937
136,077.0	204.2	143.0	122.4	367.2	326.6	285.7
500,000	715	714	714	1,429	1,429	1,429
226,795.0	218.0	217.7	217.7	435.4	435.4	435.4

<u>Notes for Table AP2.T4. (Table C9.T4.):</u>

1. (NEWQD in lbs, d in ft)

   NEWQD $\leq$ 300,000 lbs $\quad$ $d = 10*NEWQD^{1/3}$ $\qquad$ [EQN C9.T4-1]

   300,000 lbs < NEWQD $\leq$ 500,000 lbs $\quad$ $d = (13.659 - 1.6479 \times 10^{-5}*NEWQD + 1.4358 \times 10^{-11}* NEWQD^2)*$
   $NEWQD^{1/3}$ $\qquad$ [EQN C9.T4-2]

   $d \leq 669$ ft $\quad$ $NEWQD = d^3/1000$ $\qquad$ [EQN C9.T4-3]

   669 ft < $d \leq$ 715 ft $\quad$ $NEWQD = 1.50138 \times 10^8 - 6.73914 \times 10^5 *d + 1002.9*d^2 - 0.4938*d^3$
   $\qquad$ [EQN C9.T4-4]

   (NEWQD in kg, d in m)

   NEWQD $\leq$ 136,077 kg $\quad$ $d = 3.97*NEWQD^{1/3}$ $\qquad$ [EQN C9.T4-5]

   136,077 kg < NEWQD $\leq$ 226,795 kg $\quad$ $d = (5.419 - 1.4410 \times 10^{-5}*NEWQD + 2.7684 \times 10^{-11}* NEWQD^2)*NEWQD^{1/3}$
   $\qquad$ [EQN C9.T4-6]

   $d \leq$ 204.2 m $\quad$ $NEWQD = d^3/62.429$ $\qquad$ [EQN C9.T4-7]

   204.2 < $d \leq$ 218.0 m $\quad$ $NEWQD = 6.80924 \times 10^7 - 1.002764 \times 10^6*d + 4895.93*d^2 - 7.90884*d^3$
   $\qquad$ [EQN C9.T4-8]

2. (NEWQD in lbs, d in ft)

   NEWQD $\leq$ 300,000 lbs $\quad$ $d = 7*NEWQD^{1/3}$ $\qquad$ [EQN C9.T4-9]

   300,000 lbs < NEWQD $\leq$ 400,000 lbs $\quad$ $d = (1.0848 + 1.986 \times 10^{-5}*NEWQD)*NEWQD^{1/3}$ $\qquad$ [EQN C9.T4-10]

   NEWQD > 400,000 lbs $\quad$ $d = 9*NEWQD^{1/3}$ $\qquad$ [EQN C9.T4-11]

   $d \leq$ 469 ft $\quad$ $NEWQD = d^3/343$ $\qquad$ [EQN C9.T4-12]

   469 ft < $d \leq$ 663 ft $\quad$ $NEWQD = 57,424 + 515.89*d$ $\qquad$ [EQN C9.T4-13]

   d > 663 ft $\quad$ $NEWQD = d^3/729$ $\qquad$ [EQN C9.T4-14]

   (NEWQD in kg, d in m)

   NEWQD $\leq$ 136,077 kg $\quad$ $d = 2.78*NEWQD^{1/3}$ $\qquad$ [EQN C9.T4-15]

   136,077 kg < NEWQD $\leq$ 181,434 kg $\quad$ $d = (0.4303 + 1.7369 \times 10^{-5}*NEWQD)*NEWQD^{1/3}$ $\qquad$ [EQN C9.T4-16]

   NEWQD > 181,436 kg $\quad$ $d = 3.57*NEWQD^{1/3}$ $\qquad$ [EQN C9.T4-17]

   $d \leq$ 143.7 m $\quad$ $NEWQD = d^3/21.413$ $\qquad$ [EQN C9.T4-18]

   143.7 m < $d \leq$ 202.8 m $\quad$ $NEWQD = 26,048 + 767.73*d$ $\qquad$ [EQN C9.T4-19]

   d > 202.8 m $\quad$ $NEWQD = d^3/45.511$ $\qquad$ [EQN C9.T4-20]

3. (NEWQD in lbs, d in ft)

   NEWQD $\leq$ 300,000 lbs $\quad$ $d = 6*NEWQD^{1/3}$ $\qquad$ [EQN C9.T4-21]

   300,000 lbs < NEWQD $\leq$ 400,000 lbs $\quad$ $d = (-3.059 + 3.0228 \times 10^{-5}*NEWQD)*NEWQD^{1/3}$ $\qquad$ [EQN C9.T4-22]

   NEWQD > 400,000 lbs $\quad$ $d = 9*NEWQD^{1/3}$ $\qquad$ [EQN C9.T4-23]

   $d \leq$ 402 ft $\quad$ $NEWQD = d^3/216$ $\qquad$ [EQN C9.T4-24]

402 ft < d $\leq$ 665 ft	NEWQD = 148,160 + 379.7*d	**[EQN C9.T4-25]**
d > 665 ft	NEWQD = d^3/729	**[EQN C9.T4-26]**
(NEWQD in kg, d in m)		
NEWQD $\leq$ 136,077 kg	d = 2.38*NEWQD$^{1/3}$	**[EQN C9.T4-27]**
136,077 kg < NEWQD $\leq$ 181,436 kg	d = (-1.2135 + 2.6437 x 10^{-5}*NEWQD)*NEWQD$^{1/3}$	**[EQN C9.T4-28]**
NEWQD > 181,436 kg	d = 3.57*NEWQD$^{1/3}$	**[EQN C9.T4-29]**
d $\leq$ 122.6 m	NEWQD = d^3/13.485	**[EQN C9.T4-30]**
122.6 m < d $\leq$ 202.8 m	NEWQD = 67,206 + 565.05*d	**[EQN C9.T4-31]**
d > 202.8 m	NEWQD = d^3/45.511	**[EQN C9.T4-32]**

4. (NEWQD in lbs, d in ft)

NEWQD $\leq$ 500,000 lbs	d = 18*NEWQD$^{1/3}$	**[EQN C9.T4-33]**
d $\leq$ 1429 ft	NEWQD = d^3/5,832	**[EQN C9.T4-34]**
(NEWQD in kg, d in m)		
NEWQD $\leq$ 226,795 kg	d = 7.14*NEWQD$^{1/3}$	**[EQN C9.T4-35]**
d > 435.4 m	NEWQD = d^3/364.086	**[EQN C9.T4-36]**

5. (NEWQD in lbs, d in ft)

NEWQD $\leq$ 300,000 lbs	d = 16*NEWQD$^{1/3}$	**[EQN C9.T4-37]**
300,000 lbs < NEWQD $\leq$ 400,000 lbs	d = (9.9683 + 2.0135 x 10^{-5}*NEWQD)*NEWQD$^{1/3}$	**[EQN C9.T4-38]**
NEWQD > 400,000 lbs	d = 18*NEWQD$^{1/3}$	**[EQN C9.T4-39]**
d $\leq$ 1071 ft	NEWQD = d^3/4,096	**[EQN C9.T4-40]**
1071 ft < d $\leq$ 1328 ft	NEWQD = -118,180 + 390.35*d	**[EQN C9.T4-41]**
d > 1328 ft	NEWQD = d^3/5,832	**[EQN C9.T4-42]**
(NEWQD in kg, d in m)		
NEWQD $\leq$ 136,077 kg	d = 6.35*NEWQD$^{1/3}$	**[EQN C9.T4-43]**
136,077 kg < NEWQD $\leq$ 181,436 kg	d = (3.9544 + 1.76097 x 10^{-5}*NEWQD)*NEWQD$^{1/3}$	**[EQN C9.T4-44]**
NEWQD > 181,436 kg	d = 7.14*NEWQD$^{1/3}$	**[EQN C9.T4-45]**
d $\leq$ 326.6 m	NEWQD = d^3/255.709	**[EQN C9.T4-46]**
122.6 m < d $\leq$ 202.8 m	NEWQD = -53,605 + 580.89*d	**[EQN C9.T4-47]**
d > 404.7 m	NEWQD = d^3/364.086	**[EQN C9.T4-48]**

6. (NEWQD in lbs, d in ft)

NEWQD $\leq$ 100,000 lbs	d = 12*NEWQD$^{1/3}$	**[EQN C9.T4-49]**
100,000 lbs < NEWQD $\leq$ 300,000 lbs	d = (11.521 + 1.9918 x 10^{-6}*NEWQD + 2.0947 x 10^{-11}* NEWQD^2)* NEWQD$^{1/3}$	**[EQN C9.T4-50]**
300,000 lbs < NEWQD $\leq$ 400,000 lbs	d = (1.9389+ 4.0227 x 10^{-5}*NEWQD)* NEWQD$^{1/3}$	**[EQN C9.T4-51]**
NEWQD > 400,000 lbs	d = 18*NEWQD$^{1/3}$	**[EQN C9.T4-52]**
d $\leq$ 557 ft	NEWQD = d^3/1,728	**[EQN C9.T4-53]**
557 ft < d $\leq$ 938 ft	NEWQD = -193,080+526.83*d	**[EQN C9.T4-54]**
938 ft < d $\leq$ 1328 ft	NEWQD = 60,778 + 255.83*d	**[EQN C9.T4-55]**
d > 1328 ft	NEWQD = d^3/5,832	**[EQN C9.T4-56]**
(NEWQD in kg, d in m)		
NEWQD $\leq$ 45,359 kg lbs	d = 4.76*NEWQD$^{1/3}$	**[EQN C9.T4-57]**
45,359 kg < NEWQD $\leq$ 136,077 kg	d = (4.5704 + 1.7420 x 10^{-6}*NEWQD + 4.0389 x 10^{-11}* NEWQD^2)* NEWQD$^{1/3}$	**[EQN C9.T4-58]**
136,077 kg < NEWQD $\leq$ 181,436 kg	d = (0.7692+ 3.5182 x 10^{-5}*NEWQD)* NEWQD$^{1/3}$	**[EQN C9.T4-59]**
NEWQD 181,436 kg	d = 7.14*NEWQD$^{1/3}$	**[EQN C9.T4-60]**
d $\leq$ 169.8 m	NEWQD = d^3/107.877	**[EQN C9.T4-61]**
169.8 m < d $\leq$ 285.7 m	NEWQD = -87,578 + 784.00*d	**[EQN C9.T4-62]**
285.7 m < d $\leq$ 404.7 m	NEWQD = 27,568 + 380.7*d	**[EQN C9.T4-63]**
d > 404.7 m	NEWQD = d^3/364.086	**[EQN C9.T4-64]**

APPENDIX 2

Table AP2.T5. <u>HD 1.1 ILD</u> (Table C9.T5.)

NEWQD (lbs) [kg]	BARRICADED DISTANCE[1] (ft) [m]	UNBARRICADED DISTANCE[2] (ft) [m]
50[3]	33	66
22.7[3]	10.1	20.2
70	37	74
31.8	11.3	22.6
100	42	84
45.4	12.7	25.5
150	48	96
68.0	14.6	29.1
200	53	105
90.7	16.0	32.1
300	60	120
136.1	18.4	36.7
500	71	143
226.8	21.8	43.5
700	80	160
317.5	24.4	48.7
1,000	90	180
453.6	27.4	54.9
1,500	103	206
680.4	31.4	62.8
2,000	113	227
907.2	34.6	69.1
3,000	130	260
1,360.8	39.6	79.1
5,000	154	308
2,268.0	46.9	93.8
7,000	172	344
3,175.1	52.5	104.9
10,000	194	388
4,535.9	59.1	118.2
15,000	222	444
6,803.9	67.6	135.3
20,000	244	489
9,071.8	74.5	148.9
30,000	280	559
13,607.7	85.2	170.5

APPENDIX 2

Table AP2.T5. <u>HD 1.1 ILD</u> (Table C9.T5.) (continued)

NEWQD (lbs) [kg]	BARRICADED DISTANCE[1] (ft) [m]	UNBARRICADED DISTANCE[2] (ft) [m]
50,000	332	663
22,679.5	101.1	202.1
70,000	371	742
31,751.3	113.0	226.1
100,000	418	835
45,359.0	127.3	254.6
150,000	478	956
68,038.5	145.7	291.5
200,000	526	1,053
90,718.0	160.4	320.8
300,000	602	1,205
136,077.0	183.6	367.2
500,000[4]	714	1,429
226,795.0[4]	217.7	435.4
700,000	799	1,598
317,513.0	243.6	487.1
1,000,000	900	1,800
453,590.0	274.3	548.6
1,500,000	1,030	2,060
680,385.0	314.0	628.0
2,000,000	1,134	2,268
907,180.0	345.6	691.2
3,000,000	1,298	2,596
1,360,770.0	395.6	791.2
5,000,000	1,539	3,078
2,267,950.0	469.0	938.1

Notes for Table AP2.T5. (Table C9.T5.):

1. (d in ft, NEWQD in lbs)

$$d = 9*NEWQD^{1/3} \qquad \text{[EQN C9.T5-1]}$$

  (d in m, NEWQD in kg)

$$d = 3.57*NEWQD^{1/3} \qquad \text{[EQN C9.T5-2]}$$

  (NEWQD in lbs, d in ft)

$$NEWQD = d^3/729 \qquad \text{[EQN C9.T5-3]}$$

  (NEWQD in kg, d in m)

$$NEWQD = d^3/45.511 \qquad \text{[EQN C9.T5-4]}$$

2.   (d in ft, NEWQD in lbs)

$$d = 18*NEWQD^{1/3} \qquad \text{[EQN C9.T5-5]}$$

(d in m, NEWQD in kg)

$$d = 7.14*NEWQD^{1/3} \qquad \text{[EQN C9.T5-6]}$$

(NEWQD in lbs, d in ft)

$$NEWQD = d^3/5,832 \qquad \text{[EQN C9.T5-7]}$$

(NEWQD in kg, d in m)

$$NEWQD = d^3/364.086 \qquad \text{[EQN C9.T5-8]}$$

3.   For less than 50 lbs [22.7 kg], less distance may be used when structures, blast mats, and the like can completely contain fragments and debris. This table is not applicable when blast, fragments, and debris are completely confined, as in certain test firing barricades.

4.   Quantities above 500,000 lbs [226,795 kg] NEWQD are authorized only for HD 1.1 energetic liquids.

Table AP2.T6. HD 1.1 IMD Hazard Factors (Table C9.T6.)

To EXPOSED SITE (ES)		From POTENTIAL EXPLOSION SITE (PES)									
		ECM[1]				AGM[2]		Modules and/or Cells		HPM[3,9]	
		S	R	FB	FU	B	U	B	U	S	F[4]
ECM (7-Bar)	S	1 25 / 0.50	1 25 / 0.50	2 75 / 1.09	2 75 / 1.09	4 5 / 1.79	4 5 / 1.79	4 5 / 1.79	4 5 / 1.79	1 25 / 0.50	2 75 / 1.09
	R	1 25 / 0.50	1 25 / 0.50	2 / 0.79	2 / 0.79	4 5 / 1.79	4 5 / 1.79	4 5 / 1.79	4 5 / 1.79	1 25 / 0.50	2 / 0.79
	FU	2 75 / 1.09	2 / 0.79	6 / 2.38	6 / 2.38	6 / 2.38	6 / 2.38	6 / 2.38	6 / 2.38	2 75 / 1.09	6 / 2.38
	FB[5]	2 75 / 1.09	2 / 0.79	4 5 / 1.79	6 / 2.38	4 5 / 1.79	6 / 2.38	4 5 / 2.38	6 / 2.38	2 75 / 1.09	6 / 2.38
ECM (3-Bar)	S	1 25 / 0.50	1 25 / 0.50	2 75 / 1.09	2 75 / 1.09	6 / 2.38	6 / 2.38	6 / 2.38	6 / 2.38	1 25 / 0.50	2 75 / 1.09
	R	1 25 / 0.50	1 25 / 0.50	2 / 0.79	2 / 0.79	6 / 2.38	6 / 2.38	6 / 2.38	6 / 2.38	1 25 / 0.50	2 / 0.79
	FU	4 5 / 1.79	4 5 / 1.79	6 / 3.57	9 / 3.57	6 / 2.38	9 / 3.57	6 / 2.38	9 / 3.57	4 5 / 1.79	9 / 3.57
	FB[5]	4 5 / 1.79	4 5 / 1.79	6 / 2.38	6 / 2.38	6 / 2.38	6 / 2.38	6 / 2.38	6 / 2.38	4 5 / 1.79	6 / 2.38
ECM (Undefined)	S	1 25[6] / 0.50[6]; 2[7] / 0.79[7]	1 25[6] / 0.50[6]; 2[7] / 0.79[7]	4 5[6] / 1.79[6]; 6[7] / 2.38[7]	4 5[6] / 1.79[6]; 6[7] / 2.38[7]	6 / 2.38	6 / 2.38	6 / 2.38	6 / 2.38	1 25 / 0.50	4 5 / 1.79
	R	1 25 / 0.50	1 25 / 0.50	2 / 0.79	2 / 0.79	6 / 2.38	6 / 2.38	6 / 2.38	6 / 2.38	1 25 / 0.50	2 / 0.79
	FU	6 / 2.38	6 / 2.38	6 / 2.38	11 / 4.36	6 / 2.38	11 / 4.36	6 / 2.38	11 / 2.38	6 / 2.38	11 / 4.36
	FB[5]	6 / 2.38	6 / 2.38	6 / 2.38	6 / 2.38	6 / 2.38	6 / 2.38	6 / 2.38	6 / 2.38	6 / 2.38	6 / 2.38
AGM	U	6 / 2.38	6 / 2.38	6 / 2.38	11 / 4.36	6 / 2.38	11 / 4.36	6 / 2.38	11 / 2.38	6 / 2.38	11 / 4.36
	B	6 / 2.38	6 / 2.38	6 / 2.38	6 / 2.38	6 / 2.38	6 / 2.38	6 / 2.38	6 / 2.38	6 / 2.38	6 / 2.38
Modules and/or Cells	U	6 / 2.38	6 / 2.38	6 / 2.38	11 / 4.36	6 / 2.38	11 / 4.36	1 1[8] / 0.44[8]	11 / 4.36	6 / 2.38	
	B	1 25 / 0.50	1 25 / 0.50	6 / 2.38	6 / 2.38	6 / 2.38	6 / 2.38	1 1[8] / 0.44[8]	1 1[8] / 0.44[8]	1 25 / 0.50	6 / 2.38
HPM	S,F[9]	1 25 / 0.50	1 25 / 0.50	2 75 / 1.09	2 75 / 1.09	4 5 / 1.79	4 5 / 1.79	4 5 / 1.79	4 5 / 1.79	1 25 / 0.50	2 75 / 1.09

Legend for Table AP2.T6. (Table C9.T6.):

S—Side; **R**—Rear; **F**—Front: **B**—Barricaded; **U**—Unbarricaded; **FU**—Front Unbarricaded; **FB**—Front Barricaded.
ECM—earth-covered magazine (7-bar, 3-bar, or undefined, which refers to the structural strength of the headwall and door(s)).
AGM—aboveground magazine
HPM—high performance magazine

Notes for Table AP2.T6. (Table C9.T6.):

1. Descriptions of ECMs are in DoD 6055.9-STD paragraph C5.2.1.
2. AGMs are all types of above grade (non earth-covered) magazines or storage pads.

3. A description of an HPM can be found in Reference (c) at paragraph C5.2 4. Additional information is provided in Reference (c), subparagraph C9.4.1.3. The MCE in an HPM is limited to a maximum of 60,000 lbs [27,216 kg].
4. The unbarricaded front (entrance to loading area) is a factor when the HPM is the PES because the MCE includes AE in the loading area. The hazard factors have been determined accordingly.
5. Those barricades serve to mitigate both fragments and overpressure hazards. (See C5.18.17. for their requirements.)
6. Use this K-factor for NEWQD in PESs up to 250,000 lbs [113,398 kg].
7. Use this K-factor for NEWQD in PESs greater than 250,000 lbs [113,398 kg].
8. Modules and cells are defined in Reference (c), paragraph C5.2.2.
9. The storage areas in the HPM are barricaded on all sides and protected by a reinforced concrete cover. All directions are, therefore, considered to be Side (S) orientations when it is the ES. For siting purposes, an HPM has no "Rear" (R) sector. See Reference (c), Figure C9.F8., for an illustration of the front and side sectors of an HPM.

Table AP2.T7. QD For HD 1.1 AE For K = 1.1, 1.25, 2, 2.75. 4.5, and 5 (Table C9.T7A.)

NEWQD	Hazard Factor, K					
	1.1	1.25	2	2.75	4.5	5
	0.44	*0.50*	*0.79*	*1.09*	*1.79*	*1.98*
(lbs)	$(ft/lb^{1/3})$	$(ft/lb^{1/3})$	$(ft/lb^{1/3})$	$(ft/lb^{1/3})$	$(ft/lb^{1/3})$	$(ft/lb^{1/3})$
[kg]	$[m/kg^{1/3}]$	$[m/kg^{1/3}]$	$[m/kg^{1/3}]$	$[m/kg^{1/3}]$	$[m/kg^{1/3}]$	$[m/kg^{1/3}]$
100	7.0	7.0	9.3	13	21	23
45.4	*2.1*	*2.1*	*2.8*	*3.9*	*6.4*	*7.1*
150	7.0	7.0	11	15	24	27
68.0	*2.1*	*2.1*	*3.2*	*4.4*	*7.3*	*8.1*
200	7.0	7.3	12	16	26	29
90.7	*2.1*	*2.2*	*3.5*	*4.9*	*8.0*	*8.9*
300	7.4	8.4	13	18	30	33
136.1	*2.3*	*2.6*	*4.1*	*5.6*	*9.2*	*10.2*
500	8.7	9.9	16	22	36	40
226.8	*2.7*	*3.0*	*4.8*	*6.6*	*10.9*	*12.1*
700	9.8	11	18	24	40	44
317.5	*3.0*	*3.4*	*5.4*	*7.4*	*12.2*	*13.5*
1,000	11	13	20	27	45	50
453.6	*3.4*	*3.8*	*6.1*	*8.4*	*13.8*	*15.2*
1,500	13	14	23	31	52	57
680.4	*3.9*	*4.4*	*6.9*	*9.6*	*15.7*	*17.4*
2,000	14	16	25	35	57	63
907.2	*4.3*	*4.8*	*7.6*	*10.6*	*17.3*	*19.2*
3,000	16	18	29	40	65	72
1,360.8	*4.9*	*5.5*	*8.8*	*12.1*	*19.8*	*21.9*

Table AP2.T7. <u>QD For HD 1.1 AE For K = 1.1, 1.25, 2, 2.75, 4.5, and 5</u> (Table C9.T7A.)
(continued)

NEWQD	Hazard Factor, K					
	1.1	**1.25**	**2**	**2.75**	**4.5**	**5**
	0.44	*0.50*	*0.79*	*1.09*	*1.79*	*1.98*
(lbs)	(ft/lb$^{1/3}$)	(ft/lb$^{1/3}$)	(ft/lb$^{1/3}$)	(ft/lb$^{1/3}$)	(ft/lb$^{1/3}$)	(ft/lb$^{1/3}$)
[kg]	*[m/kg$^{1/3}$]*	*[m/kg$^{1/3}$]*	*[m/kg$^{1/3}$]*	*[m/kg$^{1/3}$]*	*[m/kg$^{1/3}$]*	*[m/kg$^{1/3}$]*
5,000	19	21	34	47	77	85
2,268.0	*5.8*	*6.6*	*10.4*	*14.3*	*23.5*	*26.0*
7,000	21	24	38	53	86	96
3,175.1	*6.5*	*7.3*	*11.6*	*16.0*	*26.3*	*29.1*
10,000	24	27	43	59	97	108
4,535.9	*7.3*	*8.3*	*13.1*	*18.0*	*29.6*	*32.8*
15,000	27	31	49	68	111	123
6,803.9	*8.3*	*9.5*	*15.0*	*20.7*	*33.9*	*37.5*
20,000	30	34	54	75	122	136
9,071.8	*9.2*	*10.4*	*16.5*	*22.7*	*37.3*	*41.3*
30,000	34	39	62	85	140	155
13,607.7	*10.5*	*11.9*	*18.9*	*26.0*	*42.7*	*47.3*
50,000	41	46	74	101	166	184
22,679.5	*12.5*	*14.2*	*22.4*	*30.9*	*50.7*	*56.0*
70,000	45	52	82	113	185	206
31,751.3	*13.9*	*15.8*	*25.0*	*34.5*	*56.7*	*62.7*
100,000	51	58	93	128	209	232
45,359.0	*15.7*	*17.8*	*28.2*	*38.9*	*63.8*	*70.6*
150,000	58	66	106	146	239	266
68,038.5	*18.0*	*20.4*	*32.3*	*44.5*	*73.1*	*80.8*
200,000	64	73	117	161	263	292
90,718.0	*19.8*	*22.5*	*35.5*	*49.0*	*80.4*	*89.0*
300,000	74	84	134	184	301	335
136,077.0	*22.6*	*25.7*	*40.6*	*56.1*	*92.1*	*101.8*
500,000	87	99	159	218	357	397
226,795.0	*26.8*	*30.5*	*48.2*	*66.5*	*109.2*	*120.7*
700,000	98	111	178	244	400	444
317,513.0	*30.0*	*34.1*	*53.9*	*74.4*	*122.1*	*135.1*
1,000,000	110	125	200	275	450	500
453,590.0	*33.8*	*38.4*	*60.7*	*83.7*	*137.5*	*152.1*

APPENDIX 2

Table AP2.T8. <u>QD for HD 1.1 AE For K = 6, 8, 9, 11, 18, 40</u> (Table C9.T7B.)

NEWQD	Hazard Factor, K					
	6	**8**	**9**	**11**	**18**	**40**
	2.38	*3.17*	*3.57*	*4.36*	*7.14*	*15.87*
(lbs)	**(ft/lb$^{1/3}$)**	**(ft/lb$^{1/3}$)**	**(ft/lb$^{1/3}$)**	**(ft/lb$^{1/3}$)**	**(ft/lb$^{1/3}$)**	**(ft/lb$^{1/3}$)**
[kg]	*[m/kg$^{1/3}$]*	*[m/kg$^{1/3}$]*	*[m/kg$^{1/3}$]*	*[m/kg$^{1/3}$]*	*[m/kg$^{1/3}$]*	*[m/kg$^{1/3}$]*
100	28	37	42	51	84	186
45.4	*8.5*	*11.3*	*12.7*	*15.5*	*25.5*	*56.6*
150	32	43	48	58	96	213
68.0	*9.7*	*12.9*	*14.6*	*17.8*	*29.1*	*64.8*
200	35	47	53	64	105	234
90.7	*10.7*	*14.2*	*16.0*	*19.6*	*32.1*	*71.3*
300	40	54	60	74	120	268
136.1	*12.2*	*16.3*	*18.4*	*22.4*	*36.7*	*81.6*
500	48	63	71	87	143	317
226.8	*14.5*	*19.3*	*21.8*	*26.6*	*43.5*	*96.8*
700	53	71	80	98	160	355
317.5	*16.2*	*21.6*	*24.4*	*29.7*	*48.7*	*108.3*
1,000	60	80	90	110	180	400
453.6	*18.3*	*24.4*	*27.4*	*33.5*	*54.9*	*121.9*
1,500	69	92	103	126	206	458
680.4	*20.9*	*27.9*	*31.4*	*38.3*	*62.8*	*139.6*
2,000	76	101	113	139	227	504
907.2	*23.0*	*30.7*	*34.6*	*42.2*	*69.1*	*153.6*
3,000	87	115	130	159	260	577
1,360.8	*26.4*	*35.1*	*39.6*	*48.3*	*79.1*	*175.9*
5,000	103	137	154	188	308	684
2,268.0	*31.3*	*41.6*	*46.9*	*57.3*	*93.8*	*208.5*
7,000	115	153	172	210	344	765
3,175.1	*35.0*	*46.6*	*52.5*	*64.1*	*104.9*	*233.3*
10,000	129	172	194	237	388	862
4,535.9	*39.4*	*52.5*	*59.1*	*72.2*	*118.2*	*262.7*
15,000	148	197	222	271	444	986
6,803.9	*45.1*	*60.1*	*67.6*	*82.6*	*135.3*	*300.7*
20,000	163	217	244	299	489	1,086
9,071.8	*49.6*	*66.1*	*74.5*	*90.9*	*148.9*	*331.0*

APPENDIX 2

Table AP2.T8. <u>QD for HD 1.1 AE For K = 6, 8, 9, 11, 18, 40</u> (Table C9.T7B.) (continued)

NEWQD	Hazard Factor, K					
	6	**8**	**9**	**11**	**18**	**40**
	2.38	*3.17*	*3.57*	*4.36*	*7.14*	*15.87*
(lbs)	(ft/lb$^{1/3}$)	(ft/lb$^{1/3}$)	(ft/lb$^{1/3}$)	(ft/lb$^{1/3}$)	(ft/lb$^{1/3}$)	(ft/lb$^{1/3}$)
[kg]	*[m/kg$^{1/3}$]*	*[m/kg$^{1/3}$]*	*[m/kg$^{1/3}$]*	*[m/kg$^{1/3}$]*	*[m/kg$^{1/3}$]*	*[m/kg$^{1/3}$]*
30,000	186	249	280	342	559	1,243
13,607.7	*56.8*	*75.7*	*85.2*	*104.1*	*170.5*	*378.9*
50,000	221	295	332	405	663	1,474
22,679.5	*67.4*	*89.7*	*101.1*	*123.4*	*202.1*	*449.2*
70,000	247	330	371	453	742	1,649
31,751.3	*75.4*	*100.4*	*113.0*	*138.1*	*226.1*	*502.5*
100,000	278	371	418	511	835	1,857
45,359.0	*84.9*	*113.1*	*127.3*	*155.5*	*254.6*	*566.0*
150,000	319	425	478	584	956	2,125
68,038.5	*97.2*	*129.4*	*145.7*	*178.0*	*291.5*	*647.9*
200,000	351	468	526	643	1,053	2,339
90,718.0	*106.9*	*142.4*	*160.4*	*195.9*	*320.8*	*713.1*
300,000	402	536	602	736	1,205	2,678
136,077.0	*122.4*	*163.1*	*183.6*	*224.3*	*367.2*	*816.3*
500,000	476	635	714	873	1,429	3,175
226,795.0	*145.1*	*193.3*	*217.7*	*265.9*	*435.4*	*967.8*
700,000	533	710	799	977	1,598	3,552
317,513.0	*162.4*	*216.3*	*243.6*	*297.4*	*487.1*	*1,082.7*
1,000,000	600	800	900	1,100	1,800	4,000
453,590.0	*182.9*	*243.6*	*274.3*	*335.0*	*548.6*	*1,219.4*

APPENDIX 2

Table AP2.T9. <u>Summary of HD 1.2.1, 1.2.2, AND 1.2 3 QD</u> (Table C9.T8.)

To EXPOSED SITE (ES)		From POTENTIAL EXPLOSION SITE (PES)				
		ECM		AGS		
				(H)	(H/R)	(L)
		S or R	F			
ECM (7 bar/3 bar) (IMD)	S	0 (note 1)	0 (note 1)	0 (note 1)	0 (note 1)	0 (note 1)
	R	0 (note 1)	0 (note 1)	0 (note 1)	0 (note 1)	0 (note 1)
	FU	0 (note 1)	0 (note 1)	0 (note 1)	0 (note 1)	0 (note 1)
	FB	0 (note 1)	0 (note 1)	0 (note 1)	0 (note 1)	0 (note 1)
ECM (Undefined) (IMD)	S	0 (note 1)	0 (note 1)	0 (note 1)	0 (note 1)	0 (note 1)
	R	0 (note 1)	0 (note 1)	0 (note 1)	0 (note 1)	0 (note 1)
	FU	0 (note 1)	200/300/100 *61.0/91.4/30.5*	200/300/100 *61.0/91.4/30.5*	200/300/100 *61.0/91.4/30.5*	200/300/100 *61.0/91.4/30.5*
	FB	0 (note 1)	0 (note 1)	0 (note 1)	0 (note 1)	0 (note 1)
AGS (H/R) (IMD)	U or B	0 (note 1)	0 (note 1)	0 (note 1)	0 (note 1)	0 (note 1)
AGS (H or L) (IMD)	U or B	0 (note 1)	200/300/100 *61.0/91.4/30.5*	200/300/100 *61.0/91.4/30.5*	200/300/100 *61.0/91.4/30.5*	200/300/100 *61.0/91.4/30.5*
ILD[5]		0 (Note 1)	Note 2	Note 2	Note 2	Note 2
PTRD[5]		200/300/100 *61.0/91.4/30.5*	Note 3	Note 3	Note 3	Note 3
IBD[5]		200/300/100 *61.0/91.4/30.5*	Note 4	Note 4	Note 4	Note 4

<u>Legend for Table AP2.T9. (Table C9.T8.):</u>

AGS (H)—Aboveground structure, heavy wall; buildings with wall thickness $\geq$ 12 inches [304.8 mm] of reinforced concrete; as an ES, door must be barricaded if it faces a PES.

AGS (H/R)—Aboveground structure, heavy wall and roof; AGS (H) with roof thickness > 5.9 inches [149.9 mm] of reinforced concrete; as an ES, door must be barricaded if it faces a PES; side/rear exposures may or may not be barricaded.

AGS (L)—Aboveground structure, light; light structure, open stack, truck, trailer, or railcar (open stacks—see Note 4).

<u>Notes for Table AP2.T9. (Table C9.T8.):</u>

1. Practical considerations such as firefighting and security will dictate specific separation distances as specified by ACO, PCO, and the specifics of the contract.
2. ILD = 36 percent of IBD with a minimum distance equal to the IMD given in this table for the applicable PES-ES combination.
3. PTRD = 60 percent of IBD with a minimum distance equal to the IMD given in this table for light structures, open stacks, trucks, trailers, or rail cars. Such structures are designated as AGS (L).
4. For HD 1.2.1 items in any structure, truck, trailer, or railcar, use the larger of the two applicable values given in Tables C9.T9. and C9.T10.; for HD 1.2.1 items in the open, use Table C9.T9.; for HD 1.2.2 items, use Table C9.T11.
5. See subparagraph C5.12.12. for HD 1.2.3.
6. When the NEWQD and the MCE of the packaged HD 1.2.1 items fall within the ranges specified in equation {NEWQD $\leq$ MCE $\leq$ 450 lbs [204 kg]}, the HD 1.2.1 shall be treated as HD 1.1 and the criteria of subparagraph C5.8.1.7.1., as applicable, shall be used (see subparagraph C5.12.12.).

General Comments for Table AP2.T9. (Table C9.T8.):

(a): For PES-ES combinations where three distances are given: the first refers to a PES containing HD 1.2.1 AE with an MCE < 100 lbs [45.4 kg]; the second to a PES containing HD 1.2.1 AE with an MCE ≥ 100 lbs [45.4 kg]; and the third refers to a PES containing HD 1.2.2 AE. Where three IMD are given, the IMD from a PES containing only HD 1.2.3 AE to an ES containing other than HD 1.2.3 is K11 [4.36] based on the NEWQD of a single round of the largest (greatest NEWQD) HD 1.2.3 AE in the PES.

(b) For an ES containing only HD 1.2.3 items, the IMD from any PES to such an ES is 0 (Note 1).

Table AP2.T10. HD 1.2.1 QD (IBD, PTR, ILD) for AE With NEWQD > 1.60 lbs [0.73 kg] (Table C9.T9.)

EXPLOSIVE WEIGHT[1] (lbs) [kg]	IBD[2,3,4] (ft) [m]	PTRD[5] (ft) [m]	ILD[6] (ft) [m]
2	200	200	200
0.9	61.0	61.0	61.0
3	200	200	200
1.4	61.0	61.0	61.0
4	200	200	200
1.8	61.0	61.0	61.0
5	200	200	200
2.3	61.0	61.0	61.0
7	200	200	200
3.2	61.0	61.0	61.0
10	200	200	200
4.5	61.0	61.0	61.0
15	200	200	200
6.8	61.0	61.0	61.0
20	200	200	200
9.1	61.0	61.0	61.0
30	200	200	200
13.6	61.0	61.0	61.0
50	200	200	200
22.7	61.0	61.0	61.0
70	200	200	200
31.8	61.0	61.0	61.0
100	268	200	200
45.4	81.7	61.0	61.0
150	348	209	200
68.0	106.0	63.6	61.0
200	403	242	200
90.7	123.0	73.8	61.0
300	481	288	200
136.1	146.5	87.9	61.0
500	576	346	207
226.8	175.5	105.3	63.2
700	638	383	230
317.5	194.3	116.6	70.0
1,000	702	421	253
453.6	213.9	128.3	77.0

Table AP2.T10. HD 1.2.1 QD (IBD, PTR, ILD) for AE
With NEWQD > 1.60 lbs [0.73 kg] (Table C9.T9.) (continued)

EXPLOSIVE WEIGHT[1] (lbs) [kg]	IBD[2,3,4] (ft) [m]	PTRD[5] (ft) [m]	ILD[6] (ft) [m]
1,500	774	464	278
680.4	235.8	141.5	84.9
2,000	824	494	296
907.2	251.0	150.6	90.4
3,000	893	536	321
1,361	272.1	163.3	98.0
5,000	978	587	352
2,268	298.1	178.9	107.3
7,000	1,033	620	372
3,175	314.8	188.9	113.3
10,000	1,090	654	392
4,536	332.3	199.4	119.6
15,000	1,154	692	415
6,804	351.7	211.0	126.6
20,000	1,198	719	431
9,072	365.2	219.1	131.5
30,000	1,260	756	453
13,608	383.9	230.3	138.2
50,000	1,335	801	481
22,680	406.8	244.1	146.4
70,000	1,383	830	498
31,751	421.5	252.9	151.7
100,000	1,433	860	516
45,359	436.8	262.1	157.3
150,000	1,489	893	536
68,039	453.8	272.3	163.4
200,000	1,528	917	550
90,718	465.6	279.3	167.6
300,000	1,581	949	569
136,077	481.8	289.1	173.5
500,000	1,646	988	593
226,795	501.7	301.0	180.6
>500,000	NOTE 4	NOTE 5	NOTE 6
>226,795	NOTE 4	NOTE 5	NOTE 6

APPENDIX 2

Notes for Table AP2.T10 (Table C9.T9.):

1. Explosive Weight = Number of Items x NEWQD.
2. IBD in ft, NEWQD in lbs; ln is natural logarithm
   [71 lbs < explosive weight]
   IBD = -735.186 + [237.559 x (ln(Number of items x NEWQD))] - [4.274 x (ln(Number of items x NEWQD))^2],
   with a minimum of 200 ft   **[EQN C9.T9-1]**
   IBD in m, NEWQD in kg; ln is natural logarithm.
   [18.6 kg < explosive weight]
   IBD = -167.648 + [70.345 x (ln(Number of items x NEWQD))] - [1.303 x (ln(Number of items x NEWQD))^2],
   with a minimum of 61.0 m   **[EQN C9.T9-2]**
3. IBD in ft, NEWQD in lbs; exp (x) is e^x
   [200 ft < IBD < 2016 ft]
   Number of items x NEWQD = exp[27.791 - (600.392 - 0.234 x IBD)$^{1/2}$];   **[EQN C9.T9-3]**
   IBD in m, NEWQD in kg; exp (x) is e^x
   [61.0 m < IBD < 614.5 m]
   Number of items x NEWQD = exp[27.000 – (600.287 – 0.768 x IBD)$^{1/2}$];   **[EQN C9.T9-4]**
4. Use of equations given in Notes (2) and (3) to determine other IBD-weight combinations is allowed.
5. PTRD = 60 percent of IBD with a minimum distance equal to the IMD given in Table C9.T8. for AGS (L) in. For other structures as either ESs or PESs, see Table C9.T8.
6. ILD = 36 percent of IBD with a minimum distance equal to the IMD given in Table C9.T8. for the applicable PES-ES combination. For structures other than AGS (L) as either ESs or PESs, see Table C9.T8.

General Comments for Table AP2.T10 (Table C9.T9.):

(a) The QD criteria for HD 1.2.1 items are based on the hazards from primary fragments. When stored in structures that may contribute to the debris hazard (secondary fragments), the IBD for HD 1.2.1 items whose MCE is greater than 31 lbs [14.1 kg] is determined by using the larger of two distances: those given in this table for the appropriate explosive weight or those given in Table C9.T10. for the appropriate MCE. Structures that may contribute to the debris hazard for storage of HD 1.2.1 AE include: (a) all ECMs -- frontal exposures (side and rear exposures have fixed minimum distances for IBD); (b) all AGSs -- including heavy wall (H), heavy wall/roof (H/R), and light wall (L) as defined in C9.T8., unless data/analyses are provided to show that the structural debris contribution is less. Note that ILD and PTRD are based on 36 percent and 60 percent, respectively, of the applicable IBD as determined in this note with minimum distances of: ILD minimum distances are given in Table C9.T8. for applicable PES-ES combinations; PTR minimum distances are given in Table C9.T8. for AGS (L)).

(b) See Table C9.T8. for a summary of IMD and minimum distances for ILD and PTRD.

Table AP2.T11. <u>HDD for HD 1.2.1 AE Stored in Structures</u>
<u>That Can Contribute to the Debris Hazard</u> (Table C9.T10.)

MCE	HAZARDOUS DEBRIS DISTANCE[1, 2, 3]	PTRD[4]	ILD[5]
(lbs)	(ft)	(ft)	(ft)
[kg]	*[m]*	*[m]*	*[m]*
≤ 31	200	200	200
≤14.1	*61.0*	*61.0*	*61.0*
50	388	233	200
22.7	*118.2*	*70.9*	*61.0*
70	519	311	200
31.8	*158.1*	*94.9*	*61.0*
100	658	395	237
45.4	*200.4*	*120.2*	*72.1*
150	815	489	293
68.0	*248.5*	*149.1*	*89.4*
200	927	556	334
90.7	*282.6*	*169.5*	*101.7*
300	1085	651	391
136.1	*330.6*	*198.4*	*119.0*
400	1197	718	431
181.4	*364.7*	*218.8*	*131.3*
450	1243	746	447
204.1	*378.7*	*227.2*	*136.3*
>450	1250	750	450
>204.1	*381.0*	*228.6*	*137.2*

<u>Notes for Table AP2.T11. (Table C9.T10.):</u>

1. MCE in lbs, HDD in ft; ln is natural logarithm;
    [31 lbs < MCE ≤ 450 lbs]
    $$HDD = -1133.9 + [389 \times ln(MCE)]$$
    [EQN C9.T10-1]
    with a minimum distance of 200 ft.
    MCE in kg, HDD in m; ln is natural logarithm
    [14.1 kg < MCE ≤ 204 kg]
    $$HDD = -251.87 + [118.56 \times ln(MCE)]$$
    [EQN C9.T10-2]
    with a minimum distance of 61 m.
2. MCE in lbs, HDD in ft; exp [x] is e^x
    [200 ft < HDD ≤ 1250 ft]
    $$MCE = exp [(HDD/389) + 2.914]$$
    [EQN C9.T10-3]
    MCE in kg, HDD in m; exp [x] is e^x.
    [61.0 m < HDD ≤ 381 m]

$$MCE = \exp\left[(HDD/118.56) + 2.1244\right]$$
[EQN C9.T10-4]

3. Use of equations given in Notes (1) and (2) to determine other HDD-MCE combinations is allowed.
4. PTRD = 60 percent of IBD with a minimum distance equal to the IMD given in Table C9.T8. for AGS (L). For other structures as either ESs or PESs, see Table C9.T8.
5. ILD = 36 percent of IBD with a minimum distance equal to the IMD given in Table C9.T8. for the applicable PES-ES combination. For structures other than AGS (L) as either ESs or PESs, see TableC9.T8.

General Comments for Table AP2.T11. (Table C9.T10.):

(a) The QD criteria for HD 1.2.1 items are based on the hazards from primary fragments. When stored in structures that may contribute to the debris hazard (secondary fragments), the IBD for HD 1.2.1 items whose MCE is greater than 31 pounds [14.1 kg] is determined by using the larger of two distances: those given in Table C9.T9. for the appropriate explosive weight, or those given in this table for the appropriate MCE. Structures that may contribute to the debris hazard for storage of HD 1.2.1 AE include: (a) all ECMs -- frontal exposure only. Side and rear exposures have fixed minimum distances for IBD; (b) all AGSs -- including H, H/R, and L as defined in Table C9.T8., unless data/analyses are provided to show that the structural debris contribution is less. Note that ILD and PTRD are based on 36 percent and 60 percent, respectively, of the applicable IBD as determined herein with minimum distances of (ILD minimum distances are given in Table C9.T8. for applicable PES-ES combinations, and PTR minimum distances are given in Table C9.T8. for AGS (L)).
(b) See Table C9.T8. for a summary of IMD and minimum distances for ILD and PTRD.

Table AP2.T12. HD 1.2.2 QD (IBD, PTR, ILD)
For AE with NEWQD < 1.60 lbs [0.73 kg] (Table C9.T11.)

EXPLOSIVE WEIGHT[1] (lbs) [kg]	IBD[2,3,4] (ft) [m]	PTRD[5] (ft) [m]	ILD[6] (ft) [m]
1	100	100	100
0.45	30.5	30.5	30.5
1.5	100	100	100
0.68	30.5	30.5	30.5
2	100	100	100
0.9	30.5	30.5	30.5
3	100	100	100
1.4	30.5	30.5	30.5
5	100	100	100
2.3	30.5	30.5	30.5
7	100	100	100
3.2	30.5	30.5	30.5
10	100	100	100
4.5	30.5	30.5	30.5
15	100	100	100
6.8	30.5	30.5	30.5
20	100	100	100
9.1	30.5	30.5	30.5
30	107	100	100
13.6	32.7	30.5	30.5
50	118	100	100
22.7	36.1	30.5	30.5
70	127	100	100
31.8	38.8	30.5	30.5
100	138	100	100
45.4	42.1	30.5	30.5
150	152	100	100
68.0	46.2	30.5	30.5
200	162	100	100
90.7	49.5	30.5	30.5
300	179	107	100
136.1	54.6	32.7	30.5
500	202	121	100
226.8	61.7	37.0	30.5
700	219	132	100
317.5	66.8	40.1	30.5

Table AP2.T12. HD 1.2.2 QD (IBD, PTR, ILD)
For AE with NEWQD < 1.60 lbs [0.73 kg] (Table C9.T11.) (continued)

EXPLOSIVE WEIGHT[1] (lbs) [kg]	IBD[2,3,4] (ft) [m]	PTRD[5] (ft) [m]	ILD[6] (ft) [m]
1,000	238	143	100
453.6	72.7	43.6	30.5
1,500	262	157	100
680.4	79.8	47.9	30.5
2,000	279	168	101
907.2	85.2	51.1	30.7
3,000	306	183	110
1,361	93.2	55.9	33.5
5,000	341	205	123
2,268	104.0	62.4	37.4
7,000	366	220	132
3,175	111.6	67.0	40.2
10,000	394	236	142
4,536	120.0	72.0	43.2
15,000	427	256	154
6,804	130.1	78.1	46.8
20,000	451	271	162
9,072	137.5	82.5	49.5
30,000	487	292	175
13,608	148.5	89.1	53.5
50,000	535	321	193
22,680	163.0	97.8	58.7
70,000	568	341	204
31,751	173.1	103.8	62.3
100,000	604	362	217
45,359	184.1	110.5	66.3
150,000	647	388	233
68,039	197.1	118.3	71.0
200,000	678	407	244
90,718	206.6	124.0	74.4
300,000	723	434	260
136,077	220.5	132.3	79.4
500,000	783	470	282
226,795	238.8	143.3	86.0
>500,000	Note 4	Note 5	Note 6
>226,795	Note 4	Note 5	Note 6

APPENDIX 2

Notes for Table AP2.T12. (Table C9.T11.):

1. Explosive Weight = Number of Items x NEWQD.
2. IBD in ft, NEWQD in lbs; ln is natural logarithm.
   [20 lbs < Explosive Weight]
   IBD = 101.649 - [15.934 x (ln(Number of items x NEWQD))] + [5.173 x (ln(Number of items x NEWQD))^2],
   with a minimum of 100 ft   **[EQN C9.T11-1]**
   IBD in m, NEWQD in kg; ln is natural logarithm
   [9.1 kg < Explosive Weight]
   IBD = 28.127 - [2.364 x (ln(Number of items x NEWQD))] + [1.577 x (ln(Number of items x NEWQD))^2]
   with a minimum of 30.5 m   **[EQN C9.T11-2]**
3. IBD in ft, NEWQD in lbs; exp (x) is e^x.
   [100 ft <IBD < 1240 ft]
   Number of items x NEWQD = exp [1.5401 + (-17.278 + 0.1933 x IBD)$^{1/2}$]   **[EQN C9.T11-3]**
   IBD in m, NEWQD in kg; exp (x) is e^x.
   [30.5 m <IBD < 378 m]
   Number of items x NEWQD = exp [0.7495 + (-17.274 + 0.6341 x IBD)$^{1/2}$]   **[EQN C9.T11-4]**
4. Use of equations given in Notes (2) and (3) to determine other IBD-weight combinations is allowed
5. PTRD = 60 percent of IBD with a minimum distance equal to the IMD given in Table C9.T8 for AGS (L). For other structures as either ESs or PESs, see Table C9.T8.
6. ILD = 36 percent of IBD with a minimum distance equal to the IMD given in Table C9.T8 for the applicable PES-ES combination. For structures other than AGS (L) as either ESs or PESs, see Table C9.T8.

General Comments for Table AP2.T12. (Table C9.T11.):

(a) The QD criteria for HD 1.2.2 items are based on the hazards from primary fragments.
(b) See Table C9.T8. for a summary of IMD and minimum distances for ILD and PTRD.
(c) For operational necessity, limited quantities of HD 1.2.2 may be stored without regards to QD. See subparagraph C5.12.10.

Table AP2.T13. HD 1.2.1, 1.2.2, AND 1.2.3 Mixing Rules (Table C9.T12.)

HAZARD SUB-DIVISION INVOLVED	DISTANCES TO BE APPLIED
1.2.1	Apply HD 1.2.1 distances[1]
1.2.2	Apply HD 1.2.2 distances[2]
1.2.3	Apply HD 1.2.3 distances[3]
1.2.1 + 1.2.2	Apply greater of two distances
1.2.1 + 1.2.3	Apply greater of two distances
1.2.2 + 1.2.3	Apply greater of two distances

Notes for Table AP2.T13. (Table C9.T12.):

1. HD 1.2.1 distances given in Tables C9.T8., C9.T9, and C9.T10.
2. HD 1.2.2 distances given in Tables C9.T8. and C9.T11.
3. HD 1.2.3 distances given in Table C9.T14. (See subparagraph C5.12.12.)

Table AP2.T14. <u>HD 1.3 QD</u> (Table C9.T13.)

NEWQD (lbs) [kg]	IBD & PTRD[1] (ft) [m]	Aboveground IMD & ILD[2] (ft) [m]
≤ 1000[3]	75	50
≤ 453.59[3]	22.9	15.2
1,500	82	56
680.4	25.0	17.0
2,000	89	61
907.2	27.2	18.5
3,000	101	68
1,360.8	30.7	20.8
5,000	117	80
2,268.0	35.8	24.3
7,000	130	88
3,175.1	39.6	26.9
10,000	145	98
4,535.9	44.2	30.0
15,000	164	112
6,803.9	50.1	34.0
20,000	180	122
9,071.8	54.8	37.2
30,000	204	138
13,607.7	62.3	42.2
50,000	240	163
22,679.5	73.2	49.5
70,000	268	181
31,751.3	81.6	55.1
100,000	300	204
45,359.0	91.4	62.0
150,000	346	234
68,038.5	105.3	71.4
200,000	385	260
90,718.0	117.4	79.3
300,000	454	303
136,077.0	138.4	92.5
500,000	569	372
226,795.0	173.6	113.4
700,000	668	428
317,513.0	203.8	130.5
1,000,000	800	500
453,590.0	244.0	152.3
1,500,000	936	577
680,385.0	285.3	175.8
2,000,000	1,008	630
907,180.0	307.2	192.0

APPENDIX 2

Notes for Table AP2.T14. (Table C9.T13.):

1. (NEWQD in lbs, d in ft)

    NEWQD $\leq$ 1,000 lbs

    $d_{IBD,PTRD} = 75$

    1,000 lbs < NEWQD $\leq$ 96,000 lbs

    $d_{IBD,PTRD} = \exp[2.47 + 0.2368*(\ln(NEWQD)) + 0.00384*(\ln(NEWQD))^2]$ **[EQN C9.T13-1]**

    with a minimum distance of 75 ft

    96,000 lbs < NEWQD $\leq$ 1,000,000 lbs

    $d_{IBD,PTRD} = \exp[7.2297 - 0.5984*(\ln(NEWQD)) + 0.04046*(\ln(NEWQD))^2]$ **[EQN C9.T13-2]**

    NEWQD > 1,000,000 lbs

    $d_{IBD,PTRD} = 8*NEWQD^{1/3}$ **[EQN C9.T13-3]**

    (NEWQD in kg, d in m)

    NEWQD $\leq$ 453.6 kg

    $d_{IBD,PTRD} = 22.9$

    453.6 kg < NEWQD $\leq$ 43,544.6 kg

    $d_{IBD,PTRD} = \exp[1.4715 + 0.2429*(\ln(NEWQD)) + 0.00384*(\ln(NEWQD))^2]$ **[EQN C9.T13-4]**

    with a minimum distance of 22.9 m

    43,544.6 kg < NEWQD $\leq$ 453,590 kg

    $d_{IBD,PTRD} = \exp[5.5938 - 0.5344*(\ln(NEWQD)) + 0.04046*(\ln(NEWQD))^2]$ **[EQN C9.T13-5]**

    NEWQD > 453,590 kg

    $d_{IBD,PTRD} = 3.17*NEWQD^{1/3}$ **[EQN C9.T13-6]**

    75 ft $\leq d_{IBD,PTRD} \leq$ 296 ft

    $NEWQD = \exp[-30.833 + (307.465 + 260.417*(\ln(d_{IBD,PTRD})))^{1/2}]$ **[EQN C9.T13-7]**

    with a minimum NEWQD of 1,000 lbs

    296 ft < $d_{IBD,PTRD} \leq$ 800 ft

    $NEWQD = \exp[7.395 + (-124.002 + 24.716*(\ln(d_{IBD,PTRD})))^{1/2}]$ **[EQN C9.T13-8]**

    800 ft < $d_{IBD,PTRD}$

    $NEWQD = d_{IBD,PTRD}^{3}/512$ **[EQN-C9.T13-9]**

    22.9 m $\leq d_{IBD,PTRD} \leq$ 90.2 m

    $NEWQD = \exp[-31.628 + (617.102 + 260.417*(\ln(d_{IBD,PTRD})))^{1/2}]$ **[EQN C9.T13-10]**

    with a minimum NEWQD of 453.6 kg

    90.2 m < $d_{IBD,PTRD} \leq$ 243.8 m

    $NEWQD = \exp[6.604 + (-94.642 + 24.716*(\ln(d_{IBD,PTRD})))^{1/2}]$ **[EQN C9.T13-11]**

    243.8 m < $d_{IBD,PTRD}$

    $NEWQD = d_{IBD,PTRD}^{3}/131.964$ **[EQN C9.T13-12]**

2. (NEWQD in lbs, d in ft)

    NEWQD $\leq$ 1,000 lbs

    $d_{IMD,ILD} = 50$

    1,000 lbs < NEWQD $\leq$ 84,000 lbs

    $d_{IMD,ILD} = \exp[2.0325 + 0.2488*(\ln(NEWQD)) + 0.00313*(\ln(NEWQD))^2]$ **[EQN C9.T13-13]**

    with a minimum distance of 50 ft

    84,000 lbs < NEWQD $\leq$ 1,000,000 lbs

    $d_{IMD,ILD} = \exp[4.338 - 0.1695*(\ln(NEWQD)) + 0.0221*(\ln(NEWQD))^2]$ **[EQN C9.T13-14]**

    1,000,000 lbs < NEWQD

    $d_{IMD,ILD} = 5*NEWQD^{1/3}$ **[EQN C9.T13-15]**

    (NEWQD in kg, d in m)

    NEWQD $\leq$ 453.6 kg

    $d_{IMD,ILD} = 15.2$

    453.6 kg < NEWQD $\leq$ 38,101.6 kg

    $d_{IMD,ILD} = \exp[1.0431 + 0.2537*(\ln(NEWQD)) + 0.00313*(\ln(NEWQD))^2]$ **[EQN C9.T13-16]**

    with a minimum distance of 15.2 m

    38,101.6 kg < NEWQD $\leq$ 453,590 kg

    $d_{IMD,ILD} = \exp[3.0297 - 0.1346*(\ln(NEWQD)) + 0.0221*(\ln(NEWQD))^2]$ **[EQN C9.T13-17]**

    NEWQD > 453,590 kg

    $d_{IMD,ILD} = 1.98*NEWQD^{1/3}$ **[EQN C9.T13-18]**

$50 \text{ ft} \leq d_{IMD,ILD} \leq 192 \text{ ft}$

$\quad$ NEWQD $= \exp[-39.744 + (930.257 + 319.49*(\ln(d_{IMD,ILD})))^{1/2}]$ $\qquad$ **[EQN C9.T13-19]**

$\qquad$ with a minimum NEWQD of 1,000 lbs

$192 \text{ ft} < d_{IMD,ILD} \leq 500 \text{ ft}$

$\quad$ NEWQD $= \exp[3.834 + (-181.58 + 45.249*(\ln(d_{IMD,ILD})))^{1/2}]$ $\qquad$ **[EQN C9.T13-20]**

$500 \text{ ft} < d_{IMD,ILD}$

$\quad$ NEWQD $= d_{IMD,ILD}^{3}/125$ $\qquad$ **[EQN C9.T13-21]**

$15.2 \text{ m} \leq d_{IMD,ILD} \leq 58.4 \text{ m}$

$\quad$ NEWQD $= \exp[-40.527 + (1309.19 + 319.49*(\ln(d_{IMD,ILD})))^{1/2}]$ $\qquad$ **[EQN C9.T13-22]**

$\qquad$ with a minimum NEWQD of 453.6 kg

$58.4 \text{ m} < d_{IMD,ILD} \leq 152.4 \text{ m}$

$\quad$ NEWQD $= \exp[3.045 + (-127.817 + 45.249*(\ln(d_{IMD,ILD})))^{1/2}]$ $\qquad$ **[EQN C9.T13-23]**

$152.4 \text{ m} < d_{IMD,ILD}$

$\quad$ NEWQD $= d_{IMD,ILD}^{3}/7.804$ $\qquad$ **[EQN C9.T13-24]**

3.   For quantities less than 1,000 lbs [453.59 kg], the required distances are those specified for 1,000 lbs [453.59 kg]. The use of lesser distances may be approved when supported by test data or analysis.

General Comments for Table AP2.T14. (Table C9.T13.):

(a). For reasons of operational necessity, limited quantities of items in this hazard division, such as document destroyers, signaling devices, riot control munitions and the like, may be stored without regard to QD IAW fire protection regulations in facilities such as hangars, arms rooms, and manufacturing or operating buildings.

(b) ECMs may be used to their physical capacity for this HD provided they comply with the construction and siting requirements of Chapters 5 and 9 of this Manual, respectively, for HD 1.1. ECMs used to store only HD 1.3 items must be sited for a minimum of 100 lbs [45.4 kg] of HD 1.1 items using Tables C9.T4. (ILD) and C9.T6. (IM). Use IBD and PTRD columns of Table C9.T13. for determining the IBD and PTRD associated with the HD 1.3 being placed in such ECMs.

Table AP2.T15. <u>HD 1.4 QD</u> (Table C9.T14.)

NEWQD (lbs) [kg]	IBD (ft) [m]	PTRD (ft) [m]	ILD[1] (ft) [m]	Aboveground IMD[1,2] (ft) [m]	ECM IMD[1] (ft) [m]
≤ 3000[3,4]	75	75	50	50	0 out the
≤ 1,360.8[3,4]	22.9	22.9	15.2	15.2[12]	Sides & Rear;
>3000	100	100	50 (100)	50 (100)	use AGM
>1,360.8	30.5	30.5	15.3 (30.5)	15.3 (30.5)	distance out
(No upper limit specifically required for safety reasons)			(Note: Use larger distance for combustible construction)	(Note: Use larger distance for combustible construction)	the Front

Notes for Table AP2.T15. (Table C9.T14.):

1. Magazines storing only HD 1.4 AE may be located at these IMD or ILD from all other magazines or operating buildings regardless of the HD or NEWQD authorized in those adjacent structures. Because the HD 1.4 AE may be destroyed as the result of an accident involving the assets in those adjacent structures, the ACO, PCO, and the specifics of the contract on a case-by-case basis must accept application of this provision with consideration given to the value of HD 1.4 assets at risk.

2. HD 1.4 AE may be stored in a general supplies warehouse area rather than in an AE storage area. When storing in a general supplies warehouse area, any weatherproof warehouse structure may serve as an HD 1.4 magazine. Such a structure will be separated from all other warehouses by AGM distance.

3. For reasons of operational necessity, limited quantities of HD 1.4 AE (e.g., small arms AE and riot control munitions) may be stored within facilities (e.g., hangars, arms rooms, and operating buildings) without regard to QD. Alternatively, operationally necessary HD 1.4 AE may be stored in small magazines external to those facilities without regard to QD.

4. See subparagraph C5.3.2.1.1. for the applicability of HD 1.4 QD criteria and the determination of NEWQD when HD 1.4 and other HD AE are located in the same site.

Table AP2.T16. <u>HD 1.6 QD</u> (Table C9.T15.)

NEWQD	Aboveground		ECM		
	IBD or PTRD[1,2,4]	IMD or ILD[1,3,4]	IBD or PTRD	ILD	IMD
(lbs)	(ft)	(ft)	(ft)	(ft)	(ft)
[kg]	[m]	[m]	[m]	[m]	[m]
≤100[5]	37	23	Note 4	Note 4	Note 4
≤453.9[5]	11.3	7.0			
150	43	27			
68.0	12.9	8.1			
200	47	29			
90.7	14.3	8.9			
300	54	33			
136.1	16.3	10.2			
500	63	40			
226.8	19.4	12.1			
700	71	44			
317.5	21.7	13.5			
1,000	80	50			
453.6	24.4	15.2			
1,500	92	57			
680.4	27.9	17.4			
2,000	101	63			
907.2	30.7	19.2			
3,000	115	72			
1,360.8	35.2	22.0			
5,000	137	85			
2,268.0	41.7	26.1			
7,000	153	96			
3,175.1	46.6	29.2			
10,000	172	108			
4,535.9	52.5	32.8			
15,000	197	123			
6,803.9	60.1	37.6			
20,000	217	136			
9,071.8	66.2	41.4			
30,000	249	155			
13,607.7	75.8	47.4			
50,000	295	184			
22,679.5	89.8	56.1			
70,000	330	206			
31,751.3	100.5	62.8			
100,000	371	232			
45,359.0	113.2	70.7			
150,000	425	266			
68,038.5	129.6	81.0			
200,000	468	292			
90,718.0	142.6	89.1			
300,000	536	335			
136,077.0	163.2	102.0			
500,000	635	397			
226,795.0	193.5	121.0			

APPENDIX 2

Notes for Table AP2.T16. (Table C9.T15.):

1. Applicable minimum distance:
   For IBD or PTRD, based on the NEWQD for the largest single round of AE,

   D in ft, NEWQD in lbs:
   $$D_{IBD,PTRD} = 40W^{1/3}$$ **[EQN C9.T15-1]**

   D in m, NEWQD in kg;
   $$D_{IBD,PTRD} = 15.87Q^{1/3}$$ **[EQN C9.T15-2]**

   For IMD or ILD, based on the NEWQD for the largest single round of AE,

   D in ft, NEWQD in lbs:
   $$D_{IMD,ILD} = 18W^{1/3}$$ **[EQN C9.T15-3]**

   D in m, NEWQD in kg;
   $$D_{IMD,ILD} = 7.14Q^{1/3},$$ **[EQN C9.T15-4]**

2. D in ft, NEWQD in lbs
   $$D_{IBD,PTRD} = 8W^{1/3}$$ **[EQN C9.T15-5]**
   $$NEWQD = D_{IBD,PTRD}{}^3/512$$ **[EQN C9.T15-6]**

   D in m, NEWQD in kg
   $$D_{IBD,PTRD} = 3.17Q^{1/3}$$ **[EQN C9.T15-7]**
   $$NEWQD = D_{IBD,PTRD}{}^3/31.86$$ **[EQN C9.T15-8]**

3. D in ft, NEWQD in lbs
   $$D_{IMD,ILD} = 5W^{1/3}$$ **[EQN C9.T15-9]**
   $$NEWQD = D_{IMD,ILD}{}^3/125$$ **[EQN C9.T15-10]**

   D in m, NEWQD in kg
   $$D_{IMD,ILD} = 1.98Q^{1/3}$$ **[EQN C9.T15-11]**
   $$NEWQD = D_{IMD,ILD}{}^3/7.76$$ **[EQN C9.T15-12]**

4. For HD 1.6 AE packed in non-flammable pallets or packing and stored in an ECM, provided it is acceptable to the ACO, PCO, and the DDESB, these QD apply on a site-specific basis unless a lesser distance is permitted by Table C9.T15. for aboveground sites (NOTE: These lesser distances can be applied to ECM storage):

   $D_{IBD,PTRD}$ = 100 ft [30.5 m];

   D_{ILD} = 50 ft [15.2 m];

   D_{IMD} = no specific requirement.

5. For quantities less than 100 lbs [45.4 kg], the required distances are those specified for 100 lbs [45.4 kg]. The use of lesser distances may be approved when supported by test data or analyses.

APPENDIX 2

Table AP2.T17. Hazard Classifications and Minimum QD for Energetic Liquids
(Table C9.T16.)

Energetic Liquid	OSHA/NFPA Fuel[1] or Oxidizer[2] Class	DoD Storage Hazard Class	Minimum QD[3]
Hydrogen Peroxide, > 60%	3 or 4[4]	5 1 (LA)	800[5] ft or Table C9 T20 *243.8[5] m or Table C9.T20.*
IRFNA (Inhibited Red Fuming Nitric Acid)	3	8 (LA)	Table C9 T20
Nitrogen Tetroxide/MON (Mixed oxides of nitrogen)	2	2 3 (LA)	Table C9 T20
Liquid Oxygen	N/A	2 2 (LA)	Table C9 T21
RP-1	II	3 (LB)	Table C9 T19
JP-10	II	3J (LB)	Table C9 T19
Liquid Hydrogen	N/A	2 1 (LB)	Table C9 T22
Hydrazine, > 64%	II	8 (LC)	800[5] or 300[6] ft or Note 7 *243.8[5] m or 91.4[6] m or Note 7*
Aerozine 50 (50%N_2H_4/50% UDMH) (Unsymmetric dimethylhydrazine)	I B	6 1 (LC)	800[5] or 300[6] ft or Note 7 *243.8[5] m or 91.4[6] m or Note 7*
Methylhydrazine	I B	6 1 (LC)	800[5] or 300[6] ft or Note 7 *243.8[5] m or 91.4[6] m or Note 7*
UDMH	I B	6 1 (LC)	Table C9 T19
Ethylene Oxide	I A	2 3 (LD)	H/D 1 1 QD[8] with TNT Equiv = 100%, or 800[5] or 300[6] ft *H/D 1.1 QD[8] with TNT Equiv = 100%, or 243.8[5] or 91.4[6] m*
Propylene Oxide	I A	3 (LD)	H/D 1 1 QD[8] with TNT Equiv = 100%, or 800[5] or 300[6] ft *H/D 1.1 QD[8] with TNT Equiv = 100%, or 243.8[5] or 91.4[6] m*
Nitromethane	I C	3 (LE)	Use H/D 1 1 QD with TNT Equiv = 100%[9] or Table C9 T19
Hydroxylammonium Nitrate (HAN)	2	8 (LE)	800[5] ft or Table C9 T20 *243.8[5] m or Table C9.T20.*
XM-46 (HAN Monopropellant)	N/A	1 3C (LE)	800[5] ft or use HD 1 3 QD *243.8[5] m or use HD 1.3 QD*
Otto Fuel II	III B	9 (LE)	Use H/D 1 1 QD[10] with TNT Equiv = 100%, or 150[11] ft or Table C9 T19 *Use H/D 1.1 QD[10] with TNT Equiv. = 100%, or 45.7[11] m or Table C9.T19.*
Halogen Fluorides (ClF_3/ClF_5)	4	2 3 (LE)	Table C9 T20
Liquid Fluorine	4	2 3 (LE)	Table C9 T20
Nitrogen Trifluoride	4	2 2 (LE)	Table C9 T20
Nitrate esters (e g NG, TMETN, DEGDN, TEGDN, BTTN)	N/A	1 1 D (LE)	Use H/D 1 1 QD with TNT Equiv = 100%

Notes for Table AP2.T17. (Table C9.T16.):

1. Flammable or combustible liquid classification index based on flash point and boiling point versus criteria as specified in Reference (q) and part 1910 of Reference (f). Primary descriptor is a Roman numeral, possibly with an additional letter.
2. NFPA oxidizer classification index as described in NFPA 430 (Reference (af)). Descriptor is an ordinary number.
3. Positive measures for spill containment/control shall be taken for isolated storage of energetic liquids IAW applicable OSHA and NFPA guidance (referenced in Tables C9.T19. through C9.T21.). For flammable energetic liquids and liquid oxidizers where only minimum blast or fragment distances are specified, applicable OSHA and NFPA guidance referenced in Tables C9.T19. and C9.T20., respectively, should also be used.
4. Hydrogen peroxide solutions of concentration greater than 91 percent are NFPA Class 4 oxidizers.
5. Should be used as a default value, unless otherwise hazard classified, when the material is packaged in small (non-bulk) shipping containers, portable ground support equipment, small aerospace flight vehicle propellant

tanks, or similar pressure vessels that provide heavy confinement (burst pressure greater than 100 psi [690 kPa]).

6. Should be used as a default value, unless otherwise hazard classified, when the material is packaged in small (non-bulk) shipping containers (DOT 5C or equivalent), portable ground support equipment, small aerospace flight vehicle propellant tanks, or similar pressure vessels providing a lower level of confinement (burst pressure less than or equal to 100 psi [690 kPa]) and if adequate protection from fragments is not provided from terrain, effective barricades, nets, or other physical means (lightweight building construction is not adequate). If protection from fragments is provided, use the IBD/PTRD "Protected" column of Table C9.T22.

7. For large ready, bulk, or rest storage tanks (as defined in subparagraphs C5.17.5.7., C5.17.5.9., and C5.17.5.10.), use Table C9.T22.

8. Where there is a reasonable risk of vapor cloud explosion of large quantities (for example, in bulk tank storage).

9. Technical grade nitromethane in unit quantities of 55 gallons (208.2 liters) or less in DOT-approved containers listed in Reference (g) may be stored as flammable liquids (Table C9.T19.) provided a-c apply:

    a. Packages are stored only one tier high.

    b. Packages are protected from direct rays of the sun.

    c. Maximum storage life of 2 years, unless storage life tests indicate product continues to meet purchase specification. Such tests are to be repeated at 1-year intervals thereafter.

10. For underwater static test stands, when operated at hydrostatic pressure above 50 psig [345 kPa], or for propellant tanks or other vessels having burst pressures of greater than 100 psig [690 kPa] without acceptable pressure relief devices (unless otherwise hazard classified). For underwater test stands, the TNT equivalence (i.e., MCE) should include the total energetic liquids weight in all pumps and plumbing, as well as the weight of energetic liquids held in tankage (under the test cell hydrostatic pressure) unless acceptable mitigation measures such as fuel line detonation arrestors and/or fuel tank isolation/barricading are used (as determined by hazard analysis).

11. Should be used as a default value, unless otherwise hazard classified, when the material is packaged in small vehicle propellant tanks, small (non-bulk) shipping containers, portable ground support equipment, or similar pressure vessels that provide relatively heavy confinement (burst pressure between 50 – 100 psig [345 – 690 kPa]) without acceptable pressure relief devices.

Table AP2.T18. Factors to Use When Converting Energetic Liquid Densities[1]
(Table C9.T17.)

Item	Density (lb/gal) [kg/l]	Temperature (°F) [°C]
Chlorine Pentafluoride	14.8 / 1.77	77 / 25.0
Chlorine trifluoride	15.1 / 1.81	77 / 25.0
Ethyl alcohol	6.6 / 0.79	68 / 20.0
Ethylene oxide	7.4 / 0.89	51 / 10.6
Fluorine (liquid)	12.6 / 1.51	-306 / -187.8
HAN Monopropellants	11.9 / 1.43	77 / 25.0
HAN solution (25 to 95 wt %)	10.0 to 13.4 / 1.20 to 1.61	68 / 20.0
Hydrazine	8.4 / 1.01	68 / 20.0
Hydrogen peroxide (90 percent)	11.6 / 1.39	77 / 25.0
JP-10	7.8 / 0.93	60 / 15.6
Liquid hydrogen	0.59 / 0.07	-423 / -252.8
Liquid oxygen	9.5 / 1.14	-297 / -182.8
Monomethyl hydrazine	7.3 / 0.87	68 / 20.0
Nitrogen tetroxide	12.1 / 1.45	68 / 20.0
Nitrogen trifluoride	12.8 / 1.53	-200 / -128.9
Nitromethane	9.5 / 1.14	68 / 20.0
Otto Fuel II	10.3 / 1.23	77 / 25.0
Propylene oxide	7.2 / 0.86	32 / 0.0
Red fuming nitric acid (IRFNA)	12.9 / 1.55	77 / 25.0
RP-1	6.8 / 0.81	68 / 20.0
UDMH	6.6 / 0.79	68 / 20.0
UDMH/hydrazine	7.5 / 0.90	77 / 25.0

Notes for AP2.T18. (Table C9.T17.):

1. Conversion of quantities of energetic liquids:
    From gallons to lbs [*liter to kg*]:
        lbs of energetic liquids = gallons X density of energetic liquids (lbs/gal).   **[EQN C9.T17-1]**
        kg of energetic liquids = liters X density of energetic liquids (kg/liter)   **[EQN C9.T17-2]**
        From lb/gallon to kg/liter: 1 lb/gal = 8.345 kg/liter   [EQN C9.T17-3]
        From kg/liter to lb/gal: 1 kg/ liter = 0.11983*lb/gal   [EQN C9.T17-4]

Table AP2.T19. Energetic Liquid Explosive Equivalent Explosive Weights [1, 2, 3, 4, 5]
(Table C9.T18.)

ENERGETIC LIQUIDS	TNT EQUIVALENCE	
	STATIC TEST STANDS	**RANGE LAUNCH**
LO_2/LH_2	See Note 6	See Note 6
LO_2/LH_2 + LO_2/RP-1	Sum of (see Note 6 for LO_2/LH_2) + (10% for LO2/RP-1)	Sum of (see Note 6 for LO_2/LH_2) + (20% for LO2/RP-1)
LO_2/RP-1	10%	20% up to 500,000 lbs plus 10% over 500,000 lbs
		20% up to 226,795 kg plus 10% over 226,795 kg
IRFNA/UDMH [7]	10%	10%
N_2O_4/UDMH + N_2H_4 [7]	5%	10%
N_2O_4 liquid oxidizer + PBAN solid fuel (Hybrid propellants)	15% [8]	15% [8]
Nitromethane (alone or in combination)	100%	100%
Otto Fuel II	100% [9]	
Ethylene Oxide	100% [10]	100% [10]

Notes for Table AP2.T19. (Table C9.T18.):

1. The percentage factors given in the table are to be used to determine equivalent explosive weights of energetic liquids mixtures at static test stands and range launch pads when such energetic liquids are located aboveground and are unconfined except for their tankage. Other configurations shall be considered on an individual basis to determine equivalent explosive weights.
2. The equivalent explosive weight calculated by the use of this table shall be added to any non-nuclear explosive weight aboard before distances can be determined from Tables C9.T1. and C9.T5.
3. These equivalent explosive weights apply also for these substitutions:
    Alcohols or other hydrocarbons for RP-1.
    H_2O_2 for LO_2 (only when LO_2 is in combination with RP-1 or equivalent hydrocarbon fuel).
    MMH for N_2H_4, unsymmetrical dimethylhydrazine (UDMH), or combinations of the two.
4. For quantities of energetic liquids up to but not over the equivalent explosive weight of 100 lbs [45.4 kg] of AE, the distance shall be determined on an individual basis by the ACO and PCO. All personnel and facilities, whether involved in the operation or not, shall be protected by operating procedures, equipment design, shielding, barricading, or other suitable means.

5. Distances less than intraline are not specified. Where a number of prepackaged energetic liquid units are stored together, separation distance to other storage facilities shall be determined on an individual basis by the ACO and PCO, taking into consideration normal hazard classification procedures.

6. For siting launch vehicles and static test stands, equivalent explosive weight is the larger of:

   a. The weight equal to $8W^{2/3}$ [$4.13 Q^{2/3}$] where W is the weight of LO_2/LH_2; or

   b. 14 percent of the LO_2/LH_2 weight.

   NOTE: For these calculations, use the total weight of LO_2/LH_2 present in the launch vehicle, or the total weight in test stand run tankage and piping for which there is no positive means to prevent mixing in credible accidents. When it can be reliably demonstrated that the MCE involves a lesser quantity of energetic liquids subject to involvement in a single reaction, the lesser quantity may be used in determining the equivalent explosive weight. When siting is based on a quantity less than the total energetic liquids present, the MCE and associated explosive yield analysis must be documented in an approved site plan (section C1.8.).

7. These are hypergolic combinations.

8. The equivalent explosive weight of the hybrid rocket system N_2O_4 liquid oxidizer combined with PBAN solid fuel was evaluated as 15 percent for an explosive donor accident scenario, 5 percent for a high velocity impact scenario, and less than 0.01 percent (negligible) for static mixing (tower drop) failures (AFRPL-TR-67-124 (Reference (ag))).

9. See Note 10 of Table C9.T16.

10. See Note 8 of Table C9.T16.

APPENDIX 2

Table AP2.T20. QD Criteria for OSHA/NFPA Class I – III Flammable and Combustible Energetic Liquids Storage in Detached Buildings or Tanks[1,2]
(Table C9.T19.)

Quantity	IBD/PTRD (ft) [m]	ILD/Aboveground IMD (ft) (ft) [m]
Unlimited 3	50 [4,5] 15.2 [4,5]	Note 6

Notes for Table AP2.T20. (C9.T19.):

1. Other guidelines for diking, tank or container construction, tank venting, and facility construction apply (except for Class III B combustible liquids, e.g., Otto Fuel II). Refer to Reference (p) and subpart H, part 1910 of Reference (f) for further guidance on liquid storage and fire protection.
2. Refer to References (f) and (p) for definition and explanation of OSHA/NFPA classification of flammable and combustible liquids.
3. Guidelines on interior storage configuration (for container storage inside buildings) also apply with these exceptions:
    a. If the storage building is located at least 100 ft [30.5 m] from any exposed building (under the direct jurisdiction of a fire protection organization) or property line; or
    b. If the storage building is located at least 200 ft [61 m] from any exposed building (not under the direct jurisdiction of a fire protection organization) or property line; or
    c. For combustible liquids that will not exhibit sustained burning in bulk form, e.g., Otto Fuel II, as determined through American Society of Testing and Materials D 92 Standard Test Method for Flash and Fire Points by Cleveland Open Cup or comparable testing. Refer to References (r) and (aj) for further guidance on liquid storage and fire protection.
4. For container storage inside a building, IBD/PTR distances may be less than 50 ft [15.2 m] (to a minimum of 10 ft [3.05 m]) if the storage building is constructed of fire resistive exterior walls having an NFPA fire resistance rating of 2 hours or more according to NFPA 251 (Reference (ah)).
5. For large tank storage, QD may be 25 ft [7.6 m] for tank capacities up to 100,000 gallons [378,541 liters], and 37.5 ft [11.4 m] for capacities between 100,001 gallons [378,545 liters] and 500,000 gallons [1,892,706 liters].
6. For flammable liquids container storage inside of a building, ILD/aboveground IMD is 50 ft [15.2 m] (except as in Note 4), or for adjacent incompatible oxidizer storage, distances specified for energetic liquid oxidizers (Table C9.T20.), or oxygen (Table C9.T21.). For flammable liquids storage in fixed or large portable tanks, ILD/aboveground IMD is either (1) for compatible energetic liquids, equal to one sixth of the sum of the diameters of the two adjacent tanks, or distances specified in Note 5 for adjacent container storage inside of a building; or (2) for adjacent incompatible oxidizer storage, distances specified for energetic liquid oxidizers (Table C9.T20.) or oxygen (C9T21.). ECMs may be used to their physical capacity for storing flammable energetic liquids provided they comply with the construction and siting requirements of Chapters 5 and 9 of Reference (c), respectively, for HD 1.1. ECMs must be sited for a minimum of 100 lbs [45.4 kg] of HD 1.1 items using Tables C9.T4. and C9.T6.

Table AP2.T21. QD Criteria for Energetic Liquid Oxidizer
(Excluding Liquid Oxygen) Storage in Detached Buildings or Tanks[1, 2]
(Table C9.T20.)

NFPA Oxidizer Class[3]	Quantity (lbs) [kg]	IBD/PTRD/ILD/Aboveground IMD (ft) [m]
2	up to 600,000	50
	up to 227,154	15.2
3	up to 400,000	75
	up to 181,436	22.9
4[4,5]	≤ 50	75
	≤ 22.7	15.2
	70	76
	31.8	23.1
	100	79
	45.4	24.1
	150	84
	68.0	25.7
	200	89
	90.7	27.2
	300	98
	136.1	29.9
	500	114
	226.8	34.8
	700	128
	317.5	39.0
	1,000	147
	453.6	44.7
	1,500	175
	680.4	53.2
	2,000[6]	200
	907.2[6]	60.9
	3,000	246
	1360.8	74.9
	5,000	328
	2268.0	100.0
	7,000	404
	3175.1	123.0

APPENDIX 2

Table AP2.T21. QD Criteria for Energetic Liquid Oxidizer
(Excluding Liquid Oxygen) Storage in Detached Buildings or Tanks[1, 2]
(Table C9.T20.) (continued)

NFPA Oxidizer Class[3]	Quantity (lbs) [kg]	IBD/PTRD/ILD/Aboveground IMD (ft) [m]
	10,000	510
	4535.9	155.4
	15,000	592
	6,803.9	180.4
	20,000	651
	9,071.8	198.5
	30,000	746
	13,607.7	227.3
	50,000	884
	22,679.5	269.5
	70,000	989
	31,751.3	301.5
	100,000	1114
	45,359.0	339.5
	150,000	1275
	68,038.5	388.6
	200,000	1404
	90,718.0	427.8
	300,000	1607
	136,077.0	489.7
	500,000	1905
	226,795.0	580.6

Notes for Table AP2.T21. (Table C9.T20.):

1. QD requirements do not apply to storage of NFPA Class 2 and 3 oxidizers per NFPA 55(Reference (ai)) in approved fixed tanks.
2. Other requirements for interior storage configuration, building construction, diking, container materials, facility venting, etc., also apply. Refer to Reference (af) for further guidance on oxidizer storage and fire protection.
3. Refer to Reference (af) for definition and explanation of NFPA classification of oxidizers.
4. Multiple tanks containing NFPA Class 4 oxidizers may be located at distances less than those specified in the table; however, if the tanks are not separated from each other by 10 percent of the distance specified for the largest tank, then the total contents of all tanks shall be used to calculate distances to other exposures.
5. The equations given below may be used to determine distance/weights for other quantities:
   Quantity (W) in lbs, distance in ft
   W ≤ 10,000 lbs
   $$Distance = 149.3*W^{(-0.41+0.059*\ln(W))}$$ [EQN C9.T20-1]

W > 10,000 lbs

$$\text{Distance} = 24*W^{1/3} \qquad \text{[EQN C9.T20-2]}$$

Quantity (W) in kg, distance in m

$W \leq 4,535.9\ kg$

$$\textit{Distance} = 34.2*W^{(-0.317+0.059*ln(W))} \qquad \textbf{[EQN C9.T20-3]}$$

$W > 4,535.9\ kg$

$$\textit{Distance} = 9.52*W^{1/3} \qquad \textbf{[EQN C9.T20-4]}$$

Quantity (W) in lbs, distance in ft

Distance > 75 ft

$$W = \exp[-313.18 + 206.53*(\ln(\text{Distance})) - 49.968*(\ln(\text{Distance}))^2 + 5.5354*(\ln(\text{Distance}))^3 - 0.2119*(\ln(\text{Distance}))^4]$$

[EQN C9.T20-5]

Quantity (W) in kg, distance in m

Distance > 22.9 m

$$W = \exp[-130.32 + 108.79*(ln(\textit{Distance})) - 32.587*(ln(\textit{Distance}))^2 + 4.3313*(ln(\textit{Distance}))^3 - 0.21111*(ln(\textit{Distance}))^4]$$

[EQN C9.T20-6]

6. NFPA 430 requires sprinkler protection to be provided for storage of greater than 2,000 lbs [907.2 kg] of NFPA Class 4 oxidizers inside of a building (Reference (af)).

Table AP2.T22. QD Criteria for Liquid Oxygen Storage in Detached Buildings or Tanks[1,2] (Table C9.T21.)

Quantity	IBD/PTRD (ft) [m]	ILD/Aboveground IMD (ft) [m]
Unlimited[3]	100 *30.5*	100 [4] *30.5* [4]

Notes for Table AP2.T22. (Table C9.T21.):

1. Per Reference (ah), distances do not apply where a protective structure having an NFPA fire resistance rating of at least 2 hours interrupts the line of sight between the oxygen system and the exposure. Refer to References (aj) and (al) for further guidance.
2. Additional guidelines relating to equipment assembly and installation, facility design (diking), and other fire protection issues also apply. Refer to References (aj) and (al) for further guidance.
3. QD is independent of oxygen quantity.
4. Minimum ILD/IMD distance between adjacent compatible energetic liquids storage is 50 ft [15.2 m].

Table AP2.T23. <u>QD Criteria for Liquid Hydrogen and Bulk Quantities of Hydrazines</u>[1]
(Table C9.T22.)

Propellant Weight	IBD/PTRD		ILD/Aboveground IMD[6,7]
(W) (lbs) [kg]	Unprotected[2,3] (ft) [m]	Protected[4,5] (ft) [m]	(ft) [m]
≤ 100	600	80	30
≤ 45.4	182.9	24.4	9.1
150	600	90	34
68.0	182.9	27.4	10.3
200	600	100	37
90.7	182.9	30.4	11.2
300	600	113	42
136.1	182.9	34.4	12.7
500	600	130	49
226.8	182.9	39.5	14.6
700	600	141	53
317.5	182.9	42.9	15.9
1,000	600	153	57
453.6	182.9	46.5	17.2
1,500	600	166	62
680.4	182.9	50.7	19.0
2,000	600	176	66
907.2	182.9	53.7	19.9
3,000	600	191	72
1360.8	182.9	58.2	21.5
5,000	600	211	79
2268.0	182.9	64.1	23.7
7,000	600	224	84
3175.1	182.9	68.3	25.3
10,000	603	239	90
4,535.9	183.9	72.9	27.0
15,000	691	258	97
6,803.9	210.5	78.5	29.0
20,000	760	272	102
9,071.8	231.7	82.7	30.6
30,000	870	292	110
13,607.7	265.2	89.0	32.9
50,000	1,032	321	120
22,679.5	314.5	97.6	36.1
70,000	1,154	341	128
31,751.3	351.8	103.8	38.4
100,000	1,300	364	136
45,359.0	396.2	110.7	41.0

Table AP2.T23. <u>QD Criteria for Liquid Hydrogen and Bulk Quantities of Hydrazines</u>[1]
(Table C9.T22.) (continued)

Propellant Weight (W) (lbs) [kg]	IBD/PTRD		ILD/Aboveground IMD[6,7] (ft) [m]
	Unprotected[2,3] (ft) [m]	Protected[4,5] (ft) [m]	
150,000	1,488	391	147
68,038.5	453.6	119.1	44.1
200,000	1,637	412	155
90,718.0	499.2	125.5	46.4
300,000	1,800	444	166
136,077.0	548.6	135.1	50.0
500,000	1,800	487	183
226,795.0	548.6	148.2	54.8
700,000	1,800	518	194
317,513.0	548.6	157.6	58.3
1,000,000	1,800	552	207
453,590.0	548.6	168.1	62.2
1,500,000	1,800	594	223
680,385.0	548.6	180.8	67.8
2,000,000	1,800	626	235
907,180.0	548.6	190.4	70.5
3,000,000	1,800	673	252
1,360,770.0	548.6	204.7	75.8
5,000,000	1,800	737	276
2,267,950.0	548.6	224.2	83.0
7,000,000	1,800	782	293
3,175,130.0	548.6	237.9	88.0
10,000,000	1,800	832	312
4,535,900.0	548.6	253.3	93.7

<u>Notes for Table AP2.T23. (C9.T22.):</u>

1. Positive measures shall be taken to prevent mixing of hydrogen or hydrazines and adjacent oxidizers in the event of a leak or spill.
2. Distances are necessary to provide reasonable protection from fragments of tanks or equipment that are expected to be thrown in event of a vapor phase explosion.
3. W in lbs, Distance in ft
   $W \le 10,000$ lbs
      Unprotected Distance = 600 ft
   $10,000 < W \le 265,000$ lbs,
      Unprotected Distance = $28*W^{1/3}$ **[EQN C9-T22-1]**
   $W > 265,000$ lbs
      Unprotected Distance = 1,800 ft

   W in kg, Distance in m
   $W \le 4,535.9$ kg
      Unprotected Distance = 182.9 m
   $4,535.9$ kg $<W \le 120,201.4$ kg
      Unprotected Distance = $11.11*W^{1/3}$ **[EQN C9.T22-2]**
   $W > 120,201.4$ kg

Unprotected Distance = 548.6 m

W in lbs, Distance in ft

$603 \text{ ft} \le \text{Unprotected Distance} < 1{,}798 \text{ ft}$

$$W = (\text{Unprotected Distance}/28)^3 \qquad \textbf{[EQN C9-T22-3]}$$

W in kg, Distance in m

183.9 m ≤ Unprotected Distance < 548.2 m

$$W = (\text{Unprotected Distance}/11.11)^3 \qquad \textbf{[EQN C9.T22-4]}$$

4. The term "protected" means that protection from fragments is provided by terrain, effective barricades, nets, or other physical means.

5. Distances are based on the recommended IBD given in US Department of the Interior, Bureau of Mines Report 5707 (Reference (aj)), and extrapolation of the 2 cal/cm^2 data on the 1 percent water vapor curve.

   W in lbs, Distance in ft

   $W \le 100 \text{ lbs} \qquad \text{Protected Distance} = 80 \text{ ft}$

   $100 \text{ lbs} < W$

   $$\text{Protected Distance} = -154.1 + 72.89*[\ln(W)] -6.675*[\ln(W)]^2 + 0.369*[\ln(W)]^3. \qquad \textbf{[EQN C9-T22-5]}$$

   W in kg, Distance in m

   $W \le 45.4 \text{ kg} \qquad \text{Protected Distance} = 24.4 \text{ m}$

   $45.4 \text{ kg} < W \le$

   $$\text{Protected Distance} = -30.62 + 19.211*[\ln(W)] -1.7678*[\ln(W)]^2 + 0.1124*[\ln(W)]^3 \qquad \textbf{[EQN C9.T22-6]}.$$

   W in lbs, Distance in ft

   $80 \text{ ft} \le \text{Protected Distance}$

   $$W = \exp[311.367 - 215.761*(\ln(\text{protected distance})) + 55.1828*(\ln(\text{protected distance}))^2 -$$
   $$6.1099*(\ln(\text{protected distance}))^3 + 0.25343*(\ln(\text{protected distance}))^4] \qquad \textbf{[EQN C9-T22-7]}$$

   W in kg, Distance in m

   $24.4 \text{ m} \le \text{Protected Distance}$

   $$W = \exp[122.38 - 108.8094*(\ln(\text{protected distance})) + 35.5517*(\ln(\text{protected distance}))^2 -$$
   $$4.9055*(\ln(\text{protected distance}))^3 + 0.25343*(\ln(\text{protected distance}))^4] \qquad \textbf{[EQN C9.T22-8]}$$

6. ILD/aboveground IMD distances in this column apply for adjacent compatible (ELCG LB or LC) storage; for adjacent incompatible (other ELCG) storage, use IBD distances shown in previous columns. ECMs may be used to their physical capacity for storing hydrogen provided they comply with the construction and siting requirements of Reference (c), Chapters 5 and 9 respectively, for HD 1.1. ECMs must be sited for a minimum of 100 lbs [45.4 kg] of HD 1.1 items using Tables C9.T4. and C9.T6.

7. Distances are 37.5 percent of "protected" column.

8. Extrapolations above 1,000,000 lbs [453,590 kg] extend well outside data included in Reference (aj) from which the original QD tables were derived; however, they are supported by independent calculations and knowledge of like phenomena.

Table AP2.T24. Default Maximum Case Fragment Distances
For Intentional Detonations (Table C9.T35.)

DIAMETER (in) [mm]	MAXIMUM FRAGMENT DISTANCE (feet) [m]
<1.5	1250
<38	381.0
1.5	1266
38	384.9
2.0	1626
51	497.1
2.5	1905
64	580.7
3.0	2133
76	649.3
3.5	2326
89	709.5
4.0	2493
102	761.4
4.5	2641
114	803.9
5.0	2772
127	845.0
5.5	2892
140	882.2
6.0	3000
152	913.6
6.5	3101
165	944.8
7.0	3193
178	973.8
7.5	3400
190	1033.8
8.0	3593
203	1094.3
8.5	3775
216	1151.0
9.0	3946
229	1204.4
9.5	4108
241	1251.1
10.0	4262
254	1299.1

Table AP2.T24. <u>Default Maximum Case Fragment Distances</u>
<u>For Intentional Detonations</u> (Table C9.T35.) (continued)

DIAMETER (in) [mm]	MAXIMUM FRAGMENT DISTANCE (feet) [m]
10.5	4408
267	*1344.7*
11.0	4548
279	*1384.9*
11.5	4681
292	*1426.5*
12.0	4809
305	*1466.3*
12.5	4931
318	*1504.4*
13.0	5049
330	*1538.3*
13.5	5162
343	*1573.6*
14.0	5271
356	*1607.6*
14.5	5376
368	*1637.9*
15.0	5478
381	*1669.6*
15.5	5576
394	*1700.3*
16.0	5671
406	*1727.7*
16.5	5763
419	*1756.5*
17.0	5853
432	*1784.4*
17.5	5940
444	*1809.4*
18.0	6024
457	*1835.8*
18.5	6106
470	*1861.4*
19.0	6186
483	*1886.4*
19.5	6264
495	*1908.8*
20.0	6340
508	*1932.5*
> 20	Use equations in Notes 2 & 3
> 508	*Use equations in Notes 2 & 3*

Notes for Table AP2.T24. (Table C9.T35.):

1. These calculated fragment throw distances are for individual munitions and do not apply to stacks. They also do not address "rogue" (non-case) fragments that can be produced from sections of nose plugs, base plates, or lugs. Rogue fragments can travel to significantly greater distances (i.e., > 10,000 ft [3,048 m]) than those shown. Care must be taken to properly orient the munition or take other measures to minimize rogue fragment hazards.

2. Maximum Fragment Distance (MFD) in ft, Diameter in inches; ln is natural logarithm.

$MFD = 759 + 1251*[ln(Diameter)]$	Diameter $\leq$ 7 in;	**[EQN C9.T35-1]**
$Diameter = exp[(MFD/1251) - 0.61]$;	Range $\leq$ 3193 ft;	**[EQN C9.T35-2]**
MFD in m, Diameter mm ; ln is natural logarithm.		
$MFD = -1002.08 + 381.305*[ln(Diameter)]$;	Diameter $\leq$ 178 mm;	**[EQN C9.T35-3]**
$Diameter = exp[(MFD/381.305) + 2.628]$;	Range $\leq$ 973.2 m;	**[EQN C9.T35-4]**

3. MFD in ft, Diameter in inches; ln is natural logarithm.

$MFD = -2641 + 2998*[ln(Diameter)]$;	Diameter > 7 in;	**[EQN C9.T35-5]**
$Diameter = exp[(MFD/2998) + 0.88]$;	Range > 3193 ft;	**[EQN C9.T35-6]**
MFD in m, Diameter in mm; ln is natural logarithm.		
$MFD = -3760.859 + 913.79*[ln(Diameter)]$;	Diameter > 178 mm;	**[EQN C9.T35-7]**
$Diameter = exp[(MFD/913.79) + 4.1157]$;	Range > 973.2 m;	**[EQN C9.T35-8]**

4. Use of equations given in Notes (2) and (3) to determine other Diameter/MFD combinations is allowed.
5. See subparagraph C5.18.6.3.2.2. for ranges associated with multiple munitions detonation.

Table AP2.T25. Maximum Case Fragment Distances for Selected Single Item Detonations (Table C9.T36.)

MUNITION	MAXIMUM FRAGMENT THROW DISTANCE (CASE FRAGMENTS) (ft) [m]	MUNITION	MAXIMUM FRAGMENT THROW DISTANCE (CASE FRAGMENTS) (ft) [m]
20 mm projectile	320 / 97.5	M106, 8-in projectile	3290 / 1002.8
25 mm projectile	760 / 231.6	16"/50 projectile	5640 / 1719.1
37 mm projectile	980 / 298.7	M49A3, 60-mm mortar	1080 / 329.2
40 mm projectile	1100 / 335.3	M374, 81-mm mortar	1235 / 376.4
40 mm grenade	345 / 105.2	M3A1, 4 2 -in mortar	1620 / 493.8
M229, 2 75" rocket	1375 / 419.1	M64A1 500-lb bomb	2500 / 762.0
M48, 75-mm projectile	1700 / 518.2	MK 81, 250-lb bomb	2855 / 870.2
105-mm projectile	1940 / 591.3	MK 82, 500-lb bomb	3180 / 969.3
5"/38 projectile	2205 / 672.1	MK 83, 1000-lb bomb	3290 / 1002.8
5"/54 projectile	2307 / 703.2	MK 84, 2000-lb bomb	3880 / 1182.6
155-mm projectile	2580 / 786.4	BLU-109 bomb	4890 / 1490.5
M437, 175-mm projectile	2705 / 824.5		

Notes for Table AP2.T25. (Table C9.T36.):

1. These calculated case fragment throw distances are for individual items and do not apply to detonations of multiple munitions. See subparagraph C5.18.6.3.2.2. for application to detonation of multiple munitions. In addition, shaped charge jets or slugs from directed energy munitions can travel significantly greater distances than case fragments; therefore, these munitions require specific analysis.

2. These calculated fragment throw distances are for individual munitions and do not apply to stacks. They also do not address "rogue" (non-case) fragments that can be produced from sections of nose plugs, base plates, or lugs. Rogue fragments can travel to significantly greater distances (i.e., > 10,000 ft [3,048 m]) than those shown. Care must be taken to properly orient the munition or take other measures to minimize rogue fragment hazards.

APPENDIX 2

AP3. <u>APPENDIX 3</u>

<u>ECM ORIENTATION FIGURES FROM DOD 6055.9-STD INCLUDED BY REFERENCE</u>

AP3.1. <u>ECM ORIENTATION FIGURES</u>

The figures in this appendix are extracted copies of figures found in Reference (c). The figures are provided to make this publication a more complete source of information for contractors.

AP3.2. <u>NUMBERING OF FIGURES</u>

These figures are sequentially numbered for this publication with the Reference (c) figure number shown in parentheses immediately after the figure's title.

Figure AP3.F1. <u>ECM Orientation Effects on IMD: Side-to-Side Orientation</u>
(Figure C9.F1.)

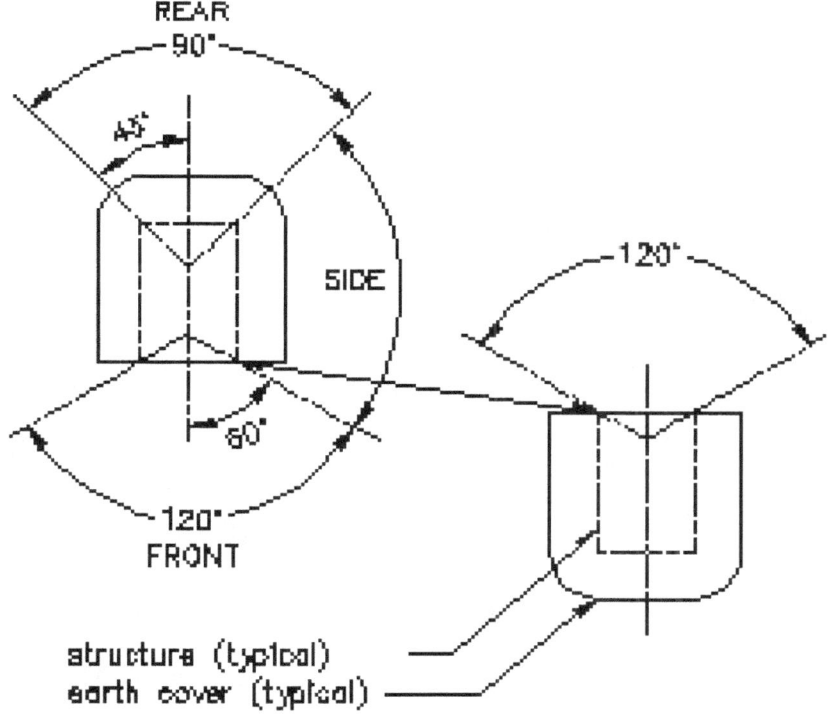

Figure AP3.F2. <u>ECM Orientation Effects on IMD: Side-to-Side Orientation</u>
(Figure C9.F2.)

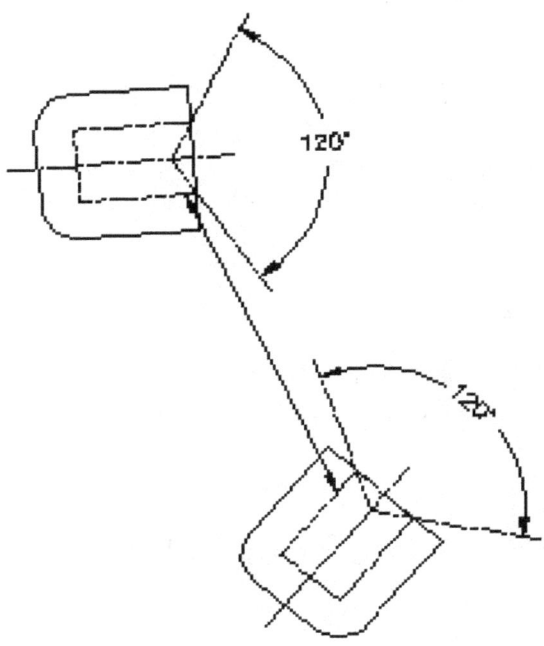

Figure AP3.F3. <u>ECM Orientation Effects on IMD</u> (Figure C9.F3.)

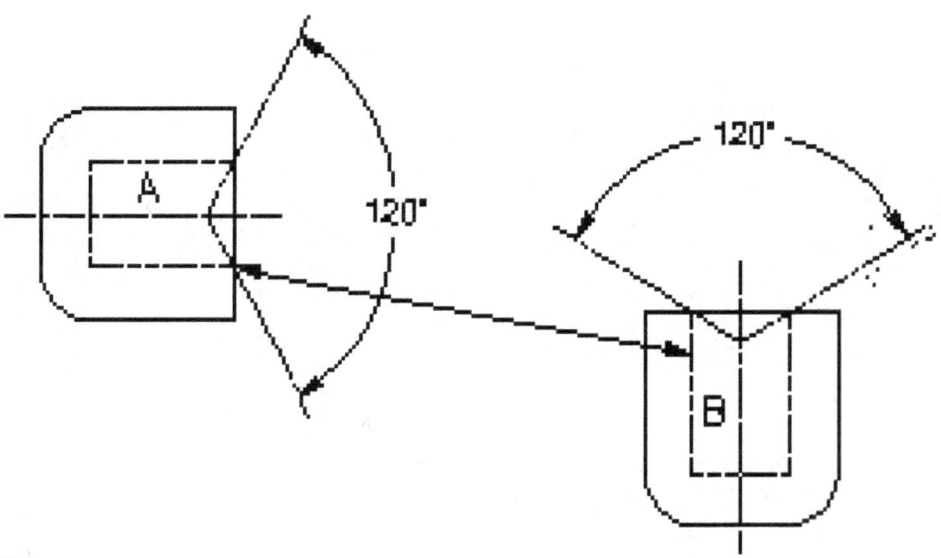

NOTES:
  1. Site A as a Side-to-Front (unbarricaded) ES.
  2. Site B as a Front (unbarricaded)-to-Side ES.

Figure AP3.F4. <u>ECM Orientation Effects on IMD</u> (Figure C9.F4.)

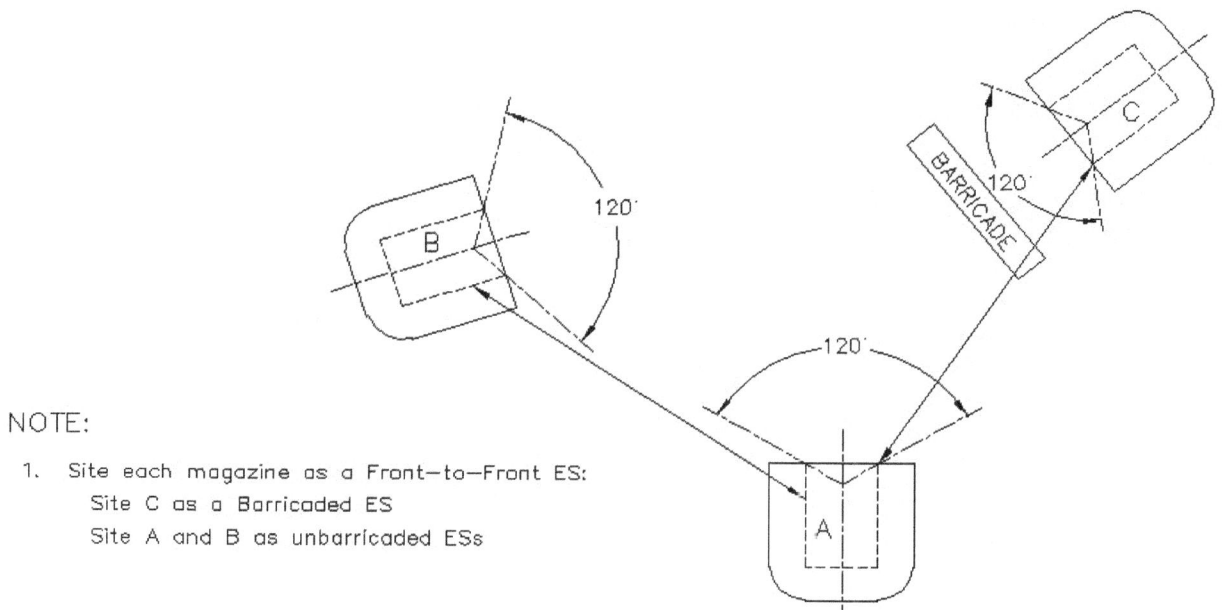

NOTE:

1.   Site each magazine as a Front—to—Front ES:
        Site C as a Barricaded ES
        Site A and B as unbarricaded ESs

Figure AP3.F5. <u>ECM Orientation Effects on IMD: Canted ECM</u> (Figure C9.F5.)

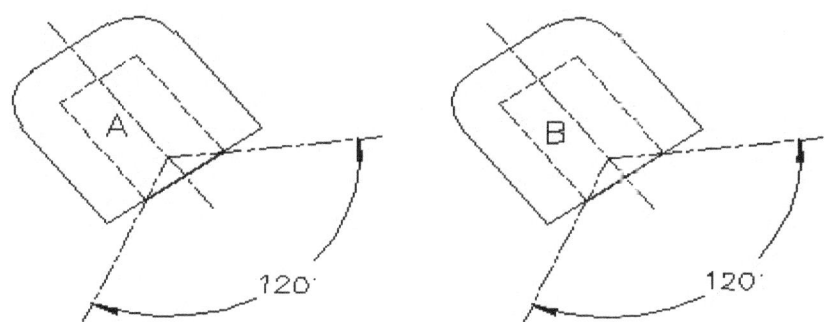

NOTES:
    1. Site A as a Side-to-Front (unbarricaded) ES.
    2. Site B as a Front (unbarricaded)-to-Side ES.

Figure AP3.F6. <u>ECM Orientation Effects on IMD: ECM of Significantly Different Lengths</u>
(Figure C9.F6.)

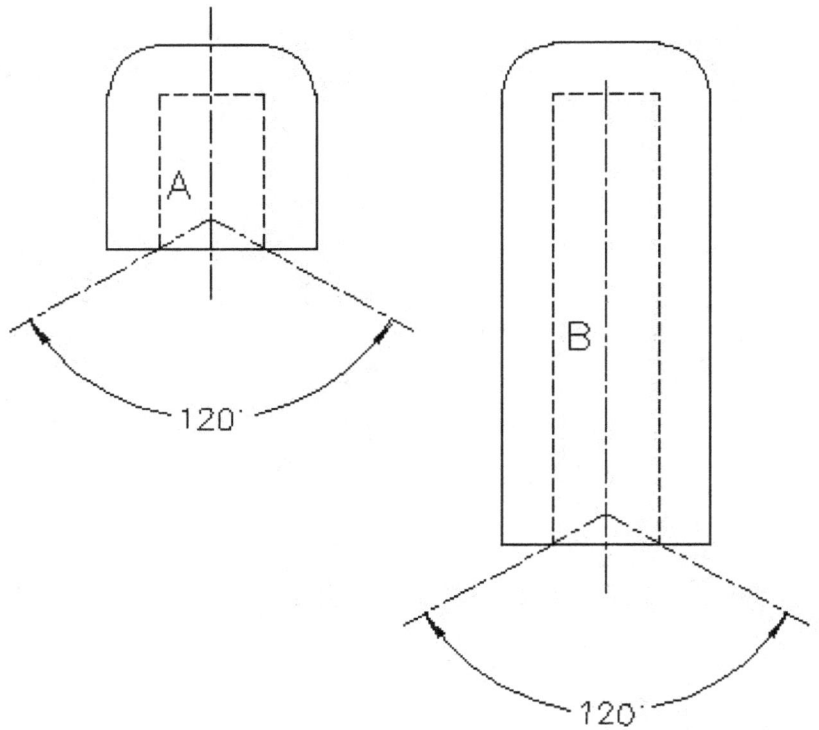

NOTES:
    1. Site A as a Side-to-Front (unbarricaded) ES.
    2. Site B as a Front (unbarricaded)-to-Side ES.

Figure AP3.F7. <u>ECM Orientation Effects on Barricaded and Unbarricaded IMD and ILD</u>
(Figure C9.F7.)

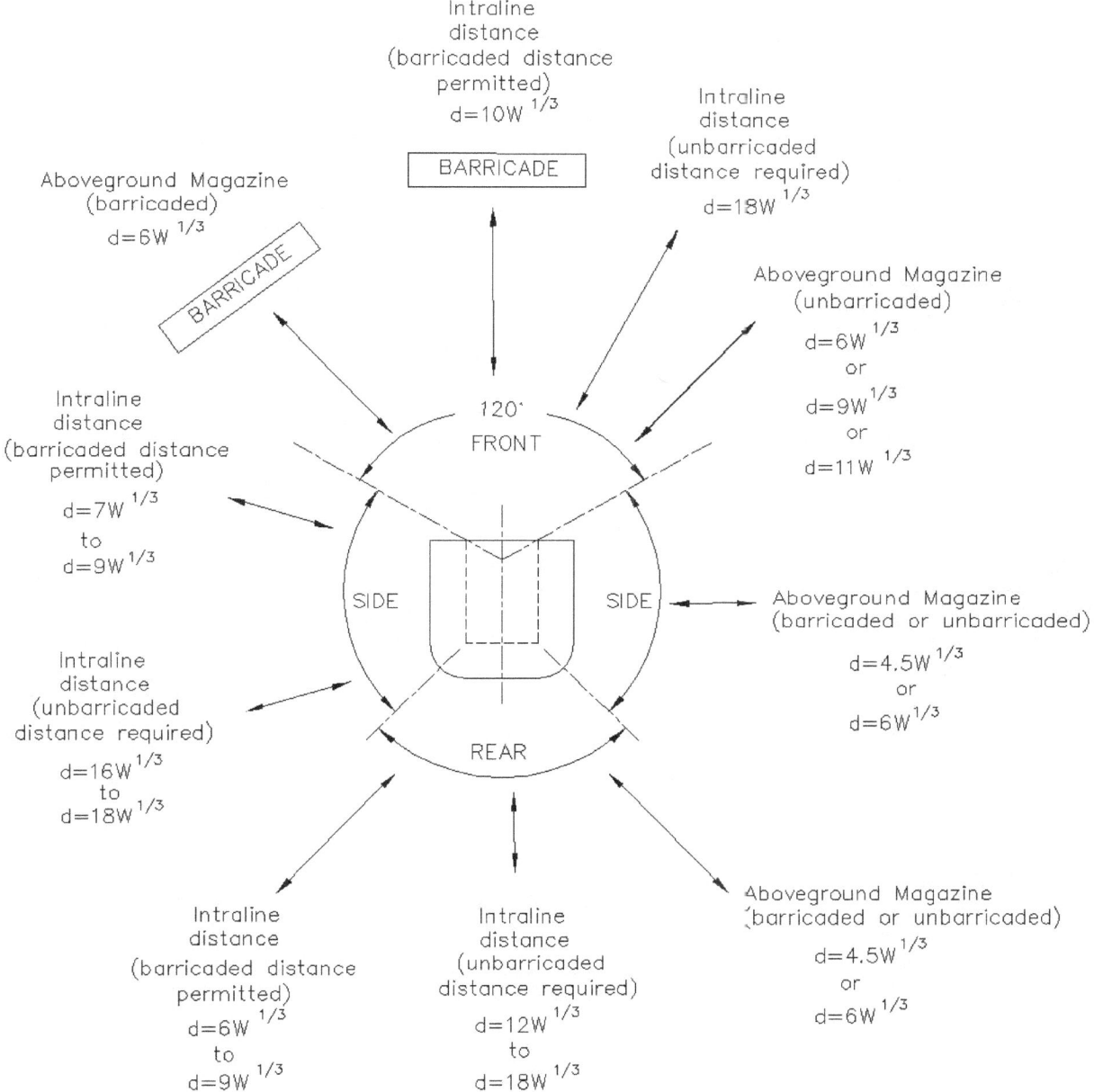

NOTES:
1. See paragraph C5.10.1 for application of ILDs from an ECM.
2. See paragraph C5.11.3 for application of barricaded IMDs and ILDs from an ECM.
3. See Table C9.T6. for application of IMDs between ECMs and AGMs.

www.ingramcontent.com/pod-product-compliance
Lightning Source LLC
Chambersburg PA
CBHW080244290526
45790CB00005B/1701